LOVE
that does
JUSTICE

LOVE
that does
JUSTICE

THOMAS L. SCHUBECK, S.J.

ORBIS BOOKS

Maryknoll, New York 10545

Founded in 1970, Orbis Books endeavors to publish works that enlighten the mind, nourish the spirit, and challenge the conscience. The publishing arm of the Maryknoll Fathers and Brothers, Orbis seeks to explore the global dimensions of the Christian faith and mission, to invite dialogue with diverse cultures and religious traditions, and to serve the cause of reconciliation and peace. The books published reflect the views of their authors and do not represent the official position of the Maryknoll Society. To learn more about Maryknoll and Orbis Books, please visit our website at www.maryknoll.org.

Manufactured in the United States of America.
Manuscript editing and typesetting by Joan Weber Laflamme.

Library of Congress Cataloguing-in-Publication Data

Schubeck, Thomas Louis, 1936–
    Love that does justice / Thomas L. Schubeck.
      p. cm.
    ISBN 978–1–57075–746–4
  1. Christian ethics. 2. Love. 3. Justice. I. Title.
    BJ1251.S38 2007
    241—dc22

                                    2007018553

*For the students at John Carroll University,
who brought me life and whose faces appear
in every chapter.*

CONTENTS

INTRODUCTION

During my first days in graduate school I became convinced, after reading William Frankena's *Ethics*, that two imperatives are essential for an adequate ethics: "Love!" and "Be just!" He reasoned that love alone, found in a type of ethics called agapism, is inadequate because the biblical command to love one's neighbor as oneself does not help persons determine how to distribute their love and other goods among their many neighbors. In his own philosophical ethics he supplements the law of love, which he calls benevolence, with the principle of distributive justice or equality. He notes that St. Paul wrote in his letter to the Romans (2:14) that the Gentiles, who do not possess the law of love, nonetheless have a moral law "written in their hearts." This suggests, Frankena said, "that agapism cannot be the whole story."[1] *Agape* needs justice as a companion.

Frankena's position, that an adequate ethic needs both love and justice, confirmed my own experience of growing up in a large family in which we ten children competed for the affection and attention of our parents. The love of our parents, Joe and Maggie, for each other and for the ten of us was rooted in a faith that believed all things and endured more things than we children could have imagined. Dad's justice insisted on honest speech, hard work, and respect for the property of others. Mom's love magnified her justice as she generously shared what little she had with needy neighbors, including food rationing stamps during World War II. Both parents managed to satisfy our basic needs in times of scarcity.

Yet we younger kids sometimes confused love with justice by questioning our mother's love when actually she was trying to be fair to all. We protested, for example, when she served breakfast first to the older brothers and laundered their shirts before serving us and helping us get dressed. We sometimes felt that we were less important and less loved than our older working brothers. She would defend her action as just: "They eat first," she said, "because they are going to work." Like many children in similar situations, we were misinterpreting her justice—which in this instance favored our older siblings—as a love that regarded them more highly than us. Consequently we younger ones began to feel that we had to earn our parents' love by going to work, or at least by being useful around the house. Professor Mark Schwehn expressed a similar question that a child might ask the parent: "Do you love me for myself, or for what I have been able to accomplish?" Schwehn then asked: "How many of us have not, at some time or another, sought an answer to this question by devising tests of love for our parents?"[2] Later, as adults, we came to realize that genuine love needs no self-justification. No one can earn a parent's love or God's, or anyone else's. Love is gift.

Even though working industriously, doing the right thing, or being just does not earn another's love, justice does express, protect, and strengthen love in relationships. This book shows how important writers in the Judeo-Christian tradition relate love and justice.

OBJECTIVES AND AUDIENCE

The author assumes that the virtues and principles of love and justice are fundamental criteria of an adequate Christian social ethics. As virtues, love and justice link up with each other and direct other virtues to help persons, friendships, families, and communities flourish. As principles, love and justice help individuals and groups to analyze and guide persons in resolving contemporary issues related to violence, war and peace, poverty, race relations, and economic issues of fair employment and trade. The book's objectives are twofold: first, it interprets and elucidates the meaning of love and justice as used by various authors and how the authors interrelate them; second, it illustrates how these two values illumine and help resolve contemporary issues. The book title suggests that love is the prime mover. By taking the initiative, love *does* something to justice; it energizes, sensitizes, and guides justice. Yet justice also affects love by giving it direction, protection, and structure. As we shall see in the following chapters, love and justice work together, sometimes as complementary companions and at other times as paradoxical partners. Precisely how love does justice and how justice shapes love varies somewhat from author to author.

Although most chapters in this book first present love and then justice, the first chapter reverses the order. It begins with injustice, then moves to justice, and ends with love. College students in Chapter 1 tell stories of their experiences of injustice. These negative experiences imply a positive dimension of justice; violation of a person's dignity makes one aware that people ought to respect the human dignity of all persons. The students' hurtful experiences helped them to appreciate the important role that the love of their mother, father, or friends played. As the student narratives consistently demonstrate, love heals the scars of injustice and helps the victim to live again.

Chapter 2 investigates the biblical love and justice that arise from within the Jewish and Christian traditions. God's love is compassionate, exceedingly generous, merciful, and forgiving. God's love, like the love of a parent or a friend, also heals. Divine justice liberates persons from slavery and frees them from sin. In its most general sense, justice means remaining faithful to the demands that arise out of a people's covenantal relationship with God. Remembering God's loving and just deeds guards people against being self-righteous.

Chapter 3 explores the meaning of love and justice in early Christianity when Jesus and his followers addressed issues of violence, nonviolence, and war. It examines what Jesus and Paul taught about loving enemies, resisting evildoers, and responding violently. It presents the perspectives of Tertullian, who opposed Christians serving in the military and of Martin Luther King, Jr., who taught his African American Christian followers to turn the other cheek by using nonviolent resistance. Although Christians in the first two centuries generally taught and practiced nonviolence, Christians in the third and fourth centuries began to serve in the Roman army and so bore arms and used them when ordered.

Chapter 3 on nonviolence sets the stage for Chapter 4 on violence and war. The author is the great theologian and bishop of Hippo, St. Augustine. Using charity as his primary reference, Augustine shows how charity and justice prohibit Christians from killing in self-defense and how the same virtues permit soldiers, under certain conditions, to kill the enemy in defense of their nation. The conditions he develops have become the core principles of today's just-war theory.

The fifth chapter concentrates on the theological ethics of Thomas Aquinas. Building on the philosophy of Aristotle and the theology of Augustine, Aquinas develops a grand synthesis of Christian theology and of an ethics of virtue that gives central roles to charity and justice. He demonstrates how charity and justice work as partners, directing persons and groups to live and act virtuously. As partners, charity and justice direct all the other virtues to help persons promote the common good and to seek their ultimate good.

Chapters 6 and 7 turn the spotlight on two contemporary figures who address social issues: Reinhold Niebuhr, American Protestant pastor, theologian, and professor at Union Theological Seminary in New York; and John Paul II, Pope of the Roman Catholic Church for twenty-seven years. Niebuhr, influenced by Augustine, sees love and justice working in a dialectical tension, each affirming and challenging the other. John Paul II, standing on the shoulders of Thomas Aquinas, sees love and justice as companions that bring persons to their full development and divine destiny. Both contemporary authors play important roles in creating an ethics that concentrates on social institutions and on social issues dealing with racism, socialist political-economies, the work place, and international trade. The book concludes with reflections on how love does justice.

ACKNOWLEDGMENTS

Researching and writing this book has been a long process. It began at the turn of the century eight years ago. Four educational institutions and a host of friends, colleagues, and students helped me launch and sustain my research and writing. I would like to acknowledge their help and support, and publicly thank them. John Carroll University generously provided me with two Grauel fellowships, in 1999 and again in 2005. Michael J. Buckley, director of The Jesuit Institute at Boston College, provided me with housing and a generous grant that supplemented my first Grauel fellowship in the fall 1999 semester. The Center of Theological Inquiry at Princeton furnished me with comfortable housing, excellent office facilities, and invited me to participate in a seminar composed of excellent scholars who met each week to discuss their writing projects. In 2004–2005 I profited greatly from my sabbatical year at the Woodstock Theological Center on the campus of Georgetown University, where I wrote three of my chapters. I am grateful to my colleagues, friends, graduate assistants, and students who read sections of my work and gave me many helpful comments. I would like to thank my colleagues at the Woodstock Theological Center and the Ethics Writers Group in Cleveland for reading, discussing, and offering me very helpful suggestions. I am especially grateful to Delores Christie, Charles Curran, Brian Daly, John Haughey, Paul Lauritzen, George Matejka, Stephen Pope, and Anthony Tambasco for their careful reading of certain chapters of the book and for their excellent suggestions. Finally, I wish to thank my graduate assistants Jodie Bowers, Michael Graskemper, and Devon Lynch-Huggins for helping me with my research and for their careful proofreading the text. From the beginning, I wanted this book to be accessible to undergraduate students, and so I asked two undergraduate students, Kristy Calaway and Alexandra Grubbs, to read the first few chapters. They did an excellent job in helping me to explain biblical and theological jargon in clearer, everyday language that will make the book an easier read.

Unforeseen events, like personal illness and heart surgery, forced me to set aside many months for recovery and rest. I am deeply grateful to my family, my rector, Howard Gray, Donna Markham, Larry Cima, Gap LoBiondo, Richard and Delores Christie, and Joseph Krall for their encouragement and for their spiritual and medical assistance.

NOTES

[1] William K. Frankena, *Ethics*, 2nd ed., Foundations of Philosophy Series (Englewood Cliffs, NJ: Prentice-Hall, 1963, 1973), 57–58.

[2] Mark R. Schwehn, "King Lear beyond Reason: Love and Justice in the Family," *First Things* 36 (October 1993): 25–33, http://print.firstthings.com/ftissues/ft9310/schwehn.html (accessed on December 7, 2006).

1

LOVE AND JUSTICE
IN NARRATIVE

Everyone talks about love and justice. All people desire to be loved and to have friendships that last. They also wish to be treated justly and insist on transactions that are fair. Workers seek justice, not a paternalistic kind of charity. In response to Pope Leo XIII's praise for the church's heroic works of mercy in the late nineteenth century, industrial laborers shouted: "We do not want benefits, but demand our rights and nothing else."[1] Upholding their dignity, these workers called for justice, not charity. Our musical lyrics, dreams, dramas, and poetry all manifest the lifelong yearning of our hearts for love as well as for justice. We search for both values in our relationships with family, friends, or fellow workers. We know the emptiness when love is absent and feel the anger when justice is denied.

Although we prize these two fundamental values and would find it impossible to live without them, we search for the appropriate words to express precisely what we mean. We may think that there is no pure essence of love or justice, though each of us has an intuitive sense of their meaning. We may feel more confident in saying what justice and love are *not* than we do in trying to define them. Intuitively we sense that justice has something to do with fairness or distributing goods equally based on certain objective criteria such as need, merit, or intrinsic qualities of human beings. When we think about justice, words like *rights, duties,* and *responsibilities* may come to mind. Justice deals with basic needs and a right to them: food, water, housing, and medicine. Justice calls forth reasons of the mind written in logical prose in the style of Aristotle: "What is just," he wrote, "will be both what is lawful and what is fair, and what is unjust will be both what is lawless and what is unfair."[2]

As for love, we may associate it with acceptance, expressed by words of affection and affirmation as well as by kind deeds.[3] Love elicits reasons of the heart, sometimes spoken in poetic language, like St. Paul's lyrical paean: "Love is patient; love is kind; love is not envious or boastful or arrogant or rude. . . . It bears all things, believes all things, hopes all things, endures all things." Paul relates this highest form of love, called *agape* (pronounced *ä GÄ pā*) to eternity: "Love never ends" (1 Cor 13:4, 7–8). Shakespeare, like Paul, sees love—which he calls the "the marriage of true minds"—holding a steady course in times when relationships encounter stormy weather. Love, he says in his sonnet, endures to "the edge of doom."

> Love is not love
> Which alters when it alteration finds,
> Or bends with the remover to remove.
> O no, it is an ever fixèd mark
> That looks on tempests and is never shaken;
> It is the star to every wand'ring barque,
> Whose worth's unknown although his height be
>   taken. . . .
> Love alters not with his brief hours and weeks,
> But bears it out even to the edge of doom.
> If this be error and upon me proved,
> I never writ, nor no man ever loved.[4]

This chapter explores the meaning of love and justice indirectly through personal narratives of college students. They tell stories in which they were either victims of injustice or vicariously witnessed unjust events and took a stand against them. My collaborator and I invited college students and alumni to share their stories of injustice.[5] We also asked whether someone like a parent, friend, clergyperson, or counselor had assisted them in working through the issue. Their responses to these questions revealed the importance of love and friendship in working through an injustice. They recount experiences of injustice where love and respect were absent. Their stories describe what justice and love are *not*. Justice is absent, our narrators said, when white students shun and taunt black students; when teachers or bosses demean students or workers; when a parent leaves children home alone while tripping on cocaine; when a coach or a teacher makes a student feel unworthy and nonexistent; or when a foreman sexually harasses his female workers and whips the male workers. The young storytellers describe a number of disorders that damaged their hearts and weighed down their souls. Their experiences left some in tears and others in shock; they felt negative about themselves, depressed, helpless, vulnerable, angry, and hurt. They also tell how they, supported by another, resisted the negative experience and in the process grew in freedom, courage, and compassion.

NEGATIVE CONTRAST EXPERIENCES

Edward Schillebeeckx (pronounced SKILL ä bākes), a contemporary Dutch theologian, calls such stories of suffering "negative contrast experiences." Surprisingly, these experiences have positive as well as negative elements. People suffer through sickness, accidents, racial discrimination, loss of a friend, loneliness, and oppression. But these negative occurrences can lead to insight when the victims resist the evil and learn from the negative experience. Personal suffering can sensitize individuals to the suffering of others. Enduring oppression can awaken them to the misery of the poor. Resisting evil and then reflecting on the encounter often provide awareness of what it means to become a free subject and not a mere object being pushed around by external forces. The oppressed person can become free, just, and loving by struggling against evil.

Negative contrast experiences also serve as a potential source for disclosing something about God; they provide insight into how God acts in human history as they reveal something about the human, or what Schillebeeckx calls the *humanum*.[6] The *humanum* is the full human being we seek to become.[7] The kingdom of God, which Jesus proclaimed and promised, symbolizes the *humanum*.[8] God calls all human beings to live in relationships with God and their neighbors, relationships that express love, justice, and peace. These qualities are called virtues, or admirable traits; they empower human beings to realize their highest potential. People arrive at this stage through the grace of God and by practicing the virtues—by being honest, kind, generous, forbearing, and just. One can come to know and imitate these excellent traits directly by listening to the teaching of a sage or simply by imitating virtuous women and men who live the virtues through their habitual way of acting.

Unfortunately we all experience directly, or learn through the media, how dishonest, greedy, violent, and unjust actions threaten the *humanum*. Yet our response to despicable deeds can also be an educative moment. We can come to understand the *humanum* indirectly by resisting these negative experiences. Schillebeeckx describes this process: "All resistance to inhumane situations reveal, if only indirectly, at least an obscure consciousness of what must be confessed positively by human integrity; it manifests in a negative and indirect way the call of and to the *humanum*."[9] Striving to become more fully human requires a process of reflecting on suffering: one's own and that of others.

Schillebeeckx uses the phrase "negative contrast experiences" because the experiences are selfish and oppressive acts that cause pain and also because they contradict the way human beings should relate to one another. Witnesses to racial or sexual discrimination or to the torture of human beings often shout in protest: "This should not be!" "Never again!" We can learn from these negative contrast experiences and be moved to resist them. Instead of blocking them from our memory, we may choose to reflect critically on them, or perhaps even publish an essay describing these happenings. Aided by a friend, counselor, or spiritual guide, we can analyze the painful event in order to understand the causes of the injustice. We may consider alternate ways of responding to the injustice, should it happen again. Encouraged by the love and support of family and friends, we can thus become more aware of our goodness, dignity, and freedom and of our potential for becoming courageous, compassionate, and just human beings.

Contrast experiences disclose the difference between the present suffering resulting from a moral evil (for example, feeling depressed because someone

maligned me) and a good (for example, awareness of my own dignity) that
calls me to affirm my true sense of self, the person I am becoming and the
internal power I possess, in order to realize fully the *humanum*. Canadian
theologian Gregory Baum illustrates the importance that negative contrast
experiences have had on the global community: "It was the revulsion from
the cruel repression and genocide practiced by a German fascist dictatorship
and the massive killing and devastation exercised by relentless bombing on
all sides that prompted the nations in 1948 to affirm human rights and commit themselves to their protection."[10] The negative contrast experience is
never one of pure negativity, because it provides the occasion for the possibility of disclosing a path to human growth, liberation, and redemption. In
light of Schillebeeckx's concepts, we turn to the narratives of the students. In
telling their stories they gained an understanding of justice through their
experience of injustice as well as an appreciation of their friends and family,
who showed them the meaning of love when they needed support.

WITH DIGNITY AND HONOR

We begin with the story of a female college student named Grace, who
grew up in a small African American village in the valley, surrounded by
white enclaves set on the hills above. In the interview, Grace talked first
about how the white residents on two of the hills sent their sewage down
pipelines into the valley below where black residents lived; then she described
her dreadful experience of going to the racist school on the hill where the
white teachers ignored her and her black friends, and white children taunted
them.

RACISM ON THE HILL

"In the early 1960s a realtor persuaded a large number of African American families, including my grandparents, to move from a large segregated
city in the Midwest to a rural district some thirty miles away. The realtor
failed to tell my grandparents and the other buyers that the two adjoining
towns, perched on the hills above our village, had replaced all the residents'
septic tank systems with sewer lines, which deposited raw sewage through
pipelines to the bottom of the hills. The bottom was where we lived. During
the spring when the snow melted and the rainy season began, the sewage
became a flood that formed a lake, caked with refuse. It covered our farm-
land. The polluted lake made it impossible for our villagers to till and to
plant. The waters flooded the barns and the coops, making it impossible to
raise cattle and chickens. Filthy and toxic water overflowed onto our road,
causing it to corrode. The stench was nauseating.

"Our villagers filed a complaint to the board of trustees of the township.
The trustees, however, refused to change anything, even turning down our

requests to clean out the ditches that collected the sewage. They defended their inaction by informing us that the township would have to pay half the cost that it would take to re-route the sewage. They did nothing; the polluted environment remains with us to this day. Dumping refuse into our village is unfair; the township's unwillingness to do anything about it is even more unjust.

"As I began school on the hill, I noticed that the all-white teachers and the white student majority would have nothing to do with us African Americans. They kept us at arms' length. Always unfriendly, the white children sometimes became hostile. They teased us and called out to us, using racist names. Some of these taunters were children of the Klu Klux Klan, which is still alive in our township. Sons of the KKK threatened my older brother. One boy attacked him with a board which had nails sticking out. In self-defense, my brother hit him. The boys threatened to shoot us in our house, though they never carried out the threat. We had no defense against the white people who ridiculed or attacked us. We had no police station in the village where we might call for help.

"The hostile school environment was so bad that my mother took me and my brother out of the local school system and sent us to a high school one hour's drive away. I liked the new school. I knew that I was there to learn, and I learned a lot. My mother drove us to school each morning and picked us up in the afternoon. The social environment was friendly, and the education was far superior to the racist school on the hill. But my older brother, even though he is quite intelligent, was already too far behind to catch up. He became discouraged, and eventually quit school.

"The racist environment was oppressive. I started to feel bad about myself. I withdrew from everyone. Racism is ugly; it's unjust, and it makes you hate yourself. I had to work hard to change the way I thought about myself. I would say things like: 'I won't get into that college because I'm black'; 'I won't qualify for that job because I'm black.' My mother challenged me when I made those negative statements about myself. She often encouraged me, like when I went away to college. During the first semester, she would call me every morning to tell me how much she loved me and believed in me. Her encouraging words and love helped me to fight off those bad thoughts and to believe in myself.

"I'm doing very well in college, and after I finish, I want to go to law school. As a lawyer I can help my family and others who face unjust situations that we have had to face. I have said that racism is unjust. So what is justice? As I see it, justice is having a fair chance and not being denied opportunities. I don't necessarily expect people to change their attitudes. I do expect them to treat others fairly and not to control other people. People should take responsibility when they cause harm to others."

Grace calls the white people's treatment of her family and the African American people in the valley racism. She also calls it unjust. Racism generally refers to a belief that "inherent biological differences among the various human races determine cultural or individual achievement." It implies that one's own race (in this instance the white race) is superior to the black race.[11] As an ideology, racism has been used to justify all kinds of discrimination, including racial segregation, beatings, lynching, and genocide.

Grace's experience of racism in her village and in elementary school echoes what Gordon Allport says about the nature of prejudice and discrimination. He defines prejudice as "an antipathy based on a faulty and inflexible generalization. It may be felt or expressed. It may be directed toward a group as a whole, or toward an individual because he is a member of that group."[12] Allport adds one more ingredient to the nature of prejudice: it "fulfills a specific irrational function" and serves as a self-gratifying end for the person who has these negative attitudes.[13] Although he analyzes prejudice from a psychological standpoint, Allport's definition suggests why prejudice is said to be unjust. The prejudgment about another human being's character is false: the overgeneralized judgment is a rash judgment to which the biased judge inflexibly clings, even after being exposed to new knowledge. The person also expresses antipathy or hatred toward a member of the group precisely because he or she is a member of that group.

Allport shows that prejudice is acted out against the "out group" according to a scale of increasing intensity, moving from antilocution (verbally rejecting the out group) to avoidance, to discrimination (including segregation), to physical attack, and finally to extermination. At Grace's school on the hill, white children taunted her and her black classmates, using derogatory names. They also avoided any association with African American children. The groups were already segregated. No blacks lived in the white neighborhoods; no whites lived in Grace's village. Grace vividly recalled the physical attack that some white boys made against her brother, who was fortunate in being able to fend them off. Finally, the white kids threatened Grace's family but stopped short of carrying out the threat.

The major discriminatory action involved the white community turning the black village into a garbage dump, as though it were simply a wasteland; worse, those in control refused to do anything about it after the village residents issued a complaint. The new families discovered the problem only after they had moved into the village. Moving again would have meant a sizeable financial loss. The realtors acted irresponsibly by failing to inform black buyers of the true situation. When the families appealed to the township's board of trustees to do something about the sewage being deposited on their land, the board refused to act.

Grace's negative experience of racial prejudice and discrimination suggests a number of injustices. First, the negative experiences caused her to hate herself. She internalized the negative feelings that her white peers projected on her and her classmates by isolating them and calling them derogatory names. As a consequence, she repeatedly doubted herself. She doubted that she would be admitted to college and get a job simply because she was black. Grace felt the hurtful attitudes, and she thinks that they are unjust. But she had little hope that they would change. By way of contrast to the injustices she experienced, Grace sees justice as equal opportunity for all people and being responsible for the harm that one has caused. The people on the hill and the board of trustees should have changed the sewage system that was ruining the land and property values of the black people's homes.

The care and love of her mother enabled Grace to grow through this harrowing experience in the valley and in the racist school on the hill. Her mother's decision to remove Grace and her brother from the hostile school environment and to enroll her in a friendly educational system was both courageous and wise. Most important, her mother taught Grace to replace the negative refrain that daily bombarded her psyche with words of love for and belief in her daughter. Grace's mother helped her to affirm herself, as Martin Luther King, Jr., urged all African Americans to do. King's mantra for his people was: "I am somebody. I am a person. I am a man, I am a woman with dignity and honor."[14] Grace possesses that dignity and honor. She has progressed in her studies, has made wonderful friends, both black and white, and is committed to working in behalf of her people.

THE RESPONSIBLE SELF

Growing up is an adventurous journey that involves pitfalls and suffering that are beyond the person's control: serious sickness, losing a parent through divorce or sickness, being isolated by cliques for refusing to conform, misunderstandings with friends, or suffering a serious injury in combat. Yet the experience of suffering can strengthen character. We may know individuals who have become great persons because they were able to work through painful encounters with parents, sickness, physical handicaps, and misunderstandings with their peers. They became more courageous and free, not simply because they walked through adversity and came out alive, but because of the way they responsibly dealt with their suffering by reflecting on what was happening to them, gaining insight, and resisting oppressive forces.

The next two stories present the journeys of two college students who met adversity early in life and responsibly dealt with it. Jennifer tells how she responded to her mother's drug addiction and to the loss of her father. Her journey was a lonely one, but through her own determination and with the help of others, she progressed toward her goals. Jason narrates his struggle against an upper-middle-class culture that threatened to mold him into its own image by forcing him to conform to its materialist values. The injustice he encountered was embedded in the culture where he grew up, an ethos that demanded conformity to a standard of dress, status, and work ethic. Jason struggled to resist these demands to conform and to follow his own values, a personal calling that said, "Be who you are!"

Addiction

"My name is Jennifer, and I would like to tell you what it was like growing up in a family broken apart by drug addiction. Although our family wasn't wealthy, my parents gave me whatever I wanted. I guess you could say that I was spoiled, that is, until troubles hit our family. Quite early in my life, my mother got hooked on cocaine. I don't remember details, but I do recall that I was only six when things began to unravel. I remember my parents often leaving the house and going to court. Soon afterward, they got divorced. I'll never forget seeing my mom leaving our house forever, saying goodbye to me and my little brother, age three. The court gave my dad custody of us because of Mom's addiction. We could visit Mom twice a week and were allowed to stay overnight; that is, until things worsened. And Mom's situation soon became worse. In our visits, we noticed that Mom acted kind of strange, and so I suspected that she was still taking drugs. Once when the police knocked on the apartment door, she told us to tell them she wasn't home.

"On another occasion, we knocked on her bedroom door. No answer. So my brother and I left the apartment to look for her, and as we departed, we heard the lock on the door snap shut. We knew that we could not return, so we had to find Mom. We walked downstairs, and not finding her, we banged on the door of a tenant who was a police officer. No response. Finding ourselves all alone at one o'clock in the morning and growing more fearful, we walked to a friend's apartment nearby. We woke her, and she let us in. The next day my dad found out about all this, and soon afterward, our overnight visitations ceased. Mom was ordered to drive us back each evening. When her drug habit became more serious (I was about eleven then), the court ruled that we could no longer visit her.

"Since that time, my brother and I have had absolutely no contact with her. I heard that she had been arrested a few times. I once saw her from a distance, but she did not see me. She did not look very good. My aunt (Mom's sister) once showed me a recent photo, and it revealed how badly her body had deteriorated. I learned that she stole money to buy drugs, and that eventually she began to use heroin. She was always on the run.

"Dad, who was a plumber, raised and supported us. He was a good father. But I missed having a mother. When I was a freshman in high school, my father began to suffer from a condition called Post-Traumatic Stress Disorder that led to a mental illness, a paranoid condition that made him afraid to go outdoors. Later we learned that he was taking a painkiller called Percocet for a period of thirteen years, which may have contributed to his physical and mental problems. As a result, he lost his job and received unemployment compensation and welfare checks to pay for housing and other expenses. My brother and I worked a little. Somehow we managed, but it was tough going. On the social side, it became increasingly difficult for my brother and me to relate to our dad as his condition worsened. I called my uncle, who contacted the Department of Social Services, who sent someone to get us. We then stayed with my aunt, which was a big improvement. But then living with her was not the best situation. She was much older than my mom; my brother and I had a difficult time relating to her.

"The whole situation was unjust. We lost our mom. Dad got sick, and so we lost him, too. It's hard to pinpoint the injustice. I'm angrier at my mom for getting into drugs, which seemed to be the root of all our family misfortunes. It definitely caused my parents to split. The divorce was traumatic for my father as well as for my mother. And it hurt us kids. Maybe her addiction was the basis of the injustice. I'm less angry with my father, but I'm not sure why. Maybe it's because he also had a very hard time.

"Somehow I managed to get through all this turmoil, graduating from high school with good grades, and then going to a prestigious university. It may seem strange to say this, but the divorce, painful as it was, gave me courage. I felt that I had to survive and to succeed on my own. I liked school, studied hard, and played on the basketball team. The guidance counselor, who began advising me when I was a junior, was definitely helpful. My teachers gave me lots of encouragement and support, even without knowing what my family situation was like. Their encouragement and my high grades helped me to realize that I could make my life better by going to a good college. Then I have been blessed with a very good friend, Ani. We played together on our high school basketball team and are today the closest of friends. Her parents have been very good to me. This year at Christmas break, for example, they invited me to stay with them. So all things considered, I have done well. When I finish college, I hope to travel and then go to law school."

To Conform or Not to Conform

"All people struggle to find their identity, and it's not easy," Jason began. "It's like swimming upstream in a river where the cultural current is almost overpowering, especially for this swimmer when I was in sixth grade. The current was swift as it moved through my upper-middle-class neighborhood and wealthy middle school. In this cultural setting where appearances and fashion really count, I struggled to find out who I was. Cliquishness and fashion do not appeal to me; but like it or not, I had to fight off these forces that tried to suck me into their way of thinking, dressing, and acting. I would like to give you two instances of my struggle, the first when I was in middle school and the second in my junior-senior years in high school.

"In middle school, cultural pressures dictated that I wear the latest style clothes with designer labels, and not the grubby, well-worn slacks I put on every day. Appearances were and continue to be most important to my peers, who seemed agitated, even threatened, when I failed to conform to their

lifestyle and to the way they dressed. They regarded anyone who was different from their norms as bad. If you didn't fit into their mold, they resented
you. They seemed afraid to relate to me. But I decided not to try to fit in with
the clique because it struck me as ridiculous and because I wanted to be who
I am—a unique individual. Being something else when my heart's not in it, I
felt, was not good.

"Do you think that I'm stubborn? Maybe I am. I know that we have to
give in to cultural norms to some extent, and in certain things I did concede.
But how much should I compromise? Of this I'm certain: I want to protect
my uniqueness, to stand on my own principles, and freely to choose my own
community. So in sixth grade, I chose to hang out with friends who didn't
feel the need to conform to fashion, appearances, and cliques.

"In high school, I continued to feel the pressure to conform, especially
when the time arrived to pick a college. Pressures came from all sides: teachers, colleges, peers, their parents, and, yes, even my family. My mom pleaded
with me to read up on possible colleges to which I might apply. She also
urged me to read a lot, so that I might at least *appear* to be an intellectual. In
the eyes of many, I seemed to be too laid back and not at all serious about
going to college. As they saw it, I wasn't working hard enough at this important endeavor. These subtle but pervasive forces were killing me. The guidance counselor was on my case, urging me to study really hard for the SAT
exam. 'Are you getting tutoring?' he would ask. Colleges also exerted pressure. Other guys' parents would inappropriately inquire, 'What were your
SAT scores?' That really got me. Everyone wanted to know whether my
friends and I were giving the appearance of doing the right thing.

"So what's unjust about all this? I'll tell you: people were infringing on
my ability to make my own decisions. They suggested that my way of doing
things was wrong. Even my mother became fearful. Eventually she apolo-
gized, and I sensed that she knew that she was intruding into my space and
decision-making process. She wanted me to be happy, but she wasn't sure I
was going about things in the right way. The uncertainty made her uncom-
fortable.

"Yet I fought off these pressures. And throughout it all, I did experience
the love and care of others. My father listened and understood what I was
saying. My close friends were also supportive. Yes, my mother, even though
she made it hard for me to make my own decision, loved me. She came to see
what I was feeling, even though at the time, I couldn't express it very well so
that she could understand. I needed to find my own way and so needed
freedom in the world beyond high school. Despite the fact that my mom and
I were often fighting over how hard I was working, or about how much I
was focusing on the process—it even got personal at times—I came to see
that she was on my side the whole time. I discovered that my mom and I
could strongly disagree about the other's actions, but that we could still love

each other. To this day, I don't agree with the way she pressured me, but I came to realize that I should not have lashed out because, in spite of appearances, she really wanted the best for me. As I look back, I think I could have made it easier for her by reassuring her that I respected and loved her even while disagreeing with her advice."

These were hard times for Jennifer and her little brother, as well as for Jason. Jennifer showed great courage and acted responsibly at a very young age, in sharp contrast to her mother, who was unable to take responsibility for her children. Jennifer took care of her brother and valiantly tried to relate to her mother until the courts finally ruled that the children were not to have further contact with her. She worked part time as she went to school, studied hard, and received good grades. As she told the story, she did not blame her mother or her father. Only after the interviewer asked whether she thought her situation was unfair did Jennifer identify her mother's addiction and irresponsible actions as unjust. Yet she had compassion for her mother and her father.

When children lose a parent, they might decide to give up. For Jennifer, giving up was not an option. The divorce, she said, actually gave her courage. She became self-reliant and free. Something inside her said, "Keep going." She credits her teachers and counselor for helping her to grow in courage through their support and direction. Friendship with Ani and loving care by Ani's family gave Jennifer life and a sense belonging to a family.

Jason struggled to grow up in very different circumstances, but like Jennifer, he learned to assume responsibility at an early age as he searched for his identity and freedom. He rightly sensed that he would never find himself by melting into the crowd, and so he resisted conforming to its values. He identified the injustice as others questioning his ability and right to make his own decisions. Both peers and adults wanted him to be like everybody else and were threatened when he resisted their pressures. Yet he knew that he had to communicate better with his mother. He opened himself to accept his mother's love even as he disagreed with her advice.

Jason was responsible in two ways. First, he was responsive; that is, he was free to exercise his option to say no to certain things and yes to others. He responded negatively to values he felt were false, like his friends' attention to fashion and appearances. At other times he responded positively to values he felt were important, such as a college education and better communication with his mother. Second, he was responsible in the sense of being accountable to others as well as to himself. He rightly sensed that he should never surrender his freedom to another by conforming to the roar of the crowd when he dissented from what the crowd was supporting. He was accountable to his parents. He shared his views with his father, who gave Jason the space and freedom he needed by listening sympathetically. Most significant, he gradually became more responsible in relating to his mother.

RESPECTING PERSONS

The next two stories are narrated by students who felt demeaned by authority figures at school and in the work place. The first narrator is Rachel, who tells of her experience as a first-year student when she visited her theology professor in his office, asking him for help in trying to understand why she did poorly on her first test. The second narrator, David, a college junior, describes his job interning at a museum as part of his academic program. He tells about his negative experience working under the supervision of the museum director. Both narrators explain why they thought the professor and director acted unjustly.

The Abusive Professor

"During my first semester in college, I experienced a painful encounter with my theology professor and learned a lesson I will never forget. I had always enjoyed the stimulation created within a religion classroom, that is, up until my first college course, called "The Problem of God." I thought I understood the materials we were studying in class, but it wasn't until I saw the low grade I received on my first test that I knew I apparently did not. I didn't want to do poorly again in the future. With exam in hand, I went to see the professor during his regular office hours.

"From the moment I entered the room, I felt a distance. Nervous about my first informal meeting with a college professor (he was a priest as well), I asked, 'Would you be able to maybe explain some of your comments on my exam?' He proceeded to read his succinct comments written in the margins of my exam. He did not elaborate or rephrase his remarks so that I might understand what he meant. Then he asked in an abrasive tone: 'What is it you don't understand?' I did not expect this sort of response from a professor, and certainly not from a religious. He communicated with short, quick answers and through his body language—distant and unapproachable, a language I certainly did not speak or understand. He made it clear to me that he did not want to help me and that I was wasting his time.

"Midway through the meeting, with hands folded across his chest and legs crossed, he sat back in his large winged chair, paused, and asked, 'I'm sorry, where *did* you go to high school?' so as to imply my lack of preparedness. I answered him with confidence, as my high school is one of the top college prep schools in the nation. So as to expedite this excruciating process, I told him that I felt I understood his comments a little better now, and thanked him for his time. I stood up and left. Upon closing his door (and with a little bit of a slam), I started to cry.

"I walked back to my dorm with tears of confusion and disgust streaming down my face. I turned to my resident adviser in my dorm, who, along with a friend of mine, listened as I told of the experience. They suggested that I see my academic dean, which I did. After listening to my experience, the dean told me she would speak with the professor.

"The professor made no attempt to contact me or talk to me after class. The class moved on, business as usual. During class discussions, I started noticing the professor paying considerable amounts of attention to the men, calling on them more frequently, allowing them to speak more freely, while virtually ignoring the women. I completed the course, passing with a good grade and with disgust for this professor. Post-graduation, I've seen him at many university events. I see him but he doesn't see me. I am invisible to him. He shows no sign of ever having met me.

"My parents helped by listening and understanding. As it turned out, 'The Problem of God' course created, for me, a true problem *about* God and about my Catholic faith. It forced me to question why it was that I allowed this man to treat me the way that he did. Multiple situations within the Catholic Church, both personal and distant, contributed to my church-going hiatus. During that time, I questioned my faith, challenged it, and made sure that it definitely is a reflection of what and who I want to be.

"Coming from a family strong in faith and dedicated to serving God, I am always ready to engage in new relationships, as long as the relationship brings out the best in both involved. I have several wonderfully established relationships with priests. I see a priest as one of the many different leaders of the church. They have earned my trust throughout the course of my life.

"I consider my professor's treatment unjust for the following reason: he abused his authority, making me feel unworthy and nonexistent. I respect authority when used appropriately. In this circumstance, it certainly was not. I went to my teacher in search of guidance. Little did I know that what I was given was not exactly guidance, but a lesson about injustice."

THE MANIPULATIVE BOSS

"In my junior year of college I accepted a job as an intern at a museum, a position which, at first, seemed to be ideal. I got along well with my boss and with the other workers. Then in the summer the situation began to deteriorate. The main problem was that the director, my boss, took on too many projects and consequently began to demand more and more work from us. My contract called for twenty hours; now I was being asked to put in between thirty and forty hours a week. Moreover, I would sometimes be expected to work weekends, and thus miss family vacations. I would be called at 2:00 or 3:00 a.m. and told to appear at work.

"Nonetheless, I decided to stick it out. I did present the situation to the boss, and for a short time, things improved. But then she resumed her former practice of over-scheduling and demanding extra hours. Consequently, some people resigned; I stayed, mostly out of a false sense of duty. I felt that it was good community work. I really did believe in the project, though I objected to how the director was administering and supervising it. Our relationship became strained, especially as she began to use hard language in speaking to me and to blame me for other people's mistakes or bad projects. I felt that I was being used as a scapegoat. The relationship was really bad.

"I consulted with a friend and then a Jesuit priest. My friend, heading off to the Army corps to do something that he did not want to do, offered me a kind of deal: 'You do this job you don't like and I'll do this job that I don't like and we will strengthen each other.' The Jesuit priest took a more developmental approach, asking me why I was staying in the job. 'What are you getting out of the experience?' He suggested I pay more attention to my interior movements and that I discuss the situation with my boss. I decided, finally, to stay because I believed the work was important and I had given my word. Since this work was part of a school project that was to be evaluated by my director, I asked to have my evaluation changed from a letter grade to credit/no-credit, because I feared that she might give me a low grade.

"In reviewing the whole experience, I have asked myself whether I would have acted differently today. Yes, I would have quit immediately! In light of that work experience, I would be far more critical of my sense of duty or honor in such a situation. I have come to learn that you can only stop destructive behavior by confronting it, and by never allowing yourself to be used by another. Later, in a visit overseas, I could see clearly how depressed I had become; how I had been working out of a sense of pleasing someone whom I did not respect, and who did not respect me. My sense of self had been depleted; I felt that I had failed. However, once I was away from the situation, I gained a healthier perspective on the whole situation. I saw clearly how irrational and punitive my boss had become. I recognized that her behavior was abnormal, like her manipulating me by calling me 'son' while gradually increasing her unreasonable demands."

Both stories illustrate how authority figures can misuse their power by demeaning persons studying or working under their direction. Both students judged that the professor's and director's actions were morally wrong. Rachel said her professor's behavior was unjust because he made her "feel unworthy and nonexistent." In the office the professor communicated to Rachel that she was not worth his time and even hinted that she was unprepared to do college-level work (which Rachel later demonstrated was false). In the classroom and later at other university events when the professor and the student were in the same room, he seemed unaware of her. She also sensed in him a bias against women by his habitual focus on the male students while ignoring the female students in classroom discussions.

David called his director's conduct manipulative. He felt manipulated in at least two ways: first, she used him as a scapegoat for all the "sins" that his fellow workers allegedly committed; second, she called him "son," perhaps to manipulate him into thinking that there was a special parental bond between them that called for his being loyal and obedient, which, in her mind, might have meant that he faithfully carry out the extra tasks she assigned him. Like a dutiful though unhappy son, he did the job in order to please his boss. It didn't work. David became depressed and acknowledged that his "sense of self had been depleted."

In both instances, the authorities affronted the *dignity* of and damaged the *self-esteem* of the students by failing to respect them as persons. In telling their stories, both students came to a new level of self-awareness. Even as they rightly pinned the blame on the authority figure, they also questioned their own reticence in tolerating the abusive treatment. As a result of their self-reflection, they gained insight into themselves as free persons who had to uphold their dignity and in the future to resist inhumane treatment. Rachel said, "It forced me to question why it was that I allowed this man to treat me the way that he did." This involved examining her faith, which she implied must develop in order to better guide and strengthen the person she wants to become. David also learned from his work experience that his strong sense of duty and desire to please must never again block him from confronting destructive behavior.

PERSONS FOR OTHERS

Like the previous narrators, the final two storytellers are concerned with their sense of self. In addition, they also came to see themselves in relation to others, especially to those others who lack the basic goods that these two students had taken for granted. Both are deeply reflective students who are sensitive to the plight of others and want to help improve others' lives.

A Different Kind of Love

Isaac came to the new awareness after a hurtful encounter with his baseball coach that led to his quitting the team in order to help care for his sick mother. Thereafter, a new world opened up. He contrasts two loves, each of which he knew would take him down a different path.

"I haven't faced that many injustices; in a way, I have been privileged. In my first year at this school I made the baseball team. Unfortunately, my mother fell seriously ill. This was a disturbing time for me because I felt that I should be with my father and family, helping them to support my mother. I admit that I was reacting out of emotion. Anyway, I told the coach that my mother was very sick, that I had to return home and so would miss some practices. The coach responded that my absence from practice meant that I was not serious about baseball. He said. 'This could hurt your playing here.' Immediately, I quit the baseball team.

"I was hurt by his reaction and his lack of understanding. Later, the coach tried to repair the situation, but it was never the same for me. I felt that I could never again fully trust him; the fun of playing the game at this school was lost.

"I recognized that I had the drive in here [Isaac pointed to his heart] to play ball, but chose not to play varsity ball here. My brother and my dad understood, and they were very supportive. My dad has been my key role model. He told me that he was proud of the decision I made to leave the team to be with the family. When I recounted this to a close friend, she said, 'You are a better person for moving off the team.' And I have done a lot of important things that I would not have done if I had stayed on the team.

"Over time, I felt that God helped me work through my negative feelings toward the coach. I came to see that there were more important things than baseball. God seemed to have widened my interests and enlarged my heart to include spiritual interests like making a retreat and volunteering to serve others. I became more deeply immersed in my studies and developed other areas of interests: doing a retreat, traveling to Ecuador, and making new friends. It's a kind of love different from that which I had, and still have in a way, for baseball. Had I stayed on the baseball team, I would have teammates, but I have now developed friendships with wonderful people whom I would otherwise never have met. When I came to the university, I majored in business, but I have switched to a religious studies major with an English minor. These experiences and studies have touched me and moved me to want to help people. I do not know exactly what I will be doing. After graduation I hope to spend a year in Ecuador. Whatever I do, it will be some kind of service. The original decision that I made to quit baseball because of the reaction of the coach, which I think was unjust, caused me to rethink my priorities. It changed my life. I still feel the hurt but realize that I gained freedom to pursue other aspects of my personality as well as spiritual interests. And so having lived with that decision, I am convinced that it was the right one for me, even though it arose from an experience that was hurtful."

WHY SHOULD I GET INVOLVED?

Justin's journey began in high school when he saw film documentaries about the dismal working situations of workers and was moved to do something. He spends time trying to help others see the injustice that he sees.

"In high school, I came to know about third-world workers—men, women, and children—laboring under oppressive conditions. I first saw them in documentaries and was shocked by how badly they were treated. I looked at films that showed how their jobs separated them from their families. Then I began to read about the terrible situation of workers. I was moved to do something. But then I asked myself: 'Why should I get involved? And what could I do?' I'm not sure what moved me, but I felt that their hard labor was in some way connected to me because through their work they produce commodities that come to my table, often as a luxury item, like cocoa or coffee. The way that the bosses degraded these people stirred something in me. I wanted to do something about this because I enjoy privileges and rights that they lack.

"Whatever my motives, and I still struggle to name them, I decided to create a social justice club in my high school. My classmates and I began to study free trade and globalization, how the open markets affect the workers abroad. One time we organized a rally in front of Starbucks to raise awareness of the workers' conditions. In my senior year I was elected vice president of the Student Council and so had the opportunity to organize a school assembly during Human Rights Week. We focused on free trade and globalization. The assembly program featured a film that I put together by using clips from documentaries. The film narrated personal stories of workers in India and the Ivory Coast, showing how free-trade policies play out for peasants working on farms and in factories. They receive low wages and work long hours on cocoa plantations, laboring under poor working conditions. Foremen abuse the workers, making them feel worthless. Employment practices keep members of families isolated from one another.

"The film also showed how interests of powerful nations and corporations shape the terms of world trade. The competitive market drives the corporations to maximize profits, which translates into low wages and pressure tactics aimed at driving the workers to produce more quality products. Employers often degrade workers by sexually harassing the women and whipping the men. They use other punitive measures, like withholding pay and forcing the employees to work longer hours with no additional compensation. The workers are vulnerable, especially because they are unorganized and lack alternatives for making a living. My sense is that the assembly had a powerful impact on many of the students.

"Now that I am in college, I continue to study how multinational corporations function and how they impact unorganized workers in the Third World. Our Licensing Oversight Committee at the university invited two Bangladeshi women to our school last semester to speak to students. As workers in a garment factory contracted to Wal-Mart, these women joined up with an NGO that pushes for labor rights for workers, and together they organized the female workers in this factory and won on the issue of maternity rights for the workers.

"The major task of changing the unjust policies of free trade to practices of fair trade and to just working conditions begins with helping people, rich and poor alike, to know what's going on. One huge obstacle that I have encountered is awakening people to their indifference. Elie Wiesel's line from one of his essays aptly sums up the problem: 'Indifference, to me, is the epitome of evil.'"

The two stories have different beginnings but similar endings. Isaac loved baseball, but when the coach forced him to make a decision whether to remain with the team or to be with his ailing mother, he chose to quit the team and to assist his family in caring for his mother. This hurtful experience became the occasion for thinking hard and long about his true values. Helped by his father and friends, he realized that his love for his mother, family, and friends was "a different kind of love" that exceeded his love for baseball. He felt that the reaction of the coach was a turning point in his life. Realigning his priorities, Isaac made changes that led him to move in the direction of serving others: making a retreat, visiting Ecuador, and changing his major to religious studies. The injustice and working through the pain it caused him, ironically, became the occasion for discovering a different kind of love that turned him to others in need—first his family and then the needs of the poor.

The turning point for Justin seems to have been his vicarious experience of injustice. Watching documentaries that graphically showed the misery of workers in third-world nations, he was moved to learn more and eventually to become personally involved. Although he does not mention love as a motive for his concern for the workers, his deep concern for them suggests that he has a heart of compassion. He sees himself linked with the workers, wants to help them, and has already taken action to make known the terrible working conditions of the laborers.

REFLECTION ON LOVE AND JUSTICE

In reading these personal accounts of negative contrast experiences, we have gained different perspectives on justice, love, and other virtues. Justice in its most general sense is a virtue that empowers a person to give everyone what is due. What is due all persons includes respecting their personhood and giving them equal treatment precisely because they are human beings. This means that discriminatory practices, racial slurs, and other forms of prejudice that unfavorably and inaccurately prejudge and isolate individuals and groups are wrong. Grace was deeply scarred by growing up and going to school in a racist township. Aided by her loving and wise mother, this courageous young woman struggled through a hostile environment and has come to believe in herself and to be free.

Rachel and David were victims of a similar form of injustice. Their self-esteem was injured by a college professor and a museum director who took advantage of their considerable power to humiliate them. Rachel was strengthened after the devastating experience with her teacher. She expressed a willingness to form new relationships "as long as the relationship brings out the best in both involved." David also grew by coming to see that his virtue of duty or loyalty needed to be balanced by other virtues, like courageously standing up for his own values and protecting his sense of self.

Why are affronts to one's dignity unjust? Immanuel Kant said that human beings, because they are endowed with a rational will, have an intrinsic worth or dignity. Human beings act in accordance with their dignity by regarding themselves and every other human being as lawmakers. As legislators, persons act morally when they make decisions based on maxims that are binding on everyone, including the legislators. If the maxim applies to some persons and not others, then the moral agent is treating someone unfairly, or in Kant's words, he or she is using them as a "mere means." We treat people with dignity by regarding them as ends by acting according to maxims that are universally applicable. This means that as a professor or boss, I should not act on maxims that discriminate between persons. Rachel's professor, for example, habitually welcomed his male students to participate in the discussion while virtually ignoring his female students. David's boss used David as a scapegoat for the failings of the other workers. Kant expressed this conviction in the second formulation of his categorical imperative: "Act so that you treat humanity, whether in your own person or in that of another, always as an end and never as a means only."[15] To violate this moral absolute is unjust.

In the Roman Catholic tradition, the Second Vatican Council likewise upholds "the sublime dignity of human person, who stands above all things and whose rights and duties are universal and inviolable." Everyone should therefore have "respect for the human person: everyone should look upon his neighbor (without any exception) as another self."[16] The church grounds human dignity in divine revelation. All men and women are created in God's image; they have the same calling and destiny. Such high regard for the dignity of the human person extends beyond religious circles. The first article of the UN Declaration of Human Rights states that "all human beings are born free and equal in dignity and rights."

The virtues of love, justice, courage, and responsibility come together in the stories of Jennifer and Jason, who became responsible persons at a young age by walking courageously, often alone, along uncharted paths. Jennifer moved through a dark valley, a void created by her mother, who became addicted, and a father who became psychologically incapable of being a parent to his two children. Jennifer quietly and courageously took responsibility for her life. Injustice ironically taught her to be fair to herself and to care for herself, which we might call a rightly ordered love of herself. Love for self, theologian Edward Vacek writes, "means both that that we affirm those dynamisms in ourselves that foster our identity as whole and that we decline to affirm those dynamisms that lead either to disintegration or degradation."[17] He calls this type of love "agapaic self-love." Love of self is illustrated in Jason's story in which he struggled to find himself by being responsible to his value system and caring for himself. This meant resisting the shallowness of his culture that pays too much attention to appearances and exerts pressure on everyone to conform to its materialistic standards. Jason felt that his mother's pressure was the hardest to bear, but he learned through their painful exchanges that she really loved him and had his best interests at heart.

Isaac and Justin came to see the bigger picture of what social justice involves and to grow in compassion for those suffering from social injustices.
Isaac, following his visit to Ecuador, felt moved to do service work that
would put him in contact with the poor. After seeing documentaries, Justin
began to connect his lifestyle with the labor of the poor, whose work brought
food and luxury items to his table. His study showed how today's global
economy with its emphasis on free trade was not fair trade when it exploited
the workers. He perceptively saw that the problem was structural, and he
wants to help change social structures, which he said were patently unjust.

Both Isaac and Justin came to be involved with the poor indirectly through
troublesome experiences: Isaac, through a painful encounter with the baseball coach, began to rethink his goals, and Justin through meaningful vicarious experiences of the suffering of poor workers, which moved him in the
direction of helping people in the First World to become aware of the unjust
treatment of the poor. While both have more studies ahead of them, we
might project that they will be involved with the poor and downtrodden in
the years ahead. Both share a conviction that they are part of a fabric of
social relationships and so must work to help others in need. Both have
concerns for the poor; this suggests that they will continue to devote part of
their future work helping them to improve their lives.

We have seen through stories of negative contrast experiences how seven
individuals came to realize their potential to become more fully human: to
achieve a greater sense of self, to become more responsible, more attuned to
what is just and loving, and to become persons who care for the poor and
downtrodden. Their reflective journeys reflect an approach to moral living
called virtue ethics. It emphasizes moral character, or what makes a person
morally good. In contrast to persons who make choices on the basis of consequences or who determine how they will chose on the basis of rules, the
virtuous individual habitually acts in accordance with virtues or moral
excellences deeply engrained in his or her character.

The foundation of the virtue approach to ethics is the person's community. The community, like each individual within it, has a story with a long
history (a meta-narrative). It expresses the people's long-term common goal
or *telos* and the institutions, customs, and virtues that help the people to
reach the goal. In the following chapter we read meta-narratives of faith
communities, which speak of liberation, justification, and reconciliation and
which give us new insight into the meaning of love and justice.

RESOURCES

Dicussion Questions

1. What does Schillebeeckx mean by a "negative contrast experience"?
   What does it disclose about the *humanum*? Could you give an example
   of a negative contrast experience from your own history?

2. What is the basic meaning of justice? Identify two types of injustice, illustrating each type from the stories found in this chapter.
3. How does love play a role for the narrators as they resisted the injustices that they encountered?
4. In light of Grace's story and Gordon Allport's ideas about prejudice, how would you approach a friend who frequently makes derogatory remarks about black people or people who are gay?
5. David's story about working for a manipulative boss suggests that there is something in us that will eventually rebel against something that is bad for us even when others try to get us to think that the bad is really good. What blocked David from seeing that he should resist the manipulative behavior of his boss?
6. Using the approach of negative contrast experience, tell of an experience in which you felt that you were treated unjustly. Or share an experience in which you assisted another who was a victim of injustice. Describe the injustice. How did it affect you? How did you respond to it? What would you do differently if you were to face the same experience today?

Suggested Readings

Allport, Gordon W. *The Nature of Prejudice*. 25th anniversary edition. Reading, MA: Perseus Books, 1979.

Burghardt, Walter J. *Justice: A Global Adventure*. Maryknoll, NY: Orbis Books, 2004.

Martin Luther King, Jr. *Where Do We Go from Here: Chaos or Community?* New York: Harper and Row, 1967.

Meilaender, Gilbert C. *The Theory and Practice of Virtue*. Notre Dame, IN: University of Notre Dame Press, 1984.

Schillebeeckx, Edward, *The Schillebeeckx Reader*. Edited by Robert Schreiter. New York: Crossroad, 1984.

Vacek, Edward Collins. *Love, Human and Divine: The Heart of Christian Ethics*. Washington, DC: Georgetown University Press, 1994.

NOTES

[1] Oswald Von Nell-Breuning, *Reorganization of Social Economy*, trans. and ed. Bernard W. Dempsey (New York: The Bruce Publishing Co., 1936), 337.

[2] Aristotle, *Nichomachean Ethics*, 5.13, quoted from *What Is Justice?* 2nd ed., ed. Robert C. Solomon and Mark C. Murphy (New York: Oxford University Press, 2000), 36.

[3] Edward Vacek, *Love, Human and Divine: The Heart of Christian Ethics* (Washington, DC: Georgetown University Press, 1994), 34.

[4] William Shakespeare, *William Shakespeare: The Complete Works,* compact ed., ed. Stanley Wells and Gary Taylor (Oxford: Clarendon Press, 1988), Sonnet 116.

[5] I am grateful to Howard J. Gray, S.J., who assisted me in conducting the interviews.

[6] Edward Schillebeeckx, *The Schillebeeckx Reader*, ed. Robert Schreiter (New York: Crossroad, 1984), 17, 100.

[7] Ibid., 17–18.

[8] Edward Schillebeeckx, *The Understanding of Faith*, trans. N. D. Smith (New York: The Seabury Press, 1974), 65.

[9] Ibid., 92.

[10] Gregory Baum, "Human Rights: An Ethical Perspective," *The Ecumenist* 1, no. 4 (May-June 1994), 64.

[11] Dictionary.com, "Racism," http://dictionary.reference.com/browse/racism (accessed on December 18, 2006).

[12] Gordon W. Allport, *The Nature of Prejudice*, 25th anniv. ed. (Reading, MA: Perseus Books, 1979), 9.

[13] Ibid., 12.

[14] Martin Luther King, Jr., "Where Do We Go from Here?" Address made to the Tenth Anniversary Convention of the S.C.L.C. Atlanta, Georgia, August 16, 1967, http://www.indiana.edu/~ivieweb/mlkwhere.html (accessed on December 20, 2006).

[15] Immanuel Kant, *Foundations of the Metaphysics of Morals*, trans. Lewis White Beck (Indianapolis: The Bobbs-Merrill Company, 1959), 56–57.

[16] Vatican Council II, *Gaudium et Spes*, in *The Conciliar and Post Conciliar Documents*, rev. ed., ed. Austin Flannery (Boston, MA: Daughters of St. Paul, 1988), nos. 26–27.

[17] Vacek, *Love, Human and Divine*, 241–42.

2

LOVE AND JUSTICE
IN COVENANT

Biblical Sources

Steadfast love and faithfulness will meet;
Righteousness and peace will kiss each other.
—Psalm 85:10–11

This chapter examines the meaning of love and justice in the Bible. It also explores how these two terms link with each other and how they provide us with a moral vision for our virtue ethics. This investigation concentrates principally, but not exclusively, on three books of the Bible: Deuteronomy, the Letter of Paul to the Romans, and parables in the Gospel according to Luke. These writings provide profound insight into love and justice. All three books address these and related virtues within a context of a covenant relationship between God and God's people. In Deuteronomy, Moses convenes his fearful, despondent, and unfaithful people in order to encourage them to recommit themselves to God as they stand on the threshold of the Promised Land. In Romans, Paul speaks of a new covenant sealed in Christ's blood that is poured out for the redemption of humankind. In Luke, Jesus journeys to Jerusalem, where he will encounter great hostility and death; on the way, he tells two remarkable parables that dramatize a father's forgiveness of a spendthrift son and a Samaritan's surprising care for a deadly enemy.

The chapter probes the meaning of love and justice within the framework of a covenant. A covenant is a solemn agreement that unites two or more parties in love and binds them in justice. (The covenant of marriage, for example, calls the couple to be faithful and love and honor each other in sickness and in health.) Enslaved by the Egyptians, the Hebrews encounter a liberating God who frees them in a revolutionary way and then invites them to form a covenant. We introduce the covenant with a modern parable that moves from enslavement to freedom to tender love. Like our narratives in Chapter 1, this parable reveals something about the *humanum,* the kind of person we wish to become, and about the virtues and relationship that empower us to become more deeply human.

A PARABLE

The Ukrainian family of eight children was struggling to survive. When a businessman from the neighborhood offered a small sum of money to the parents for one of their daughters, promising that he would get her a job and educate her in America, they took the offer and volunteered their sixteen-year-old adopted daughter Nina. She was beautiful, especially when she smiled, but most of the time she looked sad. Her parents' decision sunk her into deeper depression. For Nina, it was another sign that they never really wanted her. Her foster parents had been constantly critical of her, rarely expressing to the child any affection or tenderness. In fact, they abused her. When she was older, they made hard demands, including taking her out of school to look after the little ones while the parents worked outside the home. Nina became very unhappy and her self-confidence plummeted. Being sold to an employer was the final blow that convinced her that she was unloved. The transaction, however, gave her a glimmer of hope. She could have a better life and make lots of money in America. Gathering the few belongings that she possessed, she walked out of the house with the businessman who promised her a better life.

When she arrived in New York, however, she was devastated to learn that her job was not working with fabrics or serving as a nanny. It was prostitution. When she resisted, the slave traffickers beat her and threatened to kill her. "Besides you owe us thousands of dollars for transporting you here from Kiev." Having been duped by the businessman and still furious at her parents for selling her into bondage, she began the dark journey of the sex slave trade. Every day she would have sex with at least a dozen men, always under the scrutiny of the madams and the pimp who kept a close watch on her. Working in the brothel for a full year, she grew bitter and alienated from everyone. All the profits went to the pimp and madams who kept her imprisoned in her locked room. She seriously considered taking her life, but when one of her "regulars" slipped her a bundle of cash on the side, she began to look for opportunities to escape, fully aware that if she were caught, they would kill her.

Early one morning, while all were asleep, Nina quietly opened her bedroom door, which she had managed to keep slightly ajar after her last client left. Tiptoeing down the stairs, she moved into the kitchen and left through the back door. Once on the street she took a taxi to the Greyhound Bus terminal, where she bought a ticket for Chicago. Upon her arrival, she managed to find a job as a maid in a hotel in Chicago's loop.

One morning while having a cup of coffee in the hotel just before beginning her day's work, she saw a handsome young man sit down at an adjoining table. He smiled and then asked to borrow the sugar from her table. He thanked her and then struck up a conversation. He was courteous and kind.

But she responded coldly, trying to keep him at a distance. She was surprised that he was not put off by her heavy accent and cynical and crude way of expressing herself. Fearful that he might uncover who she was and what she had been doing, she excused herself, saying that she had to go to work.

By chance he met her later that day as they both were walking along the corridor of the hotel. He greeted her and asked if she would have dinner with him. She refused. Yet the next day, he saw her and again asked her out. She reluctantly agreed, though she was suspicious and scared, thinking that he wanted what all the men she had met wanted. But over dinner, she found herself instinctively trusting the man, who was gentle, sensitive, and refreshing, so different from the men she had slept with at the brothel in New York. Yet she grew more nervous as they talked. Trying to sever the relationship before it went too far, she told him everything about her past and how she happened to be in Chicago. "He's going to bolt after learning all this," she thought. David listened sympathetically, and to her utter amazement, he wanted to go out with her again. Sharing her story seemed to draw him closer to her. She in turn became less defensive, grew less cynical, and for the first time in her life, she felt accepted and appreciated. Gradually, she began to feel beautiful inside, and she knew the feeling came from David's love for her. She started to take better care of her appearance and to smile. His gentleness and respect made her feel like a brand new woman. They became absorbed in each other, developing a mutual love. One evening, he popped the question. "Nina, will you marry me?" She thought for a moment—an eternity for David—"Where did this good man come from? What did I do to deserve this love? Such a gift!" She looked trustfully into his eyes: "Yes! Yes!"

This modern parable has an ancient source. Ezekiel tells a folktale about a woman who symbolizes the people of Jerusalem. Regarding her as a financial liability, her parents reject her from birth and abandon her. But God passes by and, finding this unwanted girl baby exposed and near death, is moved with compassion. God becomes her foster parent, nourishes and loves her: "I passed by you and saw you flailing about in your blood. As you lay in your blood, I said to you, 'Live! And grow up like a plant of the field.' You grew up and became tall and arrived at full womanhood; your breasts were formed, and your hair had grown; yet you were naked and bare" (Ez 16:6–7). Like Nina, the maiden was unloved and vulnerable. But moved by God's unconditional and faithful love, she became a mature and dearly beloved person. The divine guardian, like David in the parable, passed by again and attracted by her beauty desires to marry her. God proposes marriage, using words of the covenant. "I passed by you again and looked on you; you were at the age for love. I spread the edge of my cloak over you, and covered your nakedness: I pledged myself to you and entered into a covenant with you," says the Lord God, "and you became mine" (Ez 16:8–9). As the allegory continues, the maiden becomes unfaithful. But in spite of all her infidelities—

she defiles herself by engaging in cult prostitution and paying homage to false gods—God nonetheless stands by her as a forgiving and faithful husband. Like Ezekiel, the Deuteronomist uses the metaphor of covenant in telling another version of the story in which God frees an enslaved people, making her the chosen one, though she is frequently unfaithful to the mutual pledge.

LOVE AND JUSTICE IN DEUTERONOMY

No book in the Bible insists so emphatically on exclusive fidelity to God as does the book of Deuteronomy.[1] This is remarkable because during the two hundred years it took to compose this book (from the mid-eighth to the mid-sixth centuries B.C.), the people of Israel encountered war, slaughter, exile, and slavery at the hands of their neighbors. Sometimes called a law book (*deuteronomy* literally means "second law"), Deuteronomy consists of a series of speeches or sermons attributed to Moses, who calls the people to become in practice what they pledged in covenant. According to the book's setting, he speaks to a disheartened, nomadic people squatting in their tents on the sandy desert and terrified at the prospect of taking possession of the land.

The book harkens back to the time of Moses in order to show continuity of the tradition. It tells people how to behave when they get into the land, but it is really a reform movement initiated after they had been in the land a long while. Deuteronomy originated in the north, when Assyrians were threatening the Israelites, but was brought south after the fall of the Northern Kingdom. The Southern Kingdom, called Judea, initiated a reform movement when Assyria was no longer a threat. The reform hoped to prevent such disasters from happening again. And so we hear Moses urging the people to halt their self-destructive lifestyle, pleading with them throughout the book to love God and to be faithful to the covenant so that they might live and enjoy a prosperous life in the Promised Land.

Deuteronomy begins: "These are the words that Moses spoke" (Dt 1:1). The words *(debārīm)* are laws that define the formal agreement or covenant between two parties, each of whom assumes certain obligations.[2] The two parties are God (Yahweh), who initiated the relationship, and the Hebrew people whom God liberated from Egypt. Their relationship, however, faces a crisis. The people are reluctant to fight the enemy occupying the territory that God promised them. It is time to move on, Moses tells them. At his bidding the Israelites climb the hill country of the Amorites, reaching Kadesh-barnea, where Moses commands them to do battle with the Amorites. They stubbornly resist his orders. Instead, they implore him to send scouts ahead, who spy on the Moabites and report back that the land God has promised is "a good land." The people nonetheless refuse to go up, fearing defeat, and so return to their tents, grumbling against God in an act of rebellion. In this anti–holy war mentality the warriors utter what are the most shocking words in the book: "It is because the Lord hates us that he has brought us out of the land of Egypt, to hand us over to the Amorites to destroy us" (Dt 1:27). The people view God through mistrustful eyes. God becomes their enemy! The Israelites at this stage of the journey not only have a bad conscience but a false consciousness. The deity, their paranoia suggests, is out to destroy them. They block out of their memory everything God had done for them. Stewing in their tents, the one-time revolutionaries are now anti–holy war renegades. Moses, prophet and mediator, is living out his last days in the wilderness. Because of his people's sins, he will never set foot on Canaanite soil. None-theless, Moses speaks hopefully and compassionately to his people. He again gathers all the people at the foot of a mountain called Horeb (Sinai) in the land of Moab, where the people had recently made a covenant with God.

REMEMBERING YOUR ROOTS

Gathering this unhappy crowd with its depressed consciousness for a sec-ond round of talks would not have been a joyous prospect for Moses. He strategizes over how to soften their hearts of stone and somehow move them to recommit themselves to the covenant and its demands.[3] His strategy is to put the people in touch with their past experiences in which Yahweh was present as their liberator and rearguard in very difficult circumstances. If Moses could successfully nudge their memories so that they could recall their past experiences in which the deity was present as a loving and just God, then perhaps they could once again become a people open, grateful, free, and courageous who could embrace their God and their mission. Invit-ing them to remember, however, would be risky. Would Moses be able to engage the memory of this people, now suffering from amnesia, and to fa-cilitate their forming a new consciousness?[4] Though their resistance is high, Moses takes the risk. As he launches into his travel narrative, showing them "film clips" of their past, he repeatedly calls out his commands, drilling them like a coach drills the team: "Remember . . . Do not forget . . . Hear, O Israel . . . Set your heart to . . . Give heed." He wants them to be aware: "But take care and watch yourselves closely, so as neither to forget the things that your eyes have seen nor to let them slip from your mind all the days of your life" (Dt 4:9).

What things? Moses wants them to remember their experiences of sla-very, exodus, fire blazing on a mountaintop, and a covenant relationship. Remember, Moses exclaims, that you once were slaves in Egypt, a "no people," but now you are a people because of your liberating God, who passionately desires to be permanently identified with you. Moses puts it this way:

Has anything as great as this ever happened or has its like ever been heard of? Has any people ever heard the voice of a god speaking out of a fire, as you have heard, and lived? Or has any god ever attempted to go and take a nation for himself from the midst of another nation, by trials, by signs and wonders, by war, by a mighty hand and an out-stretched arm, and by terrifying displays of power, as the Lord your God did for you in Egypt before your very eyes? (Dt 4:32b-34)

This kind of memory narrative that recaps the people's actual experience challenges them to move to a new understanding and to a higher form of consciousness. The new understanding involves an initial insight in which they realize that it will make a tremendous difference in their lives whether they give their allegiance to Yahweh or to other gods.[5] This insight comes only after the people have truly understood the nature of these gods—what they stand for and what they demand. They need to know what kind of justice these gods administer. And so Moses paints a portrait of Yahweh, whose justice brings forth blessings (life, land, and prosperity), and of the other unnamed gods, whose justice brings forth curses (adversity, destruc-tion, and death). He puts the finishing touches on this portrait at the conclu-sion of his sermon: "See I have set before you today life and prosperity, death and adversity. . . . Choose life so that you and your descendants may live, loving the Lord your God, obeying him, and holding fast to him; for that means life to you and length of days" (Dt 30:15, 19b-20).

Moses also has to convince the people that Yahweh loves them. Their embittered words still ring in his ears: "It is because the Lord hates us that he has brought us out of Egypt." And so he addresses their unspoken ques-tion—Does God love us?—by drawing upon their collective memory of past experiences. Moses then interprets their experiences: "He [Yahweh] loved your ancestors and chose their descendants after them and brought you out of Egypt with his own presence, by his great power, driving out before you nations greater and mightier than yourselves. . . . Therefore, acknowledge today and take to heart that the Lord is God in heaven above and on the earth beneath; there is no other. Keep his statutes and his commandments" (Dt 4:37-38, 40). Moses' persuasive type of argument moves from the in-dicative (remembering our days of liberation) to the imperative (keep the commandments). Looking at the indicative-imperative structure from an-other perspective, we hear Moses arguing: Because you have experienced God's love and justice, you ought to love God and be just to others, espe-cially to those others who are what you were: slaves, sojourners, and poor.

LOVE LINKED TO JUSTICE

What does Deuteronomy mean by God's love and God's justice? The Hebrew verb for "love" is 'ahāb, which like the noun, chesed, connotes a love that is compassionate, gratuitous, and loyal. Moses speaks of God's love as loyal or faithful *(chesed)* that lasts to "the thousandth generation of those who love me and keep my commandments" (Dt 5:10). Both terms for love express a gratuitous love that gives without expecting to get something in return; nor does the lover bestow gifts in order to exploit the people (qualities that typify the gods of ancient Greece and Rome). God's love gives for the sake of the other's good. Yet it is a commanded love, a love that makes demands that must be obeyed. Jesus also links love with obeying God's commands: "If you keep my commandments, you will abide in my love" (Jn 15:10).

In Deuteronomy, justice is similar to love in at least four ways. First, both are absolutely essential for healthy relationships, whether the relationship is between God and human beings or simply between human beings. Second, both love and justice express a loyalty to the other. Third, both are graced actions—God helps persons to love and to be just by being present and loving them. Finally, both are commands—neither is optional. God commands the people to love and to be just because God is love and because God is just and calls people who are created in God's image and likeness to become holy.

The Hebrew Bible has many terms for justice, but we shall mention only the two principal ones used in Deuteronomy, called *tsedeq* or *tsedāqâ* (fem.), which is translated "justice" or "righteousness," and *mishpāt*, which is translated "judgment." Deuteronomy also uses a related term, *nāqām*, which means either "vengeance" or "vindication." God brings about justice by vindicating those who are treated unjustly or by wreaking vengeance on Israel's enemies.

Justice as *tsedeq* or *tsedāqâ* means "fidelity to the demands of a relationship."[6] God is just in God's very being (Ps 145:17); God is just in the way that God deals with human beings. Similarly, the covenanted people are just when they act as they should; that is, when they too are faithful to the demands or obligations spelled out in the covenant. These demands taken as a whole, called Torah, form a consensus between God and all the people concerned (for example, the tribes of Israel). The consensus is a set of shared convictions about what is right, impartial, or good.[7] This then is justice in its general sense: fidelity to a relationship built on a consensus of what is right, equitable, or good. The demands are laws that God commands and that the people of Israel agree to live by, such as Deuteronomy's most general formulation, "Justice, and only justice, you shall pursue so that you may have life and occupy the land" (Dt 16:20). Or in another instance Moses tells the people, "If we diligently observe this entire commandment [Torah] before the Lord our God, as he has commanded us, we will be in the right [*tsedāqâ*]" (Dt 6:25).

In post-exilic scripture *tsedeq* becomes God's justice that acquits God's rebellious people of their infidelities by a gracious judgment that brings them salvation or deliverance. "I bring near my righteousness; it is not far off; my salvation will not tarry" (Is 46:13). As we shall see, this activity of justice is very much like St. Paul's justification by grace, whereby God through Christ acquits a sinful people and declares them to be innocent.[8]

The second term for justice, *mishpāt*, shows how justice in its general formulation is concretely implemented. Three things should be noted about *mishpāt*. First of all, *mishpāt*, like *tsedeq*, is predicated of God (Dt 10:18). Second, it is a specific type of justice that today we call a right. "Cursed be anyone who deprives the alien, the orphan, and the widow of justice" (Dt 27:19). Third, it is an ordinance or judgment that a judge orders to be done. Moses, in addressing how to select judges, says,

> They [judges and officials] shall render just decisions [*mishpāt*] for the people. You must not distort justice [*mishpāt*]; you must not show partiality and you must not accept bribes, for a bribe blinds the eyes of the wise and subverts the cause of those who are in the right. Justice [*tsedeq*] and only justice, you shall pursue, so that you may live and occupy the land that the Lord your God is giving you. (Dt 16:18b–20)

How then are love and justice related? God's love motivates and empowers the people to act justly. Justice makes love concrete by establishing conditions that will help foster the relationship (for example, liberating, providing land) and by prohibiting actions that would injure it (for example, infidelity). Justice specifies responsibilities and establishes boundaries. Love calls persons to love God with all their heart, mind, and soul; justice prohibits them from loving false gods. Love commands individuals to love their neighbor; justice specifies how they should love them and helps love set priorities, such as caring first for those with the greatest need. God's justice as spelled out in Torah makes the people just and keeps them alive (Dt 6:24–25).

LOVE YOUR GOD

Once Israel has become aware that her freedom is bound up with God's love, justice, and power and that the people are special in God's eyes, the people are predisposed to listen to the demands that will renew their relationship. Moses again formally addresses the people: "Hear, O Israel, the statutes and ordinances that I am addressing to you today; you shall learn them and observe them diligently" (Dt 5:1b). Moses then sets down the basic conditions for inclusion in the community of Yahweh—the Ten Commandments. These commandments constitute the ground floor of justice and are given to all the people living in the desert. They are like categorical imperatives, unconditional moral laws that apply to all human beings. The more specific laws of the Deuteronomic Code (Dt 12—26) would be given only to those who would enter the land.[9] These laws specify the kinds of love and justice that bind the people to Yahweh in the covenant.

Hebrew law, in contrast to Roman law, generally gives reasons or motives for obeying the law, as seen in the first five commandments. The first, for example, says, "I am the Lord your God who brought you out of Egypt, out of the house of slavery; you shall have no other gods before me (Dt 5:6–7). Thus the commandment relates the worship of false gods to slavery. One should avoid idolatrous practices because they enslave and oppress human beings, as the tribes of Israel in the Northern Kingdom painfully learned. The liberating God, having once freed the people from bondage in Egypt, absolutely forbids making any deals or alliances with neighboring tribes living under oppressive Canaanite kings, whose gods give legitimacy to the kings' rule. Aligning themselves with pagan nations, kings, and gods will inevitably enslave the people and lead to their death (Dt 30:15–20).

We should note again that the commands are almost always linked to what God has already done for the people out of love and justice. Yahweh liberated them from Egypt and nurtured and guided them through their tortuous and dangerous trek through the desert. Remembering this should elicit praise and thanksgiving from the people, thus motivating them to do for others what God has done for them. When people ask, "Why should we obey all these laws?" Moses does not say, "Because Yahweh and I say so!" Instead, covenantal law reminds them of their experience that concretely expresses God's love for them. Moshe Weinfeld relates a story from the *Mekhilta de-Rabbi Yishma'el* that illustrates this point.

Why were the Ten Commandments stated at the beginning of the Torah? They told a parable: It is like (a king) who entered into the city. He said to them, "I shall rule over you." They asked him, "Have you done us any good that you should rule over us?" What did he do? He built them the wall, he brought them water, he fought for them. Then he said to them: "I shall rule over you." They said to him: "Yes, Yes." Thus, the Omnipresent took Israel out of Egypt, parted the Sea for them, brought down manna, brought up the well, spread about the quail, and fought for them in the battle of Amalek. He asked them: "Shall I rule over you?" They answered: "Yes, Yes."[10]

For this reason Moses repeatedly impresses upon the people that they should keep alive in their consciousness God's active and liberating presence in their behalf.

Covenantal love is a two-way street. How are the people to love and do justice in response to what Yahweh has done for them? Moses responds with the solemn command called the great commandment, or Shema: "Hear, O Israel, the Lord is our God, the Lord alone. You shall love the Lord your God with all your heart, and with all your soul, and with all your might.

Keep these words that I am commanding you today in your heart" (Dt 6:4–6). The people are called to listen and then act by loving God. Love *('ahāb)* in this context means an exclusive and loyal commitment to Yahweh, expressed with reverence and praise and joyful thanksgiving.[11]

Moses captures these qualities of loyal commitment and affection in answer to a question he himself poses: "O Israel, what does the Lord your God require of you?" He replies, "Only to fear the Lord your God, to walk in all his ways, to love him, to serve the Lord your God with all your heart and with all your soul, and to keep the commandments of the Lord your God" (Dt 10:12–13). To love God with all your heart, soul, and might means embracing God with all one's faculties and powers. Loving God with all your heart symbolizes the mind and one's constant awareness of God's presence. Loving God with all your soul signifies readiness to give one's life for God. Loving God with all your might means committing to God all one's physical power and material means or wealth.[12] This great commandment calls for a total love that should exceed the love for any other.

Why should the people be willing to love this mysterious Being so totally? Initially, because it is in their best interest to do so, and eventually, because they are convinced that God loves them and vindicates them. In sum, human love for God is a free and affective acceptance of God's love, expressed through gratitude and praise, loyalty, service, and obedience to the law. This love is an affirmation of faith in which the community and each person within the community freely consent to be God's covenant partner according to the stipulations that define the relationship.

Love Your Neighbor

Justice is an attribute of God, who is faithful in executing justice for the people, especially for the needy: widows, orphans, debtors, foreigners, the destitute. Justice demands that the people of the covenant do for their neighbor what God has done out of love for them. Just as God freed them from oppression, so also they should free their servants from oppression.

The second love command (Love your neighbor as yourself) and its corresponding obligations undergo a significant change from the earlier writings (Exodus) to the later writings (Deuteronomy and Leviticus). Whereas Exodus says that the people should not *wrong or oppress* a resident alien (Ex 22: 21), Deuteronomy goes a step further, saying that the people should *love* strangers, providing them with food and clothing (Dt 10:18–19). Leviticus, written sometime after Deuteronomy, raises the love command to a higher level. Not only should the people not oppress the aliens and even love them, they should love them as they love their *very selves*. Why? Because, Leviticus says, "you were aliens in the land of Egypt" (Lv 19:34). We see a parallel development in a second example. Whereas the covenant code in Exodus insists that garments offered as security are to be returned by sunset so that poor persons may have a cloak to cover themselves at night (Ex 22:26), the code in Deuteronomy absolutely prohibits taking the cloak as collateral (Dt 24:17).[13] Thus, Deuteronomy shows a development of the love command for the neighbor and correspondingly calls for justice that requires greater equality among those neighbors who live in the Promised Land.

Deuteronomy provides an impressive list of laws in its covenant code that commands the people to establish just policies, or *mishpāt,* that will assist the poor and foreigners living on the land. This practice of righteousness and justice on behalf of the poor (slaves, Levites, alien residents, orphans, and widows) is called social justice.[14] The code presents laws not only for helping the poor, but also policies for eliminating poverty altogether. Moses makes this startling promise: "There will be no more poor among you" (Dt 15:4). While the Deuteronomist recognizes that alien workers, widows, and orphans will always be part of Israelite society, the author does not accept that they must remain indigent, landless, and without social standing.[15] The code establishes extraordinary legislation to create conditions so that these landless groups are able to change their economic conditions and social status and thus leave their life of poverty. The "land flowing with milk and honey" is mythical language that signifies that the people are "to create a just and therefore blessed society," in sharp contrast to neighboring corrupt societies.[16]

Covenantal love *('ahāb),* compassion *(chesed),* and justice *(tsedeq)* are God's gifts to the people that motivate the landowners to put these laws into practice *(mishpāt).* Remembering that they too were once slaves, landowners are required to free their own slaves every seventh year and again in the year of Jubilee (every fiftieth year).[17] But landowners, by law, are not simply to release them, leaving them to fend for themselves. They must also provide basic goods that give the freed slaves the means to grow or produce things for themselves and their family. "Provide liberally out of your flock, your threshing floor, your wine press, thus giving to him some of the bounty with which the Lord your God has blessed you" (Dt 15:14). Thus, Deuteronomic law brings about restoration to slaves and widows by moving them to a higher social status: slaves become free persons with property, and widows acquire the same level of honor as Levites, so that both are able to participate in feasts.[18]

For all its impressive emphasis on social justice for the poor, Deuteronomy also says a great deal about retributive justice within the court system. Retributive justice obliges citizens to return to society the equivalent of what they have taken or destroyed. Its purpose is to reestablish the equality according to an arithmetical equivalency. Retribution also involves denouncing the offense as society's way of disowning the crime and trying to deter others from repeating it.[19]

The court system calls for the appointment of just and righteous judges, who must be impartial and unwilling to take bribes. The code establishes a court procedure that requires two or three witnesses to testify to the guilt or innocence of the offender. If any of the witnesses gives false testimony, the lying witness is to be punished in the same manner as the accused would have been.

The court also makes a provision for sanctuary so that tribal revenge does not overtake justice. This provision is established for controlling tribal revenge, the kind of savage vindictiveness seen in today's world in Bosnia, Kosovo, Rwanda, and the Sudan. The stipulation is called the law of retaliation *(lex talionis)*, which limits the amount of punishment rendered to an approximate equivalency of the damage done. Moses states this law as follows: "Show no pity: life for life, eye for eye, tooth for tooth, hand for hand, foot for foot" (Dt 19:21). This expression of the law may seem unduly harsh, especially the command to "show no pity," which does not seem to reflect the image of the compassionate and gratuitous God, but rather a quid pro quo type of ethic.

Yet it is important to see this passage within a literary and historical context. Deuteronomy mentions it only once throughout the entire book. And it is found only in two other places of the Torah. While the law of retaliation in theory includes many capital crimes (e.g., adultery, dishonoring a parent), in practice the law has been applied only to first-degree-murder cases. One must remember that there were no prisons and scarcely any alternatives (like offering sanctuary) to protect society from repeated acts of violence. The law served to moderate uncontrolled revenge and savage brutality that would seek not only the death of a murderer but also the assassin's entire family.[20] This law, however, would be later criticized by Jesus (Mt 5:38–42).

Beware of Self-righteousness

Moses wished to reinforce an important truth in the people's consciousness; that is, that material success and self-righteousness had tended to obliterate from their memory that it was God's power that had liberated them. And in the future, when their success in the land of milk and honey might tempt them to think that their prosperity came about because of their own talents and labor, they should remember that fidelity to God's law is the cause of their success.

When the Lord your God has brought you into the land that he swore to your ancestors, to Abraham, to Isaac, and to Jacob, to give you—a land with fine, large cities that you did not build, houses filled with all sorts of goods that you did not fill, hewn cisterns that you did not hew, vineyards and olive groves that you did not plant—and when you have eaten your fill, take care that you do not forget the Lord, who brought you out of the land of Egypt, out of the house of slavery. (Dt 6: 10–12)

They must remember that these goods are God's gifts. Prosperity and riches could lead to materialistic thinking and a self-congratulatory attitude, causing a kind of amnesia that would banish from their memory how all this prosperity came to be theirs.[21]

Moses anticipates what, in fact, actually happened. The tribe of Judah eventually turned away from God and began to think of itself as a self-sufficient, autonomous agent. To ensure security and wealth, the people made deals with other nations that compromised their values and jeopardized their relation with Yahweh.[22] Moses cautioned them against being self-righteous. They should resist proudly claiming ownership for a prosperity that God made possible. "It was not because you were more numerous than any other people that the Lord set his heart on you and chose you—for you were the fewest of all peoples" (Dt 7:7).

Moses sees the amnesia arising from materialism, which spreads, like cancer, becoming a deadly hubris. "When you have eaten your fill and have built fine houses and live in them, and when your herds and flocks have multiplied, and your silver and gold is multiplied, and all that you have is multiplied, then do not exalt yourself, forgetting the Lord your God, who brought you out of the land of Egypt, out of the house of slavery" (Dt 8:12–14). Forgetting means assuming that the land, the fertile crops, and the prosperous cities that the people now possess, came to them by means of their own power and achievements. Forgetting also means erasing from their memory the fact that they were once poor and oppressed and that they were liberated by another. Forgetting finally means forgetting Yahweh. This false consciousness assumes that all the goods they possess are entitlements.[23]

Moses cautions the people: "Do not say to yourself, 'My power and the might of my own hand have gotten me this wealth'" (Dt 8:17). It was not their righteousness, but God's justice and love that had empowered them to overcome their fear of the enemy and enter the Promised Land (Dt 9:4). Forgetting manifests an arrogance that leads to selfish individualism, causing alienation in the community.[24]

Forgetting also means ignoring the destitute and weak, even kicking them should they get in the way. Fyodor Dostoevsky's parable of the peasant woman in *The Brothers Karamazov* speaks about this kind of arrogance:

> Once upon a time there was a peasant woman and a very wicked woman she was. And she died and did not leave a single good deed behind. The devil caught her and plunged her into the lake of fire. So her guardian angel stood and wondered what good deed of hers he could remember to tell God. "She once pulled up an onion in her garden," said the angel, "and gave it to a beggar woman." And God answered: "You take that onion then, hold it out to her in the lake, and let her take hold and be pulled out. And if you can pull her out of the lake, let her come

to Paradise, but if the onion breaks, then the woman must stay where she is." The angel ran to the woman and held out the onion to her. "Come," the angel said. "Catch hold and I'll pull you out." And he began cautiously pulling her out. He had just pulled her right out, when the other sinners in the lake, seeing she was being drawn out, began catching hold of her so as to be pulled out with her. But she was a very wicked woman and she began kicking them. "I'm to be pulled out, not you. It's my onion, not yours." As soon as she said that, the onion broke. And the woman fell into the lake and she is burning there to this day. So the angel wept and went away.[25]

The angel remembered the beggar woman's one good deed, which might have saved her as well as the others. As she was being lifted up, the woman forgot that what was being offered to her was a totally gratuitous act of forgiveness. In her self-absorption, she thinks of the onion as an entitlement rather than as a gift to be shared with the others. "It's my onion, not yours." Kicking her neighbors expresses her hubris, causes the onion to break, and eliminates the possibility of salvation for her and the others. Like the beggar woman, the people of the Southern Kingdom became obsessed with their own security and survival and neglected to show compassion for the poor in their midst.

LOVE AND JUSTICE IN ROMANS

The Letter to the Romans, written in the late 50s, is Paul's self-introduction to the Gentile Christians at Rome, whom he hopes to visit on his way to Spain. Paul writes them in order to explain the gospel and especially to instruct them about God's power to save all who believe. He speaks of justice and righteousness more than any other New Testament writer, using the Greek term *dikaiosynē* (righteousness) for *tsedeq*, and *krima/krisis* (judgment/justice) for *mishpāt*.[26] He calls this judgment "justification by faith" and refers to the justified persons as "righteous" *(díkaios)* or "justified ones" *(díkaioi)*.[27] Even though his audience consists of Gentiles, Paul shows a universal concern for both Jew and Gentile. He is also concerned with opposition to the gospel and to the Christian churches, an opposition that he himself had experienced firsthand and that he anticipates the Christians at Rome may soon, if not already, be experiencing.[28]

JUSTIFICATION IN THE NAME OF THE CROSS

Revelation discloses a God who loves human beings more than they could ever have imagined. Paul maintains that God's love declares human beings just or upright, a state of being that cannot be achieved by their own power. Paul teaches that righteousness comes about by being baptized in the death and resurrection of Jesus, and that this baptism comes from God as an effect of Jesus dying and rising out of love for humankind.[29] *To justify* literally means "to set right," and it is the work of God who sets us right, in relationship first to God and second to our neighbors. Paul calls this act "justification," which is achieved through the cross of Christ. Justification is an act of love for humankind that reconciles us to God through the forgiveness of our sins, gives us a judgment of acquittal in spite of our sins, and, most important, makes us free. It frees us from sin, the law, and death (Rom 6:1–14). More concretely, justification frees us from being self-serving individuals who pursue great accomplishments and boast about our achievements. Justification also involves the Spirit of God laboring in the world, creating a new people to be "ministers of a new covenant" (2 Cor 3:6). Hence, justification involves more than God reconciling individuals; it incorporates individuals into a new social structure or covenant called the body of Christ.[30] On the positive side, it transforms our consciousness so that we come to think of ourselves as servants of one another, bearing one another's burdens, and showing concern for the vulnerable and the suffering.[31]

St. Paul's concept of justification is like Deuteronomy's metaphor of liberation in many respects, but it is unlike it in others. They are alike, first of all, inasmuch as justification and liberation are processes that entail a double dynamic of freeing persons from sin and the slavery that sin brings, and then of bonding persons in relationships with God and their neighbors. Second, both metaphors insist that freedom comes as a gift not as a result of individual effort—it is God's justice and love that cause the transformation. Third, liberation and justification are eschatological processes, which means that the salvation we are striving for is happening right now but will not be completed until some time in the future. While we are on the journey moving toward full justification and freedom, we recognize that we are still flawed human beings who sin; yet we are no longer enslaved by selfish passions. Fourth, justification and liberation are brought about by means of a covenant relationship with God that expands the meaning of neighbor.

Yet there are a couple of differences. First, whereas the covenant of the Old Testament demands that the neighbors we are commanded to love as ourselves eventually come to include resident aliens, the New Testament covenant makes a quantum leap by insisting that in Christ we must love Gentiles as well as Jews, foes as well as friends, and slaves as well as free persons (Gal 3:28).

Second, there is an important difference between Pauline justification and Deuteronomic liberation. In the Pauline salvific process, God justifies people through the cross of Jesus rather than through Torah.[32] Paul teaches that persons become just or righteous not simply by loving God and neighbor as the law directs, but by being "made just" through the Christ-event that makes possible our loving God and neighbor. Paul thinks that fidelity to the law, which commands unqualified love for God and neighbor, cannot save or redeem anyone because no one can fulfill these commands. He does not argue that the law per se is an ineffective means to salvation, but he insists that keeping the law is an impossibility for both Jew and Gentile. As we saw in Deuteronomy, the great commandment calls people first to hear and then to love. While hearing God's revelation is a prerequisite, performance (loving God and neighbor) is the decisive criterion for salvation. But performance by Jew and Gentile falls far short of the mark. Brendan Byrne nicely summarizes Paul's thought on this issue: "If sin has been the pattern of life, possession or non-possession of the law makes no fundamental difference."[33] All human beings need God's justice; that is, they need to be justified by divine grace.

For Paul, justice is not a principle for guiding one's conduct, but rather a spiritual power, or virtue, given to persons that transforms their behavior. By conferring the spirit on sinners, God empowers persons with an interior freedom that enables them to listen, love, and live in loving and just relationships with others. Even though in practice the justified fall short of keeping the law (Gal 5:13), they nonetheless have peace with God, have access to God's abiding favor *(charis)*, and possess hope of obtaining the glory of God (Rom 5:1–5). This hope does not rest on human achievement but on what God has done for us through Christ and continues to do through God's love—a love, Paul says, that "is poured into our hearts through the Holy Spirit" (Rom 5:5).[34]

GENUINE LOVE AS A RADICAL OPTION

Paul probes the depth of Christ's love, arguing that Jesus' death on the cross manifests the profundity of his love. He makes his case using an a fortiori argument: If while we were enemies, we were reconciled by God through the death of his Son, how much more, now that we are reconciled, shall we be saved by his life (Rom 5:10). Paul asks, "Who will separate us from the love of Christ? Will hardship, or distress, or persecution, or famine, or nakedness, or peril, or sword?" (Rom 8:35). No, he answers, nothing in all of creation can "separate us from the love of God in Christ Jesus our Lord" (Rom 8:39). This reconciliation of sinners (whom Paul calls "enemies of God" [Rom 11:28]) by means of the cross shows extraordinary love and serves as the basis for Paul's teaching that the followers of Jesus must love their enemies. Just as Jesus forgave his enemies who persecuted him, so also should followers of Jesus do the same by blessing those who persecute them (Rom 12:14–21).

Paul says many things about love and justice that reinforce the teaching in Israel's covenant with Yahweh. He tells the Thessalonians that they do not need further instruction on loving their brothers and sisters because they "have been taught by God to love one another" (1 Thes 4:9). He describes in beautiful lyrical verse the qualities of love: what it is and what it is not.

"Love is patient; love is kind; love is not envious or boastful or arrogant. . . . It bears all things, believes all things, hopes all things, endures all things. Love never ends" (1 Cor 13:4–8).

In his exhortation to the Christians at Rome, Paul says, "Let love be genuine" (Rom 12:9). Genuine love *(agapē anypókritos)*, stands in opposition to love that is hypocritical *(agapē hypókritēs)*, which is a make-believe love, akin to the kind of love performed on stage.[35] Genuine love in Romans follows the trajectory of the neighborly love expressed in Deuteronomy and Leviticus where love and justice for members of one's own tribe become expanded to include aliens living on the land, even to the point of loving the resident aliens as self. Paul's love and justice continue this trajectory toward universalizing the meaning of neighbor by inviting Christians to accept Gentiles into the community and by loving and being just to enemies. "Do not repay anyone evil for evil" (Rom 12:17), Paul says to the Christians at Rome. "Never avenge yourselves, but leave room for the wrath of God" (Rom 12:19). This new consciousness flows from the example of Jesus and from the inspiration of the Holy Spirit. Jesus died at the hands of enemies, yet he died for them with forgiveness on his lips. So also should we, as members of Christ's body forgive our enemies. This then is genuine love: a radical option for the good of another.[36] It is an *option* not in the sense of it being optional; it is rather a firm commitment to the good of the neighbor, friend and foe alike. It is *radical* because it transcends self-interest by blessing those who oppress us and by feeding and giving drink to our enemies, and by pursuing peace. Vengeance must be deferred to God, who, as ruler of the universe, has the prerogative and wisdom to make the final judgment.[37]

LOVE AND JUSTICE IN PARABLE

In the Lukan account of the gospel, Jesus inaugurates his ministry by proclaiming good news to the poor (Lk 4:16–21). In his Sermon on the Plain, Jesus calls the poor blessed because the kingdom of God is theirs. He utters woes to the rich and powerful because the materials things that give them consolation will not last (Lk 6:20, 24–26). He speaks and eats with, even touches, the so-called untouchables of Jewish society: tax collectors, lepers, and prostitutes, and preaches about the great banquet that will be celebrated with "the poor, the crippled, the blind and the lame" (Lk 14:21).[38]

This compassionate teacher is a master storyteller, who uses the literary genre called parable to explain what he means by the kingdom of God. The kingdom, he says, is like a mustard seed that someone sowed in the garden; it grew and became a tree. And then he makes a second comparison: The kingdom is "like yeast that a woman took and mixed in with three measures of flour until all of it was leavened" (Lk 13:21). C. H. Dodd defines the New Testament parable as "a metaphor or simile drawn from nature or common life, arresting the hearer by its vividness or strangeness, and leaving the mind in sufficient doubt about its precise application to tease it into active thought."[39] Though Jesus uses folksy, homespun language, his parables often startle the audience. Theologian Michael Cook suggests that a good way to listen to parables is to ask oneself: "What is it about this parable that I don't like? What shocks me or upsets my comfortable ordered world?"[40]

In Matthew's parable of the workers in the vineyard (Mt 20:1–16), Jesus tells such a story. A landowner, after agreeing to pay workers the usual wage for a day's work, gives latecomers the same pay as those who worked the full day. Those who worked the whole day expected to be paid more than those who worked only one hour, and so they grumble against the landlord when everyone receives a denarius: "You have made them equal to us" (Mt 20:12). They want equal pay only for equal work. But the kingdom of God does not operate according to strict law-court justice. The unexpected conclusion challenges listeners to consider a deeper meaning of justice.

While the language is familiar, the parable stretches the imagination and invites the mind to think more intuitively, as koans of Zen Buddhism do. The Zen master asks his disciple: "We are all familiar with the sound of two hands clapping. What is the sound of one hand clapping?"[41] Jesus ends a parable with a paradox: "So the last will be first, and the first will be last" (Mt 20:16). Like koans, such sayings defy our ordinary logic; like poetry, the words are polyvalent, challenging the imagination to unlock their meaning and intuitively to grasp the point of the story. Parables describe in vivid language the effect that the kingdom produces, such as compassion, righteousness, and peace. We shall look at two well-known Lukan parables to see what insight they present about how love leads to justice: the prodigal son and the good Samaritan.

A MAN HAD TWO SONS

The traditional title given this parable—the prodigal son—focuses on the younger son, the recklessly extravagant individual, who, after devouring his father's capital, returns home and is reconciled with his father. Other interpreters call it the parable of the two sons because both sons are objects of the father's affection and generosity in spite of their sinful ways. A third interpretation, and the one followed here, puts the spotlight on the father; hence the parable is called simply a man had two sons, following the opening words of the parable. It gives top billing to the father because of his surprisingly magnanimous and loving response to his sinful sons. This interpretation suggests that the parent is God incarnate, a model for what all fathers and mothers, indeed for what all of us should strive to become—compassionate and forgiving human beings who welcome home the wayward and then try to reconcile them to resentful members of the community.

The father divided his property between the two sons. While the younger son took his share of the inheritance and traveled to a distant land where he foolishly squandered his money, the elder son dutifully continued to work for his father. Although the father must have been crushed by the younger son's disrespectful and irresponsible action, he did not do what the parents in Deuteronomy are told to do to a stubborn and rebellious son who is "a glutton and a drunkard"; that is, denounce him before the elders, who then will stone him to death (Dt 21:20–21).

After the son's life hit rock bottom, when he could no longer bear the hunger and misery in feeding pigs, he decided to go home. He rehearsed what he would say. "I have sinned against heaven and before you; I am no longer worthy to be called your son; treat me like one of your hired hands" (Lk 15:18–19). Back bent in defeat and head drooping with guilt, the young man began his long trek home. The father, upon catching sight of his son's distinct gait, "was filled with compassion; he ran, and put his arms around him and kissed him" (Lk 15:20–21). A father running to meet his son would be shocking to onlookers in this society, and even more so because the son had made a mockery of the father's generosity. No sooner had the son begun his rehearsed speech—"I am no longer worthy to called your son"—than his father, delirious with joy over his son's return, calls to the servants to give his son the best robe, ring, and sandals. These gifts, symbols of reconciliation and authority, suggest that the son is not only forgiven and reinstated as son, but that he is empowered to act as a co-owner in the affairs of the estate.[42] His father restores his full dignity. This is the genuine love of which Paul speaks.

Two other remarkable things about the father should be underscored: first, he is "filled with compassion" for the younger son. The Greek root for compassion *(splagchna)* connotes "being stirred in one's gut," the kind of feeling a pregnant mother might feel for the fetus within her.[43] Compassion is an extraordinary gift, and it impels the father to do extraordinary things. Second, the father, exhilarated at his son's return, never admonishes him. There is no hint of criticism for the way he messed things up. The father can only shout for joy: "Let us eat and celebrate, for this son of mine was dead and is alive again; he was lost and is found" (Lk 15:23–24).

Meanwhile, the elder son returns home after working in the field, hears about the party, becomes enraged, and refuses to join the celebration. The father comes out to plead with his son to join the festivities, an initiative by the father that would again surprise people living in a patriarchal society. The elder treats his father with disrespect, complaining that for many years he worked "like a slave" for him. "But when this son of yours comes back, who has devoured your property with prostitutes, you killed the fatted calf for him" (Lk 15:29–30). But the father is not put off by the elder son's disdain and defiance. He tenderly calls him "son," thus upgrading the son's self-identification as a slave. The father talks to him as though he were an equal partner. "Son, you are always with me, and all that is mine is yours" (Lk 15:31). He counters the elder son's words—"But when this *son of yours* came back"—with "this *brother of yours* was dead and has come to life" (Lk 15:32).

The parable implies that this is the way God welcomes all sinners—both the self-righteous and the prodigal. It also suggests that God's justifying love intends to transform the sinners' poor self-image and their image of God, and in effect, to transform the nature of the relationship from one of master and slave to one of parent and son, from a social contract written in terms of servile obligations to a covenant grounded in grace.[44] The parable also sketches an image of a God whose compassionate face and warm embrace of both sons model a distinctive type of justice called reconciliatory justice or what is called today "restorative justice."[45] This type of justice invites us to envision ourselves not only as beloved sons and daughters of God in a vertical or God-human direction, but also as brothers and sisters to one another in a horizontal direction.

How different is the father's response to his sons from that of King Lear, who disowns his daughter Cordelia for not praising him with the kind of exaggerated protestations of love given by her disingenuous sisters Goneril and Regan. To Cordelia, the wounded Lear says:

> Here I disclaim all my paternal care,
> Propinquity and property of blood,
> And as a stranger to my heart and me
> Hold thee from this for ever.[46]

Filled with anger and hubris, Lear throws Cordelia out of the house and exiles her to a foreign land, which gives the wicked sisters a free hand in completely dispossessing their father and destroying the kingdom. How unlike the father of the two sons, who humbly and patiently absorbs the irresponsible deeds of the younger and the hostility of the elder, as he compassionately calls them to become true and righteous sons and brothers to each other in the kingdom of God.

Parable of the Good Samaritan

This parable brings us full circle from the commandments stated in Deuteronomy and Leviticus to Paul's Letter to the Romans and finally to the Gospel according to Luke. The questioner, a lawyer, asks Jesus what he must do to inherit life in the age to come. Jesus poses a counter question, "What is written in the law?" The lawyer responds by reciting the Shema, the centerpiece of the covenant: "You shall love the Lord your God with all your heart" (Lk 10:27); then he adjoins to it the command to love the neighbor as oneself. Jesus affirms his answer and encourages him to do this and he will live.

The lawyer, however, is not satisfied. In an effort to justify himself, he asks Jesus: "And who is my neighbor?" (Lk 10:29). Wishing to justify himself should not be read as a desire to compensate for his naive question about how to gain eternal life. A more plausible interpretation is that the lawyer wanted to know the boundary line of the covenant command that required a Jew to love the neighbor as oneself. As we saw earlier, the Torah says that neighbor includes all Jews and those foreigners who live on the land.[47] Rather than responding with a concrete answer, Jesus creates through parable an imaginary world that affords the lawyer an opportunity of thinking expansively, to enlarge his consciousness by broadening his conception of the meaning of neighbor.

Jesus begins his story with stark simplicity: "A man was going down from Jerusalem to Jericho, and fell into the hands of robbers, who stripped him, beat him, and went away, leaving him half dead" (Lk 10:30). Other travelers came upon this victim, presumably a Jew, and, crossing over to the other side, passed him by. No motives are given for their ignoring the man.[48] Jesus mentions that the two travelers were a priest, the highest religious leader among the Jews, and a Levite, one who performed secondary priestly functions. Jesus then introduces a third traveler. The audience might have expected that this person would be an Israelite, thus completing the triadic formula of priest, Levite, and Israelite (Jewish layperson) that represents a classical division of the Jewish people.[49] Jesus jolts his audience by introducing a long-time foe of the Jews, a Samaritan, whom the listeners might have expected to have acted just as coldly, if not scornfully, to the man dying in the ditch.[50] In the chapter preceding this parable, Luke narrates an incident in which the Samaritans refused to receive Jesus on his way to Jerusalem. Two disciples, James and John, manifest the prevailing Jewish animus toward Samaritans by asking Jesus for permission to avenge this snub by commanding fire from heaven to consume them (see Lk 9:51–55).

The parable gives the audience a shock. The Samaritan, unlike the priest and the Levite, did not cross to the other side of the road. He saw the half-dead man and "was moved with pity" (Lk 10:33). He dismounted and attended to the victim's injuries. After cleansing and bandaging his wounds, the Samaritan put him on his own animal, took him to an inn, cared for him, and, when he had to leave, paid the innkeeper to care for him until his return.

Turning to the lawyer, Jesus shifts the lawyer's question. He does not ask, "Who is my neighbor?" which focuses on the object of love, that is, on those whom we are commanded to love. Instead he asks, "Which of these three, do you think, was a neighbor to the man?" (Lk 10:36). This question looks to the neighbor as subject, the one who sees another's need and responds. Jesus, by emphasizing the neighbor as subject, suggests that one becomes neighbor when one responds to anyone in need, whether that person is Jew or Gentile, man or woman, friend or foe. The lawyer gets the point and answers without further questioning: "The one who showed him mercy" (Lk 10:37). This parable expresses Jesus' conviction that there are no outsiders in God's kingdom, that all men and women, whatever their ethnic group, race, or class, are potentially neighbors, and that they actually become neighbors when they serve those in need, like the dying, the hungry, the imprisoned, and the homeless.

As in the previous parable, love in this parable relates to justice. The Samaritan's compassion moves him to care for the victim's immediate needs and then to set up conditions for his full recovery and freedom. In order to ensure that he would not be victimized again (say, by the innkeeper), the Samaritan pays the innkeeper to care for him and lets the innkeeper know that he will return to check back on the victim. John Donahue sees in this parable a nexus between love and justice: "It is not enough simply to enter the world of the neighbor with care and compassion; one must enter and leave it in such a way that the neighbor is given freedom along with the very help that is offered."[51] We may speak of this example of justice as social or contributive justice, which deliberately acts to establish structural conditions that enable persons to be free, active, and productive participants in society.[52] We saw this kind of justice in Deuteronomy, where a debtor is not only relieved of his debt every seven years, but upon his release is given land so that he may earn a living and so not become enslaved again.

LOVE THAT DOES JUSTICE

This chapter examined the meaning of love and justice through the lenses of two covenants. Both concepts played significant roles in defining the relationship between God and the people of Yahweh and between God and the followers of Jesus. In both covenants love and justice are intricately linked. Both are gifts of God that gradually take root in the people as virtues that empower them to respond to God's call and mission.

Both testaments understand that love and justice are divine attributes and that God calls the people to be imitators of their creator, who made them in God's image and likeness. They are, therefore, commanded to love as God loves, to do justice as God does justice, and to be holy as God is holy. Moreover, the image that human beings have of God influences how they relate to God and their neighbor. Seeing God as the liberator of the enslaved impels liberated people to free their oppressed neighbor. The image of God as a compassionate father or mother calls people, like the two sons, to see themselves as sons or daughters and not as slaves.

The Bible does not define justice and love in the manner of the ancient philosophers like Plato and Aristotle. These philosophers define justice as a virtue that renders to others what is their due. It is a justice achieved by repeated practice, and it is measured in terms of equal exchange and proportional distribution. For Aristotle, justice is based on merit. In contrast, covenantal justice is birthed by God's gracious giving or love, which shapes and empowers the innermost core of persons and shapes them more and more into God's likeness. God's love for persons creates the possibility of their loving God and others in return. God needs no motive for loving but does seem to attend especially to those in dire need crying out for help.

Aristotle's justice does not require loving God, but covenantal justice does. Plato and Aristotle also restrict love to friendship between equals, which rules out relationships with God and relationships between the rich and the poor. Within the Judeo-Christian tradition, love and justice connect with each other in the covenant. God initiates the relationship with unequal human partners, loving us with a passionate love and insisting that this love be reciprocated. Our response calls for a radical commitment to God and to our neighbors, with a special option that calls for loving and doing justice for needy and vulnerable neighbors. Micah captures the way we should respond: "O mortal, what is good; and what does the Lord require of you but to do justice, and to love kindness, and to walk humbly with your God?" (Mi 6:8).

RESOURCES

Discussion Questions

1. How does Deuteronomy define love? How does it differ from the way that contemporary society defines it?
2. The Hebrew Bible distinguishes between justice as *tsedeq* and justice as *mishpāt*. What does each term mean?
3. Deuteronomy identified the most needy or most vulnerable groups of people in ancient Israel to be strangers *(gerim)*, because they had no clan or family to protect them, and then widows and orphans, because they had no husband/father to support them. What specific groups of people would you say are the most needy or vulnerable in today's society? Why? What measures could be taken to assist them?
4. What does St. Paul mean by justification by faith? What are the effects of a person being justified?
5. If doing justice for others is born out of a realization that we who were once poor, sick, oppressed, and enslaved are now materially secure, healthy, and free from oppression, thanks to the help of God and others, what should motivate us to love our enemies, who, let us suppose, have never done us any good? What theological conviction lies behind St. Paul's injunction: "Vengeance is mine, I will repay, says the Lord. . . . If your enemies are hungry, feed them; if they are thirsty, give them something to drink, for by doing this you will heap burning coals on their heads" (Rom 12:19–20)?
6. In Luke's Gospel, a lawyer asks Jesus, "Who is my neighbor?" After answering the question by telling the parable of the good Samaritan, Jesus changes the point of reference from neighbor as object (which

groups of people must we love?) to neighbor as subject (how are we called to be neighbor?). If you were to take on this new consciousness that Jesus suggests, what difference would it make in your everyday life?

7. The parable of a man who had two sons suggests that both sons acted irresponsibly. What were the sins of the younger and elder sons? The father seems more concerned about the *relationship* with his two sons than about the sins themselves. How does the father try to improve the relationship with his sons? Would the new way of seeing the relationship be more freeing?

8. As we have seen, scripture sees a very close connection between love and justice. If you were to accept the fact that you are blessed with both gifts—that you are a loving and just person—how would you see love and justice working together, guiding your relationships and your social life?

Suggested Readings

Brueggemann, Walter. *Deuteronomy*. Nashville, TN: Abingdon, 2001.

Byrne, Brendan, S.J. *The Hospitality of God: A Reading of Luke's Gospel.* Collegeville, MN: The Liturgical Press, 2000.

Donahue, John R., S.J. "What Does the Lord Require: A Bibliographical Essay on the Bible and Social Justice." Rev. and exp. Saint Louis: The Institute of Jesuit Sources, 2003.

Harrelson, Walter J. *The Ten Commandments and Human Rights.* Rev. ed. Macon, GA: Mercer University Press, 1997.

Malarek, Victor. *The Natashas: Inside the New Global Sex Trade.* New York: Arcade, 2004.

Malchow, Bruce V. *Social Justice in the Hebrew Bible: What Is New and What Is Old?* Collegeville, MN: The Liturgical Press, 1996.

Shklar, Judith N. *The Faces of Injustice.* New Haven, CT: Yale University Press, 1990.

NOTES

[1] Richard Clifford, S.J., *Deuteronomy*, With an Excursus on Covenant and Law (Wilmington, DE: Michael Glazier, 1982), 1.

[2] Jeremiah Unterman, "Covenant," in Paul J. Achtenmeier, ed., *Harper's Bible Dictionary* (San Francisco: Harper and Row, 1985), 190.

[3] Clifford, *Deuteronomy*, 4–5. Like its neighboring nations in the Near East, Israel made pacts or covenants with other nations or groups within its own territory. These covenants included (1) an invocation of the deity; (2) historical prologue that recounted the history of the relationship between the leaders or kings; (3) stipulations or laws which would define the transaction; and (4) names of witnesses of the transaction, and sanctions (curses and blessings) for upholding the terms of the covenant.

[4] Walter Brueggemann, *Deuteronomy* (Nashville, TN: Abingdon, 2001), 113.

[5] J. P. M. Walsh, S.J., *The Mighty from Their Thrones* (Philadelphia: Fortress Press, 1987), 112.

[6] John R. Donahue, S.J., "Biblical Perspectives on Justice," in John C. Haughey, ed., *The Faith That Does Justice* (New York: Paulist Press, 1977), 69.

[7] Joseph A. Fitzmyer, S.J., "What Do the Scriptures Say about Justice?" in Martin R. Tripole, ed., *Jesuit Education 21: Conference Proceedings on the Future of Jesuit Higher Education* (Philadelphia: Saint Joseph's University Press, June 25–29, 2000), 99–112 at 100.

[8] Ibid., 100, 104.

[9] Moshe Weinfeld, *Deuteronomy 1–11*, The Anchor Bible (New York: Doubleday, 1991), 5:246.

[10] Moshe Weinfeld, *Social Justice in Ancient Israel and in the Ancient Near East* (Jerusalem: Magnes Press, 1995), 246.

[11] W. L. Moran, "The Ancient Near Eastern Background of the Love of God in Deuteronomy," *Catholic Biblical Quarterly* 25 (1963), 77–87 at 78. Moran cites many passages in Deuteronomy that show that love *('ahāb)* expresses loyalty (Dt 11:1, 22; 30:16), obeying or heeding God's voice (Dt 11:13, serving God (Dt 10:12; 11:1, 13).

[12] Weinfeld, *Deuteronomy*, 338–39.

[13] Bruce V. Malchow, *Social Justice in the Hebrew Bible* (Collegeville, MN: The Liturgical Press, 1996), 22–23.

[14] Weinfeld, *Social Justice in Ancient Israel*, 8–9.

[15] Norbert Lohfink, S.J., "Poverty in the Laws of the Ancient Near East and of the Bible," *Theological Studies* 52 (1991), 34–50 at 44.

[16] Ibid., 42.

[17] Weinfeld, *Social Justice in Ancient Israel*, 167–68.

[18] Lohfink, "Poverty in the Laws," 44–45.

[19] Christopher D. Marshall, *Beyond Retribution: A New Testament Vision for Justice, Crime, and Punishment* (Grand Rapids, MI: William B. Eerdmans Publishing Company, 2001), 85.

[20] Clifford, *Deuteronomy*, 106.

[21] Brueggemann, *Deuteronomy*, 86.

[22] Micah spoke of the fall of Jerusalem, condemning its leaders, who abhorred justice: "Therefore because of you Zion shall be plowed as a field; Jerusalem shall become a heap of ruins" (Mi 3:12).

[23] Walsh, *The Mighty from their Thrones*, 117–18.

[24] Ibid., 114–16.

[25] Fyodor Dostoevsky, *The Brothers Karamazov*, ed. Ralph E. Matlaw, trans. Constance Garnett (New York: W. W. Norton and Company, 1976), 330–31.

[26] Fitzmyer, "What Do the Scriptures Say," 100–102.

[27] Paul uses various forms of dikaiosynē for justice and righteousness to replace the two Hebrew terms *tsedeq* and *mishpāt*; for love, he uses *agapē*, *charis*, and *philia* in place of the Hebrew terms *'āhāb* and *chesed*.

[28] Gordon Zerbe, "Paul's Ethic of Nonretaliation and Peace," in Willard M. Swartley, ed., *The Love of Enemy and Nonretaliation in the New Testament* (Louisville, KY: Westminster/John Knox Press, 1992), 188–89.

[29] Joseph A. Fitzmyer, S.J., "The Letter to the Romans," in Raymond Brown, S.S., Joseph A. Fitzmyer, S.J., and Roland E. Murphy, O.Carm., eds., *The New Jerome Biblical Commentary* (Englewood Cliffs, NJ: 1990), 40:24, 840.

[30] Ibid, 95.

[31] Donahue, *Biblical Perspectives*, 94.

[32] Richard B. Hays, "Justification," in David Noel Freedman, ed., *Anchor Bible Dictionary* (New York: Doubleday, 1992), 3:1130.

[33] Brendan Byrne, S.J., *Romans, Sacra Pagina* Series, vol. 6, ed. Daniel J. Harrington, S.J. (Collegeville, MN: The Liturgical Press, 1996), 88.

[34] Byrne, *Romans*, 165.

[35] Ibid., 378n9.

[36] Ibid., 376.

[37] Gordon Zerbe, "Paul's Ethic of Nonretaliation and Peace," in Willard M. Swartley, ed., *The Love of Enemy and Nonretaliation in the New Testament* (Louisville, KY: Westminster/John Knox Press, 1992), 205.

[38] Donahue, "What Does the Lord Require?" 50–51.

[39] C. H. Dodd, *The Parables of the Kingdom* (New York: Scribner, 1961), 5.

[40] Michael L. Cook, S.J., "Jesus' Parables and the Faith That Does Justice," *Studies in the Spirituality of the Jesuits* (St. Louis: The Seminar on Jesuit Spirituality, 1992), 24, no. 5: 11.

[41] Huston Smith, *The World's Religions* (San Francisco: Harper SanFrancisco, 1991), 134.

[42] Ibid., 19.

[43] Ibid.

[44] John R. Donahue, S.J., *The Gospel in Parable* (Philadelphia: Fortress Press, 1988), 157.

[45] Howard Zehr, *Changing Lenses* (Scottdale, PA: Herald Press, 1995).

[46] William Shakespeare, "The Tragedy of King Lear," in Stanley Wells and Garry Taylor, eds., *William Shakespeare: The Complete Works* (Oxford: Clarendon Press, 1988), 1.1, 113–16.

[47] N. T. Wright, *Jesus and the Victory of God* (Minneapolis: Fortress Press, 1996), 306.

[48] Kenneth E. Bailey, *Poet and Peasant* and *Through Peasant Eyes*, combined ed. (Grand Rapids, MI: Eerdmans, 1983), 2:44–46; and J. Duncan M. Derrett, *Law in the New Testament* (London: Darton, Longman and Todd, 1970), 211–17. Commentators speculate that the priest and Levite wanted to avoid contamination by contact with a dead or dying man. Contact with a corpse would have made them unclean and thus impeded their participation in the ceremonies in the temple at Jericho.

[49] Bernard Brandon Scott, *Hear Then the Parable* (Minneapolis: Fortress Press, 1989), 198.

[50] Donahue, *The Gospel in Parable*, 130.

[51] Ibid., 133.

[52] National Conference of Catholic Bishops, *Economic Justice for All* (Washington, DC: United States Catholic Conference, 1997), par. 71.

3

LOVE AND JUSTICE
AMONG ENEMIES

Jesus of Nazareth

"But I say to you, Do not resist an evildoer. . . .
Love your enemies and pray for those who persecute you,
so that you may be children of your Father in heaven."
—Matthew 5:39, 44–45

The gospel commands Christians to love their enemies. This distinctively Christian love seeks to transform enemies so that they are no longer enemies. As children of their heavenly Father, Christians are to be brothers or sisters to all their neighbors. The gospel, however, also enjoins believers not to resist evildoers. This poses a problem: how can we actively love those bent on doing us harm and yet not resist them? A short answer is that Christians should actively love the doers of evil and not resist by paying them back; but they should resist the *evil* of the perpetrators in a creative, generous, and nonviolent manner. Jesus' love of enemies is a nonviolent expression of love and justice that is called an ethics or spirituality of nonviolence.

A longer answer calls for carefully reading the gospel to see how Jesus lived and how his life faithfully reflected what he taught about nonviolence, love of enemies, and a non-retaliating justice. The chapter first develops the thesis that Jesus loved his enemies and resisted their evil deeds nonviolently. It demonstrates this first by examining the deeds of Jesus and then his teaching.

Biblical scholars generally affirm that Jesus was nonviolent both in his actions and in his teaching.[1] Yet certain scholars have qualified the meaning of Jesus' nonviolence. Jesus, they claim, was nonviolent in practice but not in principle. He used nonviolence as a strategy to convert the powerful foe or to reconcile the oppressors and their victims. It would have been foolhardy to do otherwise. Jesus and his first followers knew that if they were to confront the enemy with force, the Roman regime would have destroyed the movement.[2] Given different circumstances in a future age, the followers of Jesus might have justified or at least tacitly approved the use of force. As we will see in the following chapter, Augustine argued that, since John the Baptist and Jesus never admonished soldiers for serving in the Roman army, they implied by their silence that it was morally legitimate to serve in the military (Lk 3:14; Mt 8:5–13).

The chapter then investigates two important followers of Jesus who serve as bookends of this two-thousand year tradition. The first is an early Christian theologian, Tertullian (160–220), who expressed loyalty to and prayed for the Roman emperor even as he resisted the emperor by opposing Christians doing military service in his army. The other is a twentieth-century Baptist minister, Martin Luther King, Jr. (1929–68), who urged his African American people to love the white segregationists while they nonviolently resisted their discriminatory laws and practices. We examine how faithfully they followed Jesus' example and teaching in their dealing with enemies and violent situations and structures.

Tertullian and King, although separated by many centuries and vastly different cultures, read the same gospel and were inspired by many of the same biblical texts, and they used them to guide their Christian communities. Both leaders held that Jesus was nonviolent. These two leaders and those Christians who agreed with their teaching represented a minority group within a powerful empire in which the majority was generally hostile toward them. While both men may be called nonviolent, neither one was a sectarian pacifist who set himself and his people apart from the rest of society. Their frequent references to the nonviolent love of Jesus present us with this question: how faithfully did Tertullian and King follow Jesus' life and teaching on nonviolent resistance and love of enemies?

The chapter concludes with a reflection on whether Jesus' example and teaching on love of enemies and nonviolent resistance constitute a universal mandate for Christians in all ages.

NONVIOLENCE, PACIFISM, AND PEACE

Before investigating these questions, we should first clarify the meaning of three key concepts that arise in this discussion, namely, nonviolence, pacifism, and peace. Generally speaking, nonviolence means refraining from all violent acts, including inflicting physical injury on persons, killing them or threatening to do so, as well as intentionally damaging the property of another.[3]

Pacifism is a contemporary term, which would have been an anachronism in Jesus' time. The term comes from the Latin verb *pacificare*, which means "to make peace," and so pacifism denotes an active involvement to promote peace.[4] In this sense, Jesus may be called a pacifist because he proclaimed peace as an integral part of the kingdom of God. Pacifism, however, generally refers to opposition to war and has many shades of meaning. Pacifist theologian John Howard Yoder constructed a typology of sixteen forms of pacifism that range from an absolute type that allows no exceptions to the command "thou shall not kill" to a relative and contextual type that deliberates about the morality of war on a case-by-case basis. While an absolutist type of pacifism prohibits all use of violence, including war, physical force by police, and individual self-defense, a more restricted type defines pacifism simply as opposition to all war.[5]

Both Tertullian and King acknowledged that their nonviolence was inspired by the teaching of Jesus; both men, like Jesus, acknowledged the authority of the state even as they resisted some of its policies and unjust laws. Neither Jesus nor Tertullian and King were absolute pacifists. Tertullian's nonviolence was closer to the absolutist end of Yoder's pacifist spectrum; King's was closer to the relativist end, though it should be noted that toward the end of his life, he strongly opposed the war in Vietnam and all use of nuclear weapons.[6] Tertullian opposed all use of force by Christians, even as he acknowledged Rome's right to use force and to maintain an army. King called his type of nonviolent resistance a "realist pacifism": "realist" because it accounted for the reality of sinfulness in the hearts and actions of the oppressor and even in the hearts of the oppressed; it was a "pacifism" because love or *agape*, which he says rejects using violence against persons, must be its motivating force.[7]

Peace *(šālōm)* in the Hebrew Bible means a state of living in harmony with oneself, with others, with nature, and with God.[8] The New Testament builds on the Hebrew concept of peace as harmony and emphasizes the element of reconciliation. For Jews and Christians alike, reconciliation means reestablishing mutually loving relations with God and with one's neighbor following a period of estrangement. St. Paul taught that peace is a gift, made possible through the cross of Christ. His death and resurrection reconcile people to God and to one another (Rom 5:1–11; Col 1:20). The risen Jesus greeted his disciples with "Peace." Hence, peace is not simply the absence of war, although the elimination of war is a minimum condition for peace. It is a gift enabling people to live in harmonious relationships, a harmony that comes about by respecting the dignity of one's neighbors, by building trust through communication and negotiation, and by making policies and laws that are fair to all concerned. Peace, therefore, is the fruit of love and justice.

THE WORLD OF JESUS

Before exploring Jesus' way of life, it will be helpful to tour the world in which Jesus lived and taught. He was born and lived in a society where Jews were a colonized and therefore dependent people. He traveled and preached in Galilee, Judea, and Samaritan territory occupied and controlled by the Roman Empire. The wars of conquest and revolts had subsided before Jesus' birth, ending with Pompey's successful invasion of Jerusalem in 67 B.C. When Jesus was born (c. 4 B.C.), the Roman government under Caesar Augustus had achieved political unity in Western Europe, the Near East, and Northern Africa. But the unity Rome forged brought an external peace, called the *Pax*

Romana, which was, for the most part, free from regional wars, highway robbery, and pirating on the seas. This relatively tranquil period enabled Jesus and his followers to move about freely and to preach openly, although eventually they encountered persecution.[9] The territories were tightly controlled by the Roman emperor, whose local rulers (Herod Antipas and Pilate) exploited the people by heavy taxation, forced donations, and confiscation of property. These agents of Rome would from time to time provoke the people, pushing them to the brink of rebellion. Jesus, however, kept a critical distance from both the governors and from the various and diverse groups that wished to overthrow the Roman occupation as he went about proclaiming the reign of God.

There were rumblings of insurrection against imperialistic Rome during Jesus' lifetime. But an actual revolt would only come about thirty years after Jesus' death, beginning with the Jewish revolt in A.D. 66–67, when the Zealots conquered Jerusalem and occupied the fortress at Masada, and ending in A.D. 73, when the Roman army recaptured the fortress and crushed the insurrection.[10] Except for this unsuccessful Jewish revolution and early persecutions of Christians (for example, Nero's persecution in 64–67), there were no major military conflicts in the first century that would have provided an occasion for Jesus' and his first followers to reflect on the rightness or wrongness of Jewish revolutionaries engaging in military action. Aside from Jesus' allusion to the future destruction of Jerusalem (Lk 21:20ff.), the Gospels are silent regarding war. And yet, as the Gospels attest, Jesus and his followers ran into conflict with religious leaders and eventually with Roman leaders, which led to his arrest, condemnation, and death.

JESUS' PRACTICE OF NONVIOLENT LOVE

This section focuses on Jesus' virtue ethic based on what he *does*; that is, how he habitually responds to people, especially to those who oppose him or are hostile toward him, and finally to those who kill him. Since Jesus claimed to be acting in accordance to the will of his heavenly Father, whom he addressed as Abba, we may assume that the way Jesus responded to friend and foe manifested something about the nature of God and about how God wishes to relate to human beings. The actions of Jesus, in other words, reveal something about God's mode of being. If Jesus loves his enemies and labors to reconcile them, so also does his Father. God, Jesus says, "makes his sun rise on the evil and on the good, and sends rain on the righteous and on the unrighteous" (Mt 5:45).

Jesus had enemies. As he went about his mission preaching that the kingdom of God was at hand, he encountered stiff opposition. He was accused of blaspheming for forgiving a paralytic's sins (Mk 2:5ff.) and of violating the Sabbath by healing the blind man (Jn 9:14ff.). Religious leaders angered him by asserting that he had driven demons out of people by the power of

Satan (Mk 3:22–30). In each case Jesus not only responded nonviolently, but he patiently clarified what he did and sometimes why he did it in order to help his critics understand the meaning of his actions. When certain scribes and Pharisees, for example, criticized Jesus for eating with tax collectors and sinners, he replied, "Those who are well have no need of a physician, but those who are sick; I have come to call not the righteous but sinners" (Mk 2:17).

Jesus was gentle and merciful; he was never punitive in his relationships with sinners and adversaries. Yet he opposed sinful acts, including the sin of self-righteousness (Lk 7:36–50). In the story of the woman caught in adultery (Jn 8:2–11), the scribes and the Pharisees brought the woman to the Temple, where Jesus was teaching, and said, "The law of Moses commanded us to stone such women. Now what do you say?" (Jn 8:5). They thought that they had pinned Jesus on the horns of a dilemma. If Jesus were to reply, "Yes, do what the law commands and stone her," they could accuse him of opposing local Roman authority that forbade the Jews to put anyone to death (Jn 18:31). But if Jesus were to say, "Let her go," the Pharisees could have charge him with contempt of the Mosaic law. He avoided the trap by challenging the woman's accusers: "Let anyone among you who is without sin be the first to throw a stone at her." When none accepted the challenge, he forgave the woman: "Go your way, and from now do not sin again" (Jn 8:1–11). Like the Father who makes the sun rise on the evil and on the good, Jesus acted nonviolently toward the self-righteous accusers while protecting the adulterous woman from a violent end.

Nowhere in the Gospel accounts does Jesus ever employ violence to defend himself or his disciples. Nor does he allow his disciples to defend him by use of force. When Jesus is confronted at Gethsemane by the Sanhedrin's police force, one unnamed disciple (identified as Peter in John 18:10) cut off the ear of the high priest's servant (Mt 26:51).[11] Jesus criticized this violent act: "Put your sword back into its place." Then, speaking to the sword-wielding disciple as well as to the armed guards, Jesus continued, "for all who take the sword will perish by the sword" (Mt 26:52). He did not threaten but simply informed his disciples and the armed guards that they should change their violent ways because violent actions eventually come around like a boomerang to whack the perpetrator.[12]

The strongest evidence supporting Jesus' nonviolent commitment, found in all four Gospels, is Jesus' willingness to suffer condemnation and death on the cross without retaliating or threatening to do so. This redemptive act most powerfully demonstrated his merciful love, nonviolence, and forgiveness of enemies.[13] As he was about to be arrested, Jesus considered asking his Father to send twelve legions of angels to rescue him in what might have been a violent intervention. Yet he discerned that this was not God's will (Mt 26:53–54). He courageously faced the Jewish and Roman authorities and accepted his death sentence. During his trial before the Sanhedrin, Jesus was struck by a guard. He did not literally "turn the other cheek" but resisted in a way that was neither violent nor submissive. He simply questioned the justice of the guard's action: "If I have spoken wrongly, testify to the wrong. But if I have spoken rightly, why do you strike me?" (Jn 18:23).

Jesus carried out in practice what he taught his disciples; namely, that they should not try to save their lives by securing their perimeters and refusing to take risks and that they should not seek to maximize their earnings by building larger barns to store their grains. They should, instead, share their goods and be willing to risk their lives as an integral part of proclaiming and living the gospel. Jesus forewarned his followers that bearing witness to the gospel would lead to their persecution (Mk 8:34–35). Jesus himself bore witness to God's reign with total commitment by healing and forgiving people, exposing evil deeds, and speaking the truth—actions that he foresaw would lead to his own death. His refusal to use physical force to promote his mission did not mean surrendering to the enemy and to the power of evil. He resisted evil by nonviolent love and by reconciling sinners. He called to a tax collector, "Zacchaeus, hurry and come down; for I must stay at your house today" (Lk 19:5).

Paul described Jesus' death on the cross as a form of execution that involved a humbling and self-emptying of himself (Phil 2:5–11). It was a scandalous and degrading type of capital punishment intended for insurrectionists and other criminals of low socioeconomic status.[14] But God exalted Jesus from the depths of humiliation and shame, giving him a name above every other name. Henceforth, Jesus would be acclaimed as "Lord, to the glory of God the Father" (Phil 2:11). The unsurpassed power and authority of Jesus came about, not by his exercising enormous physical force, but by a radical emptying of self in obedience to God's call.

OBJECTIONS RAISED

There are, however, other decisions and actions of Jesus that appear to suggest that he used or permitted violence. Jesus seems to have acted violently when he cleansed the Temple, for example; in another instance he appears to have permitted violence by allowing his disciples to carry swords, even telling them to buy a sword. These passages seem to contradict, or at least to qualify the nonviolent lifestyle of Jesus. Let us examine them.

In the Temple incident, Jesus forcefully drove out sellers and buyers and overturned tables of the moneychangers (Mk 11:15–19). If violence includes intentionally destroying another's property (as earlier defined), we might be inclined to say that Jesus acted in a violent manner. Exegetes, however, generally regard the cleansing of the Temple as a prophetic, symbolic act in which Jesus protested against "the misuse of the sanctuary to enrich the leading priestly families."[15] Although his actions certainly brought about temporary disorder and possibly financial loss that day, the chaos was not sufficiently grave to cause the Roman guards to intervene. Moreover, Jesus directed his action toward the tables more than toward the people. Here is the passage of the Temple cleansing narrated by Mark. What do you think?

> Then they came to Jerusalem. And he entered the temple and began to drive out those who were selling, and those who were buying in the temple, and he overturned the tables of the money changers and the seats of those who sold doves; and he would not allow anyone to carry anything through the temple. He was teaching and saying, "Is it not written,
>   My house shall be called a house of prayer for all the nations?"
>   But you have made it a den of robbers.
> And when the chief priests and the scribes heard it, they kept looking for a way to kill him; for they were afraid of him, because the whole crowd was spellbound by his teaching. And when evening came, Jesus and his disciples went out of the city. (Mk 11:15–19)

As for bearing arms, the Gospel accounts say that at least one of the disciples carried a sword and used it to defend Jesus. If indeed Jesus permitted his disciples to carry a sword for self-defense, then we might conclude that Jesus was not absolutely opposed to violence. But as we have seen, Jesus admonished the disciple for using the sword against persons, even against his enemies. Earlier in Luke's Gospel, Jesus sent his disciples to various towns in order to proclaim the reign of God. As they were about to depart, he cautioned them that he was sending them like lambs moving out among wolves. One may reasonably infer that the disciples, like lambs, were defenseless in the midst of a hostile people and against robbers along the way. They carried no weapons to fend off the "wolves." They were told to travel simply, leaving behind purse, bag, and sandals (Lk 10:3–4).

Later in the Lukan account, when resistance stiffened, he reminded his disciples of their first missionary journey: "When I sent you out without a purse, bag, or sandals, did you lack anything?" "No," they replied. "But now, the one who has a purse must take it, and likewise a bag. And the one who has no sword must sell his cloak and buy one" (Lk 22:35–36). The literary context of Luke-Acts implies that "sword" in this passage is symbolic. It suggests an impending crisis in which the disciples must prepare themselves to deal with severe hostility and persecution. The disciples, interpreting Jesus' words literally, thought that they would actually need swords to defend themselves: "Lord, look, here are two swords." Jesus, seeing that his disciples had missed the point, responded, "It is enough!" It becomes clear when the whole Gospel account is read that Jesus did not want them to respond violently to their enemies. They were commanded to love their enemies (Lk 6:27) and if the enemy continued to be unreceptive, they were to move on to another town. He rebuked James and John for requesting permission to send fire from heaven to consume the inhospitable Samaritans (Lk 9:51–56), and he admonished one of his disciples for cutting off the right ear of the high priest's slave with a sword: "No more of this" (Lk 22:51). In the Acts of the Apostles, Luke says that Paul and other missionaries never used swords.[16]

The evidence examined so far, the objections to the contrary notwithstanding, supports the thesis that Jesus related to people, including enemies, in a consistently nonviolent and loving manner, even as he resisted their evil actions. Next we investigate Jesus' teaching in the Matthean and Lukan gospel accounts and letters of Paul and Peter to see whether his teaching is consistent with his actions.

THE TEACHER OF NONVIOLENCE

In Matthew's Sermon on the Mount, Jesus taught his disciples and a large crowd of people the meaning of the law, including how they should apply God's commandments in conflict situations. He began his instruction by congratulating those among them who were poor in spirit, merciful, and pure in heart. He also singled out the peacemakers, calling them "happy ones," because they had become both recipients of God's peace and agents of peace by loving and being merciful to their neighbors. Henceforth, they would be called God's children (Mt 5:9).

Jesus then presented a mini course on the meaning of the law. He emphasized that he did not intend to abolish or even diminish the law; he intended to fulfill it by opening up its deeper meaning. He stated six theses related to murder, adultery, divorce, swearing, retaliation, and love of enemies. Interpreters sometimes called them antitheses because Jesus presents these teachings in a "point-counterpoint" manner, first stating a traditional expression of the law, then countering or qualifying it with a counter thesis or antithesis. Each antithesis begins with a pattern similar to the rabbinic style of teaching—"You have heard, but I say to you"—a formula that implies that Jesus was teaching in an authoritative and solemn manner, something like a naval commander who issues orders to his subordinates with the ritualistic expression, "All hands on deck, now hear this!"

We consider only three of the six antitheses that speak to issues related to murder, retaliation, and treatment of enemies. In the first antithesis, Jesus affirmed the prohibition against murder and then cut to the heart of the matter: "You have heard that it was said to those of ancient times, 'You shall not kill; and whoever kills shall be liable to judgment.' But I say to you that if you are angry with a brother or sister, you will be liable to the council; and if you say, 'You fool,' you will be liable to the hell of fire" (Mt 5:21–22). Anger or rage, Jesus suggests, is the emotional prelude to insulting and murderous acts.[17] Restraining yourself from killing your neighbor while allowing the rage to fester in your gut does not fulfill the law. Jesus taught that his followers must deal with the anger by becoming reconciled with the neighbor.

The fifth antithesis states the principle of retaliation *(lex talionis)*, then counters it: "You have heard that it was said, 'An eye for an eye and a tooth for a tooth.' But I say to you, Do not resist an evildoer" (Mt 5:38–39a). As we saw in the previous chapter, *lex talionis* permits an individual or clan to claim proportionate compensation for damages done to oneself or to one's clan. While the Torah does not justify this principle, it includes it as a practical way of controlling retaliation. This principle was an important advance over the savage practice of one tribe destroying a second tribe in retaliation for its killing one or two of its members. In theory, the principle seems fair: eye for eye and life for life. In practice, it tends to foster a spirit of vindictiveness. Jesus virtually abrogated the principle of retribution; it should no longer be their guide. Vengeance is God's prerogative and responsibility. In place of retaliation, Jesus commanded them not to resist the evildoer, and if the unjust aggressor did them physical harm, they were not to respond in kind. They should transcend their desire to make any claim against the transgressor and, instead, respond in a manner that is nonviolent, forgiving, and generous. Jesus illustrated what resisting nonviolently meant:

> But I say to you, Do not resist an evildoer. But if anyone strikes you on the right cheek, turn the other also; and if anyone wants to sue you and take your coat, give your cloak as well; and if anyone forces you to go one mile, go also the second mile. Give to everyone who begs from you, and do not refuse anyone who wants to borrow from you. (Mt 5:39–42)

At first glance, the three illustrations appear to suggest a passivity: (1) "turn the other cheek"; (2) "walk a second mile"; and (3) "give up your cloak." Did not resisting mean that his followers should surrender their dignity, clothes, and purse to the enemy?

Martin Luther King, Jr., answered, "Absolutely not!" When Jesus said do not resist, he meant that we should resist, but nonviolently.

> The phrase "passive resistance" often gives the false impression that this is a sort of "do-nothing method" in which the resister quietly and passively accepts evil. But nothing is further from the truth. For while the nonviolent resister is passive in the sense that he is not physically aggressive toward his opponent, his mind and emotions are always active, constantly seeking to persuade his opponent that he is wrong. The method is passive physically but strongly active spiritually. It is

not passive non-resistance to evil; it is active nonviolent resistance to
evil.[18]

Biblical scholars agree with King. Martin Hengel says that the refusal to
use violence is far from being a weakness; it demonstrates Jesus' sovereign
power. "This power is demonstrated in the fact that, instead of adding to
another's suffering, it is unconditionally prepared to take the suffering upon
itself. . . . The power of nonviolence, which proceeded from Jesus, manifests
itself for us therefore in a special way in the two great martyrs of our century, Mahatma Gandhi and Martin Luther King, Jr."[19] Walter Wink points
out that Jesus' command "do not resist the evildoer" has been wrongly interpreted to mean that the victim should be totally passive to the enemy's aggression.[20] Like King, Wink says that Jesus seeks to transform the ways of
the evildoer. The Greek verb for "resist," *antistēnai*, has a second meaning,
namely, to "withstand" or "rise up" against the enemy, that is, to resist with
armed force. In other words, disciples of Jesus are commanded neither to
pay back in kind for the injustice inflicted nor to resist violently. But they
should resist! Wink notes that a variant form, *anistēmi*, which is virtually
interchangeable with *antistēnai*, means "to rise up against someone" in a
revolt or war. The latter form is used ninety-four times in various places of
the Greek translation of the Hebrew Bible (Septuagint).[21] In Deuteronomy,
for example, Moses tells his people to fight the enemy: "No one will be able
to stand against you *[antistēnai]* until you have destroyed them" (Dt 7:24).[22]
By telling his followers not to resist, Jesus was commanding them not to
retaliate in the violent manner that the *lex talionis* permits ("eye for eye,
tooth for tooth, and life for life").

They should resist in a different way and for a different reason. The different way is *nonviolent* ("turn the other cheek"), *imaginative* ("give him
your inner garment as well as the outer garment"), and *generous* ("walk a
second mile"). The different reason or aim is to enlarge the enemy's and the
victim's consciousness so that they may dispel hatred for the other. Nor-
mally, violated persons instinctively think of revenge, and the perpetrators
ready themselves for a counterattack. But the three illustrations suggest a
resistance that is neither retributive nor violent. This type of nonviolent resistance, in Wink's words, "goes beyond inaction and overreaction, capitu-
lation and murderous counter violence to a new response, fired in the cru-
cible of love, that promises to liberate the oppressed from evil even as it frees
the oppressor from sin."[23]

The reader might object that this kind of resistance doubles the victim's
injustice by allowing the aggressor to strike twice and the Roman soldier to
double the compulsory service by making the oppressed carry his bags a
second mile. The victim risks getting both cheeks slapped, and the debtor
allows the creditor to violate God's law by taking his cloak as well as his

inner garment. In the oppressive world of prisoners, this kind of ethic may seem like folly, as the following story illustrates.

The new prison chaplain, making his rounds on the fourth tier of the North Cell Block at San Quentin, stopped to talk to prisoners locked down twenty-four hours a day because of bad behavior in the yard. In one of first conversations with these tough inmates, the chaplain was asked, "Are you a Christian?" When the chaplain nodded affirmatively, the inmate inquired, "Do you believe what Jesus said that you should turn the other cheek." "Yes," the chaplain replied, "Jesus taught us to forgive our enemies and turning the other cheek is one expression of forgiveness." The inmate then cynically scoffed at the idea, explaining that at San Quentin and even "in the streets" turning the other cheek would mean enslavement or death. "Here you have to fight or you're a dead man." The prisoner identified Christianity with what he thought was an absurd nonviolent teaching. The prisoner's perspective taught the chaplain that biblical commandments need to be interpreted within a social context. It also prompted him to ask other "cons" outside of the North Cell Block how they would apply "turning the other cheek" to confrontations in the yard. While many agreed with the first prisoner, others thought confrontation leading to violence was not the right way to respond.

What could justify allowing one's dignity to be affronted by accepting a blow and even inviting the bully to strike again? The books of Matthew, Romans, and Proverbs suggest a number of reasons. First, refusing to strike back, even offering the other cheek, frees the victim from the sin of vengeance and anger that otherwise would, like a poison, consume the person. Second, it expresses a prophetic symbolic response that says in effect, "I do not seek vengeance from you because that is God's responsibility; and God surely will judge you." This response is neither a curse nor a personal vendetta aimed at hurting the oppressor.[24] It is simply witnessing to Jesus' conviction that retribution falls within the domain of God's justice, not of human justice. St. Paul's instruction to the Christians in Rome reinforces Jesus' teaching: "Do not," he says, "repay anyone evil for evil." They should never avenge themselves, "for it is written, 'Vengeance is mine, I will repay, says the Lord'" (Rom 12:17, 19). Paul is convinced that we are neither wise enough nor good enough to judge our enemies justly. Third, by one's refusal to respond violently, the disciple raises the consciousness of the evildoer, which may ultimately lead to his or her conversion. Quoting a verse from the book of Proverbs (25:21–22), Paul cites another reason why the disciple should express love to the enemy: by feeding and giving drink to hungry and thirsty enemies (analogous to turning the other cheek), "you will heap burning coals on their heads" (Rom 12:20). This means that by meeting evil deeds with genuinely loving acts, the disciple helps the enemies to come to their senses and to feel ashamed of their evil actions.

The sixth antithesis, in which Jesus called his followers to love their enemies, is closely related to the previous antithesis about resisting counter violence. The text says,

> You have heard that it was said, "You shall love your neighbor and hate your enemy." But I say to you, Love your enemies and pray for those who persecute you, so that you may be children of your Father in heaven; for he makes his sun rise on the evil and on the good, and sends rain on the righteous and on the unrighteous. (Mt 5:43–45)

In fact, the Bible does not say "hate your enemy." On the contrary, the book of Leviticus states: "You shall not take vengeance or bear a grudge against any of your people, but you shall love your neighbor as yourself: I am the Lord" (Lv 19:18). In this sixth antithesis Jesus was correcting a common, but erroneous, understanding of this commandment that allowed Israelites to hate their enemies. Jesus, perceiving good even in enemies, commanded his followers to love them as well as their compatriots.[25] The teacher and model of such magnanimous love is their Father in heaven, who loves evildoers as well as doers of good.

As the reader might suspect, biblical experts have differed over their interpretations of Matthew 5:38–48. Richard Horsley has disagreed with Walter Wink, first of all, over the meaning of nonresistance, contending that Jesus in this passage was not teaching nonviolent resistance at all. He also differs with Wink over the identity of the enemies, insisting that they were compatriots or fellow Jews and not Romans, as Wink suggests. Third, he objects to Wink's making direct application of Jesus' teaching about not resisting violently to contemporary situations, such as King's civil rights movement and to the nonviolent resistance against apartheid in South Africa.

As for the first objection, it is paradoxical that Horsley, a self-acclaimed pacifist, would argue that Matthew's passage "do not resist against the evildoer" does not refer to resisting physical violence; and that Wink, who is not a pacifist, maintains that it does. Horsley contends that Matthew, who in fact used the same source as Luke (called the "Q" source), inserted the antithesis that states "do not resist an evildoer (violently)" into the original text as well as one of the three illustrations: "If anyone forces you to go one mile, go with him two miles."[26] Neither of these verses is found in Luke, and Horsley says Luke is more faithful to the original "Q" source. Without these two verses, Horsley argues, it would be difficult to prove that Jesus was commanding his disciples never to employ counter violence. Horsley thinks that this text is not presenting a nonviolent strategy that the disciples are to follow, but that it is teaching a new kind of social relations that would renew local communities. He concludes, "We must look elsewhere for indications of whether Jesus' approach was nonviolent. Aside from his announcement of imminent divine judgment, it appears to have been nonviolent."[27]

In response, Walter Wink argues that Luke, not Matthew, has deleted these two verses from its Palestinian context and has "applied it to the wandering preachers in the early church."[28] Given the literary context of Luke, the author suggests that the blow on the cheek and taking the creditor's cloak were the dirty deeds of robbers; hence, the reference to carrying the soldier's pack a second mile (found only in Matthew) makes no sense and so Luke dropped it. Wink also notes that Horsley argues in another publication that Jesus, though not a pacifist, "actively opposed violence, particularly institutionalized oppressive and repressive violence, and its effects on a subject people. Jesus was apparently a revolutionary but not a violent political revolutionary."[29] Wink asks Horsley how he would know this inasmuch as he rejects one of the best texts for demonstrating Jesus' teaching on counter violence.

In his second objection Horsley says that Wink is wrong in holding that the enemies refer to Romans; rather, Horsley says, they are compatriots engaged in local disputes on an interpersonal level. Roman soldiers, he says, would not have a presence in Galilee, where Jesus addressed the crowd. Therefore, Jesus would not have been talking about resistance against the Roman army because such resistance, spearheaded by Zealots after the death of Jesus, was nonexistent. Other biblical scholars disagree. N. T. Wright supplies much historical evidence that demonstrates the existence of Jewish resistance movements against the Romans by groups of Pharisees during Jesus' time.[30] Wright says, "Revolution of one sort or another was in the air, and often present on the ground, both in Galilee and (particularly) in Jerusalem, throughout the period of Roman rule. It was not confined to one group, whether the Zealots properly so called, the Sicarii, or any other."[31]

Agreeing with Wright as well as with Wink, Marcus Borg says that "enemies" must have included the non-compatriots or the non-Jewish enemy because Jesus said, "You have heard that it was said, 'You shall love your neighbor and hate your enemy,' but I say to you, Love your enemy." This contrast between neighbor and enemy implies that the enemies were non-Jews, because Jesus would not have quoted a Jewish saying that would have implied that you love your Jewish neighbor and hate your other Jewish compatriots to whom you owe debts. Borg says that the command, "Love your enemies," had an "inescapable and identifiable political implication: the non-Jewish enemy above all, was Rome."[32] While the identity of "enemies" in Matthew's account is not expressly stated, Jesus' instructions about how to respond to enemies could be applied to other comparable situations, which, as the illustrations suggest, would include the Romans and non-Christian Jews. In Luke's account Jesus refuses to curse Samaritans for their inhospitality and in a parable speaks of a Samaritan as being a neighbor par excellence.[33]

Finally, Horsley objects to applying these verses directly to situations of oppression today, such as the racial discrimination in the United States that Martin Luther King, Jr., faced, or the apartheid in South Africa that Nelson Mandela and his organization nonviolently resisted. In response, Wink says that applying the Bible's general commands, such as "do not resist violently," is legitimate, just as Jews and Christians today apply the Ten Commandments. Yet he concedes that the three illustrations of Jesus are simply examples to give concreteness to the meaning of the general command; hence, one should determine anew how to act nonviolently in contemporary situations. The illustrations, Wink says, exemplify creative responses of nonviolent resistance that "break the cycle of humiliation with humor and even ridicule, exposing the injustice of the system."[34] Other kinds of creative, nonviolent responses could achieve the same end.

In his declaration of loyalty to Caesar, "Give to Caesar the things that are Caesar's," Jesus qualified this loyalty by adding the second clause, "and to God the things that are God's" (Mt 22:21). Giving God what is due means being faithful to the demands of the covenant, which prohibit turning Caesar and the things of Caesar into idols. Concretely this meant refusing to recognize the false gods of the Romans, who warred against each other and who functioned as militant, self-aggrandizing models for leaders and citizens. In contrast, Jesus proclaimed the reign of God that stressed peace, not war, and serving one another out of love for one's neighbor, not competing for the highest places of honor.[35]

Jesus clearly instructed his first disciples not to respond to their unjust enemies according to the principle of retaliation but in a prophetic way by declaring the retribution of God. Paul taught the same nonviolent message, urging the Christians at Rome to "bless those that persecute you" so that they might "overcome evil with good." They are commanded to shun retribution of all kinds, especially violent vengeance (Rom 12:14–21).

The nonviolent love of Jesus gives his justice a distinctive character. Jesus relates openly and in an evenhanded way to the righteous and the unrighteous. He welcomes to the table both sinners and saints, tax collectors and Pharisees, men and women. An essential part of his table fellowship involves remedying the situation, which is the work of justice. In one instance the remedy involves helping Simon the Pharisee understand forgiveness and to free him from prejudice toward the sinful woman who had entered his home unannounced (Lk 7:36–50). In another instance Jesus told a story in which a father welcomed home his prodigal son and then tried to reconcile him to his dutiful son, who was enraged by his brother's royal reception (Lk 15:11–32). Nonviolent love moves justice from retribution to reconciliation.

CHRISTIANS AND GOVERNING AUTHORITIES

Yet when Paul shifts the discussion away from individual Christians to the rights of governing authorities, he introduces a new dimension that qualifies the nonviolent teaching of Jesus. Paul wrote to the Christians at Rome that they must be subject to the governing authorities. They should pay taxes and revenues, as well as respect those in authority because "the authorities are God's servants" (Rom 13:6–7). Therefore everyone should be subject to earthly sovereigns, and anyone who resists their authority resists God. As God's agents, civil authorities have the obligation to maintain order and work for the good of the community.

This includes the right of the state to punish those who break the law, even though Paul had written in the previous chapter that Christians should never "repay anyone evil for evil" (Rom 12:17–21). But in chapter 13 Paul writes, "But if you do what is wrong, you should be afraid, for the authority does not bear the sword in vain" (Rom 13:4). This affirmation of the state's right to use the sword reflects Jewish teaching and is affirmed by both Paul and by the First Letter of Peter (1 Pt 2:13–17; 3:13). The sword, Paul implies, is a symbol of power for inflicting punishment, a power that ultimately comes from God.[36] Hence the servant of God can execute God's wrath on the wrongdoer (Rom 13:4). While recognizing the state's right to use the sword to enforce its laws, neither Paul nor Peter says anything about the right of the Roman Empire to wage war against its enemies. But three centuries later, Augustine, using Paul's teaching, will make a case for a Christian empire doing battle with its enemies inside and beyond its borders. Christian nonviolence will give way to just-war theory.

TERTULLIAN AND THE EARLY CHRISTIAN WITNESS

We move into the late first to the early third centuries to learn how faithfully Christians in general and Tertullian in particular applied Jesus' teaching of love of enemies and nonviolent resistance. The enemies were the Roman emperors, governors of provinces, and citizens who persecuted and sometimes executed members of the small band of Christians for refusing to renounce their faith by paying homage to the gods. Those who suffered death because of their resistance included bishops (Ignatius of Antioch and Polycarp), philosophers (Justin Martyr), soldiers (Martin of Tours), and catechumens (Perpetua). Enemies also included the military establishment, which the Christian writers Tertullian, Origen, Lactantius, and others resisted, especially when some Christians began to join the Roman army. While these theologians gave good reasons why Christians should not serve in the military, none of them carried on any sustained discussion of the morality of war during the second and third centuries.[37]

CHRISTIAN PERSECUTION

Roman persecutions of Christians were spasmodic and involved relatively few people until the second and third century, when repression came in waves.

In the first century Nero (54–68) was the first emperor to persecute Christians. According to Roman historian Tacitus, Nero blamed the Christians for the burning of Rome, though it was widely believed that the emperor himself had set fire to the city. While Nero charged Christians with arson, Tacitus indicated that the real reason for persecuting them was the whim of the emperor, not justice.[38]

Emperors in the second and third centuries arrested, tortured, and killed Christians because they refused to worship the Roman gods and the emperor himself. Later persecutions of Christians, especially in the third century, were brutal military operations in which emperors Marcus Aurelius (161–80), Decius (249–51), and Diocletian (284–305) ordered their armies to destroy churches and scriptures, confiscate property, and prohibit Christian worship. Governors arrested clergy and bishops, ordering them to sacrifice to the Roman gods under penalty of torture or execution.[39] Christians not only refused to worship the Roman gods, but they denied their existence, even speaking of them as malevolent demons.[40]

Although the reasons for Rome's persecution of Christians varied, the chief reason was religious; Christians refused to worship the gods. This refusal had political implications. Historian G. E. M. de Ste. Croix expands on Rome's concerns. "The monotheistic exclusiveness of the Christians was believed to alienate the goodwill of the gods, to endanger what the Romans called the *pax deorum* (the right of harmonious relationship between gods and human persons), and to be responsible for disasters which overtook the community."[41] According to Rome's perspective, Christians were not only viewed as atheists for their unwillingness to pay homage to the gods, but insurrectionists because they were undermining Rome's foundation.[42]

Yet Christians were never revolutionaries. Even under the duress of horrible persecution, Christians, unlike the Zealots, did not organize resistance movements or engage in guerrilla warfare in retaliation for the murderous actions of their persecutors. On the contrary, they guided their conduct in accordance with Jesus' teaching of love, nonviolence, and forgiveness of enemies. Roman authorities and pagan writers labeled Christians stubborn and recalcitrant, because they held fast to what the Romans considered superstitious beliefs. But they never charged them with terrorism even at the height of the persecutions.

In the midst of an unfriendly environment, Christians prayed for the emperor, obeyed the authorities, and paid their taxes. They were not sectarian pacifists, like Anabaptists, who separated themselves from mainline society. Justin Martyr, writing in A.D. 150, reiterated the nonviolent teaching expressed in Matthew, Luke, and Paul: Christians do not wage war with their enemies but turn the other cheek and pray for them. Justin, commenting on Isaiah's prophecy that nations in a future age will reject war by turning their swords into plowshares and spears into pruning hooks, said that this prophecy had already been realized in the coming of Christ. He wrote:

You can believe that this prophecy, too, was fulfilled. For twelve men, ignorant and unskilled in speaking as they were, went out from Jerusalem to the world and with the help of God announced to every race of men that they had been sent by Christ to teach the word of God to everyone, and we who formerly killed one another not only refuse to make war on our enemies but in order to avoid lying to our interrogators or deceiving them, we freely go to our deaths confessing Christ.[43]

Later executed by a Roman governor, Justin expressed what some contemporary historians judge to have been the dominant view in his age; most Christians were pacifists who refused to kill human beings and to participate in war.[44] But as we will see, other Christians began to dissent from that strong pacifist view by entering military service.

Tertullian and the Military

Born in Carthage (present-day Tunisia), Tertullian was the son of a Roman centurion who worked in his early years for the proconsul of Africa. Living a self-indulgent life as a young man, he shared with his fellow Romans the pagan prejudices against Christianity; following his conversion to Christianity, however, he became an instructor of catechumens. He was touted as a literary genius and was perhaps the greatest Christian Latin writer of his time.[45] Generally regarded as a pacifist, he nonetheless thought that war was necessary, even though he deplored war's destruction and carnage. He interpreted quite literally Jesus' commands that his disciples ought to love the enemy and not retaliate for any injury received.[46] He taught that Christians living in the empire should be loyal to Caesar by praying for him: "We pray without ceasing for all emperors, for their prolonged life, for a secure empire, for protection of the imperial palace, for brave armies, a loyal Senate, an upright citizenry, a peaceful world and for everything that the emperor desires as a man and as a Caesar."[47] But he urged his fellow Christians to resist the dominant pagan Roman culture and particularly to resist participating in the "brave armies" that Tertullian and other Christians prayed for. In response to the Roman establishment, which charged that Christians were enemies of the state, he acknowledged that "we are enemies, that is, not of the human race, but of human error."[48] He meant that Christians resist the evil that humans do (human error) but do not reject the people themselves (the human race). This statement was consistent with what Jesus taught. Tertullian opposed Christians serving in the military, which increasingly became a major issue during his lifetime. He opposed military service for two reasons: first, the Roman army required that soldiers participate in rituals of offering sacrifices to pagan gods and to the emperor himself; and second, military officers had to issue the death sentence to those convicted of capital crimes and to order their legions to engage in battle.[49] Invoking the gospel, he stated that killing convicted felons and enemy warriors is wrong. Christians must never use arms.

Because Christians generally refused to serve in the Roman army, they were disliked, sometimes even scorned by the military establishment. Roman author Celsus, writing in 176, severely took them to task for shunning the army: "If all men were to do the same as you, there would be nothing to prevent the king from being left in utter solitude and desertion and the forces of the empire would fall into the hands of the wildest and most lawless barbarians."[50] Celsus did not know that some Christians had in fact entered the army and had even played a decisive role in praying for victory for the Roman army's "Thundering Legion" in A.D. 173.[51]

Tertullian, like Justin, was a Christian apologist. He was the first theologian to address the issue of Christians serving in the military. In his *Apology,* written around 197, Tertullian found himself somewhat torn between his conviction that the Roman Empire had to secure its own borders against foreign invaders and his equally strong conviction that Christians' serving in defense of the borders was incompatible with the gospel. This tension between loyalty to the state and opposition to the army remained a constant. He had previously commended the Christian community's loyalty to Rome, even mentioning that Christians were serving in the governor's army. Yet in this work he expressed his strong misgivings about their doing military service because military camps professed the pagan rituals and veneration of standards carrying images of the gods (*Apology* 16.8).

In his *Treatise on Idolatry,* written fourteen years after the *Apology,* Tertullian addressed two questions: first, whether Christians could hold public office in the state; and second, whether they could serve in the army without compromising their faith. His response to both questions was negative. Both civil magistrates and soldiers sooner or later must participate in idolatrous practices and the shedding of blood. Magistrates and military officers must offer sacrifices to deities or authorize others to do so, and they issued sentences to execute or torture prisoners.[52] As for the soldiers of lower rank, they too would have to participate in rituals honoring the pagan gods and, if ordered, carry out executions.

Tertullian gave additional reasons why Christians should not serve in the army. Even in peacetime the soldier had to wear military dress, which symbolized idolatrous actions forbidden to a Christian, and to carry a sword, which symbolized a willingness and readiness to kill.[53] Roman military life was a total institution that required participation in practices that were offensive to Christians. By yielding to these demands, the soldier seriously compromised his Christian faith. If the Christian soldier refused to carry out these duties, he would likely be subject to court martial.

Tertullian *asserted* that killing human beings is wrong, but he never gave reasons or developed an argument demonstrating its intrinsic wrongfulness. Moreover, he failed to distinguish between different kinds of killing: murder, self-defense, capital punishment, killing on the battlefield. By holding that all killing is wrong, he implied that he was an absolute pacifist. In fact, he was not. He supported the Roman army's defense of its borders against foreign intruders, even as he denounced Christian participation in its defense. In addition, he made one exception to Christians serving in the military. Soldiers who had converted to Christianity could remain in the army as long as they did not perform any act of violence. Why? Deserters would be court-martialed, and if they managed to escape the death penalty, they would likely lose severance pay and all other benefits that came to soldiers who retired from service in good standing.[54]

Yet the contradiction remained. If it is wrong for Christians to use the sword, why would it be permissible for pagan soldiers to kill? Following Paul (Rom 13:1–7), he recognizes that the emperor is God's servant: "We respect in the emperors the decision of God, since he has placed them over the people."[55] He might have argued that killing in defense of the empire and at the behest of the governor was justifiable because the governor is God's agent. Yet he did not. Respecting the emperor meant praying for him, not fighting for him. Tertullian held fast to his conviction that shedding blood and killing human beings are at odds with Christian love. Yet he held that military defense, although a moral evil, was necessary. But if military defense was necessary, why should Christians be exempted from engaging in it, when in fact they benefited from the military's protection? Tertullian never addressed this apparent contradiction. He simply supported his pacifist claim on the basis of his literal interpretation of the teachings of Jesus. His ethics followed what contemporary ethics calls divine-command theory, which says that something is right if God (and Jesus as the Son of God) commands it; it is wrong if God forbids it.

Part of Tertullian's resistance to Christians serving in the military sprang from his strong opposition to idolatrous practices. But he also stood firmly against Christians committing violent acts. He regarded killing as a serious transgression, as the following rhetorical questions suggest: "Will a son of peace, who should not even go to court, take part in battle? Will a man who does not avenge wrongs done to himself have any part in chains, prisons, tortures and punishments? Will he perform guard duty for anyone other than Christ, or will he do so on the Lord's Day when he is not doing it for Christ Himself? (*On the Crown* 11, 1–7). His answer to these questions is a firm no. He adamantly held to the biblical command "you shall not kill" and to Jesus' reinforcement of the command: "Put away the sword."

Tertullian had to wrestle with the fact that the God of the Old Testament permitted the law of retaliation, which calls for the death sentence for specific capital crimes, and, under certain conditions, demanded that Israel wage war against its enemies. While not denying the authority of the Old Testament, he argued that the New Testament superseded it. In accord with Justin Martyr, he held that with Jesus' announcement of the kingdom, military weapons are transformed into weapons for farming and peace shall reign (Is 2:4). After the coming of Jesus, wars sanctioned in the Old Testament would no longer be justified. The love of neighbor in the Old Testament was extended to include the enemy in the New Testament, and the law of retaliation yielded to the New Testament teaching that vengeance belongs to the Lord.[56]

His literalist interpretation also included understanding the Gospel accounts as chronological developments, so that Jesus' later sayings and actions in the Gospels expressed his final position on violence; in certain instances they corrected perspectives stated earlier in the same Gospel account. For example, in arguing against Christians serving in the military, Tertullian said that Jesus' prohibiting his disciples from using a sword (Lk 22:50–51) trumped John the Baptist's allowing Roman soldiers to remain soldiers after they were baptized (Lk 3:14). Jesus, by disarming his disciple, disarmed every soldier thereafter.

In summary, Tertullian, along with other theologians like Origen and philosophers like Justin Martyr, argued that Christians ought to be pacifists. They should refuse to serve in the military, not only because they would be forced to engage in idolatrous practices, but also because they might be ordered to torture or execute prisoners or be commanded to engage in warfare. While Tertullian was faithful to the teachings of Jesus on nonviolence, he did not address the teaching to love one's enemies.

Although we find abundant evidence that Christians did not take up arms to defend themselves when persecuted and generally refused to serve in the military in defense of the Roman Empire, pacifism was neither an explicit church teaching nor a universal practice during the first three centuries of Christianity. Clement of Alexandria, Tertullian's Greek contemporary, was much more ambiguous about war. While he spoke of wars as the inspiration of pagan deities, he also praised Moses as a military commander. He compared Christians to warriors and Christ to the military commander who "directs his troops on the line with eye to their safety."[57] Lisa Sowle Cahill concludes her excellent analysis of pacifism in the early church with this balanced summary: "Although the theologians of early Christianity upheld pacifism as an ideal and exhorted their hearers to lay hold of the new life possible in Jesus Christ, we have seen that not all Christians actually realized this ideal, and that a thinker like Origen communicates a subtle resignation to the incomplete accessibility of genuine discipleship."[58] The same could be said of Tertullian.

KING AND NONVIOLENT RESISTANCE

Eighteen centuries later a Baptist preacher living within the belly of another powerfully armed behemoth galvanized a black church resistance movement called the Southern Christian Leadership Conference (SCLC). People hailed this renowned charismatic leader of the civil rights movement as a prophet. What U.S. President Lyndon Johnson said about the "American Negro" in this nonviolent movement for civil rights would certainly apply to Martin Luther King, Jr.: "And who among us can say we would have made the same progress were it not for his persistent bravery and his faith in American democracy?"[59] King and his people were indeed brave, and they did believe in American democracy. But his ethics of nonviolent resistance was more deeply rooted in Jesus' teaching on love and nonviolence. In presenting King with the Nobel Peace Prize in 1964, the Chairman of the Nobel Committee, Gunnar Jahn, said:

> It was not because he led a racial minority in their struggle for equality that Martin Luther King achieved fame. Many others have done the same, and their names have been forgotten. Luther King's name will endure for the way in which he has waged his struggle, personifying in his conduct the words that were spoken to mankind: "Whosoever shall smite thee on thy right cheek, turn to him the other also." Fifty thousand Negroes obeyed this commandment in December, 1955, and won a victory. This was the beginning.[60]

The beginning was actually a few days earlier, December 2, 1955, when Rosa Parks, a black seamstress headed home on a Montgomery, Alabama, city bus, courageously refused to yield her seat to a white passenger. Her arrest roused the black community to take action. Its leadership called for a city-wide boycott of the city's busses on the following Monday. On that same Monday, Martin Luther King, Jr., at the age of twenty-six, was chosen president of the Montgomery Improvement Association and was asked to address a large gathering of black Christians that evening. As he prepared his talk, he pondered how to reconcile two diverse groups in this city-wide gathering at the Holt Street Baptist Church—people who he knew would surely differ over continuing the boycott and disagree about how it should be conducted. King would have to allay the fears of the first group, which tended to be passive, nonpolitical, and fearful of losing jobs. He won over this passive group by convincing the people that their self-respect was at stake and that their backing off after the day's successful boycott would compromise "their own sense of dignity and the eternal edicts of God himself."[61] He also had to channel the anger of the second group, whose militancy might quickly escalate from peaceful protest to violent action. He cautioned this militant group to be calm and nonviolent, as Jesus was in his preaching and action.

King contrasted his proposed nonviolent approach with the well-known methods of the White Citizens' Council and the Klu Klux Klan. These groups used public protest for maintaining injustice. Their protests led to cross burnings, abduction of black folks from their homes, and lynchings. That shall not be our way, King concluded; no, we shall protest for justice; our method will follow the highest principles of love and nonviolence. "No white person will be taken from his home by a hooded Negro mob and brutally murdered."[62] Our faith and love calls us to a method of persuasion that Jesus taught us by word and example. King quoted the words of Jesus: "Love your enemies, bless them that curse you, and pray for them that despitefully use you" (Lk 6:27–28). He concluded with a stirring statement: "If you will protest courageously, and yet with dignity and Christian love, when the history books are written in future generations, the historians will have to pause and say, 'There lived a great people—a black people—who injected new meaning and dignity into the veins of civilization.' This is our challenge and our overwhelming responsibility."[63] By basing his nonviolent resistance on the principles of Jesus and the strategy of Gandhi, Martin Luther King, Jr., assumed (as did Gandhi) that Jesus was nonviolent and that his nonviolence involved an *active* resistance against the evildoer. King had to convince his civil rights followers that they, like Jesus, must love the white segregationists while they opposed their laws and practices.

King accurately interpreted and aptly applied Jesus' teaching on love and nonviolence to the civil rights movement in the United States. How well King applied the teaching may be summarized in five points: (1) *agape* as foundational to his ethics, (2) avoidance of hatred of the enemy, (3) distinguishing between evil and evildoers, (4) the strategy of nonviolent resistance, and (5) applying the strategy to groups.

King, first of all, grounded his principles and strategy in God's love, or *agape*. God's creative and redemptive love and Jesus' teaching of love that embraced sinners and enemies motivated and guided King's principles of justice, freedom, and responsible use of power, as well as his strategy of nonresistance. *Agape*, in its New Testament sense, connotes expressing good will, esteem, and affection for the other, even enemies. King agreed wholeheartedly with this understanding of love. He defined *agape* as understanding, creative, redemptive good will toward all men.[64] He saw nonviolent response in the face of adversity to be virtually synonymous with love.[65]

Second, King opposed hatred toward the enemy. Jesus' teaching and practice of *agape* taught him to avoid internal violence of the spirit as he and the people protested against racial discrimination. Jesus, as we saw earlier, not only condemned murder but also the internal anger that impelled persons to kill. "The nonviolent resister," King said, "not only refuses to shoot his opponent, but he also refuses to hate him."[66] Jesus' *agape*, King taught, does not discriminate between friend and enemy because *agape* loves others for their own sake, and not because they have admirable qualities or because they have done good things for us. "The Samaritan who helped the Jew on the Jericho Road was 'good' because he responded to the human need that he was presented with. . . . The Negro must love the white man, because the white man needs his love to remove his tensions, insecurities, and fears."[67] In a Christmas sermon at Ebenezer Baptist Church, King spoke eloquently about resisting hatred even under the duress of suffering at the hands of the oppressor. The sermon clearly demonstrates that the ground of King's ethics is the gift or virtue of love.

> I've seen too much hate to want to hate, myself, and I've seen hate on the faces of too many sheriffs, too many white citizens' councilors, and too many Klansmen of the South to want to hate, myself; and every time I see it, I say to myself, hate is too great a burden to bear. Somehow we must be able to stand up before our most bitter opponents and say: "We shall match your capacity to inflict suffering by our capacity to endure suffering. We will meet your physical force with soul force. Do to us what you will and we will still love you. We cannot in all conscience obey your unjust laws and abide by the unjust system because noncooperation with evil is as much a moral obligation as is cooperation with good, and so throw us in jail and we will still love you. Bomb our homes and threaten our children, and, as difficult as it is, we will still love you. . . . But be assured that we'll wear you down by our capacity to suffer, and one day, we will win our freedom. We will not only win freedom for ourselves; we will so appeal to your heart and conscience that we will win you in the process, and our victory will be a double victory."[68]

Third, King, like Jesus, distinguished between evil and the evildoer. He correctly understood that Jesus resisted by refusing to submit to an evil power and even actively worked to eliminate the evil, while refusing to act aggressively toward the evildoer. King and his people tried to do the same. Nonviolent resistance, he said, is a "courageous confrontation with evil by the power of love."[69] His nonviolent resistance, like the action of Jesus, did not intend to defeat or humiliate the opponents but to win their understanding and eventually their friendship. The nonviolent protests, marches, and sit-ins were intended to demonstrate that the policies were unjust because they violated the U.S. Constitution by discriminating against a group of citizens simply because they belonged to the black race.

Fourth, an essential element in King's strategy of nonviolent resistance called for a willingness to accept suffering and verbal and physical abuse at the hands of the enemy without retaliating. This again follows the example of Jesus, as demonstrated in the accounts of his being tried, beaten, sentenced to death, and executed. King's nonviolent protests sometimes involved physical abuse by the opponent. He tried to avoid injury to his people, but when police or anti-demonstrators used violence against the demonstrators, King insisted that his people not respond in kind. When Bull Connor's firefighters and police attacked the children in Birmingham, the black people became enraged (see case below). The following day, some black protesters equipped themselves with guns and knives. One of King's leaders, James Bevel, called out to the people through a policeman's bullhorn: "Okay, get off the streets now. We're not going to have violence. If you're not going to respect policemen, you're not going to be in the movement."[70]

Fifth, King rightly interpreted Jesus' ethics of turning the other cheek and loving enemies to be applicable to conflicts with groups as well as with individuals. Although Jesus never sent his disciples on mission to protest an unfair policy of the Roman and Jewish leaders, he did send them in pairs to groups of people throughout Galilee to proclaim God's reign, a mission that involved a kind of protest. Anticipating that they would encounter hostility, Jesus forewarned them: "See, I am sending you out like lambs into the midst of wolves; so be wise as serpents and innocent as doves" (Mt 10:16). And should the disciples receive a hostile reception, Jesus instructed them to protest the rejection by shaking the dust off their sandals as a prophetic symbolic witness that this people refused to accept the reign of God. King took this passage to heart, commenting that workers in the civil rights movement "must combine the toughness of the serpent and the softness of the dove, a tough mind and a tender heart."[71] The toughness of the serpent symbolized a just use of power and the softness of the dove symbolized love and grace.

It should also be noted that King and his followers, like Jesus and his disciples, were aware that they were a marginal people, made so by discrimination from and domination by the established power. As marginal people, African American people lacked the means of legal redress that the majority possessed. They lived on the boundary of society, which meant dwelling in segregated housing, going to separate and inferior schools, riding in the back of the bus, and being impeded from registering to vote. Members of the white majority expressed hostility to King. They bombed his home, vilified, imprisoned, and finally assassinated him.

THINKING ETHICALLY ON THE STREETS

Not all things go well in nonviolent protests. Even with police protection, protesters face the possibility of being beaten or shot. But King and his people often engaged in public demonstrations without police protection because the very laws they were protesting were ones the police were enforcing. Decisions to go ahead with planned protests under threats weighed heavily on King's conscience. In one protest in Selma, called Bloody Sunday, the Alabama state troopers charged the marchers, knocking the first ten rows of people off their feet. People, young and old, screamed and struggled to break free as their belongings were scattered across the Edmund Pettus Bridge. The troopers then fired tear gas and rode their horses into the crowd of old people and young children, knocking them down with their clubs. King, who was absent from that march, asked that U.S. District Court Judge Frank Johnson forbid Governor George Wallace from interfering with the next march, planned for the following Tuesday. The judge refused the request and ruled against the march.

King responded, "We have gone too far to turn back." Organizing fifteen hundred people from all over the country, he led the march, even against the wishes of the Justice Department, which had asked him to reconsider. King said, "I would rather die on the highway in Alabama than make a butchery of conscience by compromising with evil."[72] That Tuesday, two days after Selma's Bloody Sunday, King led the marchers out of the church and across the Edmund Pettus Bridge. They again encountered state troopers who ordered them to stop. The marchers stopped, joined hands, and sang "We Shall Overcome." Then King knelt and asked Rev. Ralph Abernathy to lead the demonstrators in prayer. King knew that many of the demonstrators wanted to continue the march. The violent scenes from Bloody Sunday's violence flashed through his consciousness. What should he do? He rose and directed the marchers to turn back.

Later King explained the dilemma on the bridge and how he resolved it. One alternative was not to march at all. This, he said, was unthinkable, because it would be caving in to the injustice (violation of voting rights). A second alternative would be to go forward recklessly when it became clear that the state troopers would again use force. This would be irresponsible. It would mean knowingly putting his people in harm's way. It would also cause supporters to lose confidence in his leadership. He chose a middle course: to march until it was clear that the troopers were going to use force.[73] King felt that they had arrived at that crisis point, and so he halted the march. The goal of dramatizing the injustice had been achieved.

NONVIOLENCE: A UNIVERSAL ETHIC?

While Martin Luther King, Jr., faithfully followed Jesus' ethics of nonviolent love of enemies, one may ask whether the pacifism of Jesus constitutes a universal ethic that Christians today should apply in all circumstances involving violence. Emmanuel Charles McCarthy, a Roman Catholic priest, gives an emphatic yes.

Does the Son of God come down from heaven so His followers can create hell on earth with a clear conscience? Does it not take an elephantine indifference to the Divinity of Jesus to lead people in His name to where Jesus never would have led them? When Jesus says, "follow me" He never, never means, "Follow Me" in committing homicidal violence. Never! What does "follow Me" mean if it does not mean to teach what Jesus taught, to live what Jesus lived, to love as Jesus loved and to die as Jesus died? If Jesus is nonviolent, then to follow Him is to live and die nonviolently.[74]

McCarthy, a radical Christian pacifist, poses a challenging question, one that would require a great deal of research and analysis. At most, we can make a few observations based on this study of the gospel and the two historical figures. First, Tertullian and King were both faithful to Jesus' principles of nonviolence, yet neither was an absolute pacifist. Both Christian strategists adapted the teaching to their circumstances. Tertullian saw the necessity of the Roman Empire having a standing army and of engaging in military conflict, even though he opposed Christian participation in armed conflict. As we have seen, he justified converts remaining in the military.

King applied nonviolence to the civil rights movement, but he justified the use of police force to quell riots in cities. He also justified the federal use of force for getting James Meredith admitted to the University of Mississippi.[75] But in his later years King came to see the folly of war. "Many men cry, 'Peace! Peace!' but they refuse to do the things that make for peace!"[76] He denounced the U.S. intervention in the Vietnam conflict, which he said was basically a civil war, as morally wrong. But he did not condemn all war.

It should also be noted that Tertullian and King, like Jesus, proclaimed a nonviolent resistance on behalf of a weak and dependent people. Some observers argue that Jesus' ethics of nonviolence may be applied only by minority groups who choose to resist the oppression of a dominant group. Biblical scholar Luise Schottroff cites the fittingness of King applying Jesus' teaching to the civil rights movement. "The love of enemy is an attitude adopted by groups which have no means of legal redress as the rest of society does."[77] She concludes that the commandment to love one's enemies and to resist oppressors' unjust laws should not be taken as a universal ethic. In a similar vein, patristic scholars Helgeland, Daly, and Burns ask, "Is this [nonviolent teaching] a universal ethic for everyone, or only for Christians in a situation of powerlessness?"[78] Like Schottroff, they imply that it is an ethics for the powerless. It is clear that in the powerless church within the first three centuries of Christianity, the people of God for the most part rejected serving in the military. The reasons, as noted earlier, were both religious and moral. Christians objected to sacrifices to the gods, worshiping the emperor, and participating in the cult of the military standards. They strongly objected to a military life that was morally loose and that would require killing the enemy and those convicted of capital crimes.

In the next chapter, we shall see how St. Augustine reinterprets and adapts Jesus' and Paul's teaching on violence for Christian communities in the fourth and fifth centuries as they face invading armies.

RESOURCES

DISCUSSION QUESTIONS

1. What does nonviolent resistance within a Christian perspective mean?
2. What is the ordinary way people understand peace? What deeper meaning does the Bible add to peace?
3. What are the key points of disagreement between Richard Horsley and Walter Wink on Jesus' teachings "do not resist evildoers" and "love your enemies?" (Mt 5:38–48)
4. In the same Matthean passage, Jesus commands his listeners to love their enemy. Does the text suggest that this kind of love will transform the enemy or transform the disciple who loves in this heroic manner? Or does the text suggest that the intended outcome is that both parties will be changed?
5. How does Paul's teaching in Romans 13:1–7 (that governing authorities are servants' of God and that they do not bear the sword in vain) begin to shift Christian nonviolence to a new level of interpretation?
6. Tertullian saw war as a necessary evil and prayed for the "brave army." At the same time he argued strongly that it was wrong for Christians to serve in the Roman military because they were not permitted to kill. Do you see anything inconsistent in his position?
7. How well did Martin Luther King, Jr., embody the spirit of Jesus' teaching on love of enemies?
8. The great American Protestant theologian Reinhold Niebuhr has criticized pacifists, like the Quakers, for talking about power as contradictory to love; he says that they thereby leave out the whole problem of how to attain justice. "Justice," Niebuhr says, "may be the servant of love, and power may be the servant of justice. Every historic form of justice has been attained by some equilibrium of power. Force in the narrow sense may be an element in the arsenal of power, but power is wider than force."[79] Did King have a realistic sense of using power to attain justice, or do you think he is subject to the same criticism made by Niebuhr of the Quakers?
9. The case that follows, in which King uses children as nonviolent protesters, presents us with the dilemma: whether to risk putting people in harm's way. The new dimension is whether the leaders ought to have risked using children. His detractors opposed his doing so. Did King make a good decision?

   In March 1963, Martin Luther King, Jr., together with a coalition of Southern black ministers and black women, organized a series of protests in Birmingham, Alabama. Their immediate goal was to desegregate lunch counters, rest rooms, and drinking fountains, and change the hiring practices in the business and industrial community that would afford blacks opportunities to work and to be upgraded in their jobs.

The live drama began with nonviolent sit-ins and marches, which brought them face to face with Eugene "Bull" Connor, Commissioner of Public Safety, who arrested them and sent them off to jail. The national media, some black leaders, and local white clergymen criticized the movement and King, saying that the protests were ill timed. The protesters should have waited until the newly elected mayor of Birmingham, Albert Boutwell, could bring about reforms that he had promised in his campaign. King, however, knew that the new mayor was a segregationist and would therefore do little, if anything, about desegregating public facilities and changing hiring policies. Writing the clergymen from a Birmingham jail, King said, "Justice too long delayed is justice denied."

With King and many of his protesters in jail, the demonstrations limped along through most of April. Meanwhile, the Reverend James Bevel came up with a daring and brilliant idea: ask Birmingham's black children to participate in the demonstrations. Bevel argued that many adults were reluctant to march because they would be arrested, lose their jobs, and be unable to pay their rent, utility bills, and support their families. But children are free of those responsibilities. The coalition leaders were soon to discover that the children were eager to help. Bevel convinced King that photos and television footage of young children being hauled off to jail would stir the nation's conscience.

When the strategy to use children in the demonstrations became public, Robert Kennedy phoned King to warn him that the children could be hurt. Newspaper critics deplored the idea of "using" children to further the demonstrations. King responded, "Where had these writers been during the centuries when our segregated social system had been misusing and abusing Negro children?"[80] The young people, seven to eighteen years old, responded enthusiastically to their training to march in a nonviolent demonstration. One teenage boy resisted his father's command forbidding him to participate in the marches. "Daddy," the boy said, "I don't want to disobey you, but I have made my pledge. If you try to keep me home, I will sneak off. If you think I deserve to be punished for that, I'll just have to take the punishment. For, you see, I'm not doing this only because I want to be free. I'm doing it also because I want freedom for you and Mama, and I want it to be before you die." After further reflection, the father gave the son his blessing.[81]

On May 2, 1963, over one thousand black children marched through town. Bull Connor was there to arrest them. Herding them into paddy wagons, the police carted the kids off to jail. At the day's end, 959 children were incarcerated. The next day, a thousand more children stayed out of school and assembled at a church. Television cameras were focused on the drama as Bull Connor stood with firefighters and cops with city police dogs. Hoping to nip the march in the bud, he ordered the firefighters to turn their hoses on the young boys and girls, shooting them with canons of water with 100 pounds of pressure per square inch, which knocked the children down and slammed them into curbs and parked cars. Black businessman A. G. Gaston, who had opposed King's demonstrations, witnessed the event from his office across the street. Strategizing over the phone with a lawyer about how to stop the protests, he stopped in mid-sentence, watching in horror the street scene. He saw the children being hosed and others being bitten by the police dogs. He said to the lawyer: "They've just turned the fire hoses on a black girl. They're rolling that little girl right down the middle of the street. I can't talk to you no more."[82] *That night the major television networks spent fifteen minutes on the nightly news showing and commenting on the grisly scene in Birmingham. The city's black population became enraged. U.S. public sentiment changed overnight. This single event turned the tide for the civil rights movement. King and the coalition won a desegregation settlement, which laid the groundwork for the U.S. Civil Rights Act passed the following year.*

While the news media criticized King and the movement for using children, King thought this strategy was the wisest moves that SCLC ever made. Were Bevel and King right to use children in the protest movement?

Suggested Readings

Harnack, Adolf. *Militia Christi*. Edited and translated by David McInnes Gracie. Philadelphia: Fortress Press, 1981.

Helgeland, John, Robert Daly, and J. Patout Burns. *Christians and the Military: The Early Experience*. Edited by Robert Daly. Philadelphia: Fortress Press, 1985.

King, Martin Luther, Jr. *Stride toward Freedom: The Montgomery Story*. New York: Harper and Row, 1958.

Stassen, Glen, ed. *Just Peacemaking: Ten Practices for Abolishing War*. Cleveland: The Pilgrim Press, 1998.

Wood, John A. "Pacifism." Chapter 6 in *Perspectives on War in the Bible*. Macon, GA: Mercer University Press, 1998.

NOTES

[1] C. John Cadoux, *The Early Christian Attitude to War* (New York: The Seabury Press, 1982); Roland H. Bainton, *Christian Attitudes toward War and Peace* (Nashville, TN: Abingdon, 1960); Peter Brock, *Pacifism in Europe to 1914* (Princeton, NJ: Princeton University Press, 1972), 3–24.

[2] Adolf Harnack, *Militia Christi*, trans. and ed. David McInnes Gracie (Philadelphia: Fortress Press, 1981); Albert Nolan, *Jesus before Christianity* (Maryknoll, NY: Orbis Books, 1992), 134–35.

[3] The Albert Einstein Institution, "A Journalist's Brief Glossary of Nonviolent Struggle" (Cambridge, MA: The Albert Einstein Institution, 2005), 1–5, http://www.hermanos.org/nonviolence/jourglos.html (accessed on April 1, 2005).

[4] Glen Stassen, ed., *Just Peacemaking: Ten Practices for Abolishing War* (Cleveland: The Pilgrim Press, 1998), 2–4.

[5] John Howard Yoder, *Nevertheless: Varieties of Religious Pacifism* (Scottdale, PA: Herald Press, 1992).

[6] Martin Luther King, Jr., "Conscience and the Vietnam War," in *The Trumpet of Conscience* (New York: Harper and Row, 1967), chap. 7.

[7] Martin Luther King, Jr., "A Christmas Sermon on Peace," in James Melvin Washington, ed., *A Testament of Hope: The Essential Writings of Martin Luther King, Jr.* (San Francisco: Harper & Row, 1986), 256.

[8] Xavier Léon-Dufour, ed., *Dictionary of Biblical Theology,* 2nd ed. (New York: The Seabury Press, 1967, 1973), s.v.

[9] Victor Paul Furnish, "War and Peace in the New Testament," *Interpretation* 38 (October 1984), 363–79.

[10] Martin Hengel, *Victory over Violence: Jesus and the Revolutionists*, ed. Robin Scroggs, trans. David E. Green (Philadelphia: Fortress Press, 1973), 33–34.

[11] Luise Schottroff, "Give to Caesar What Belongs to Caesar and to God What Belongs to God," in William M. Swartley, ed., *The Love of Enemy and Nonretaliation in the New Testament* (Louisville, KY: Westminster/John Knox Press, 1992), 231–33.

[12] Ibid., 233.

[13] Robert A. Seeley, *The Handbook of Non-Violence* (Westport, CT: Lawrence Hill and Company, 1986), 16.

[14] Richard J. Cassidy, *Paul in Chains: Roman Imprisonment and the Letters of St. Paul* (New York: Crossroad, 2001), 180–82.

[15] Hengel, *Victory over Violence,* 54; Cadoux, *Early Christian Attitudes to War,* 34–35.

[16] Robert J. Karris, "The Gospel according to Luke," in Raymond E. Brown, Joseph A. Fitzmyer, and Roland E. Murphy, eds., *New Jerome Biblical Commentary* (Englewood Cliffs, NJ: Prentice Hall, 1990), sec. 43:183.

[17] Benedict T. Viviano, "The Gospel according to Matthew," in Brown, Fitzmyer, and Murphy, *New Jerome Biblical Commentary*, sec. 42.29.

[18] Martin Luther King, Jr., "An Experiment in Love," in Washington, *A Testament of Hope,* 17–18.

[19] Martin Hengel, *Was Jesus a Revolutionist?* trans. William Klassen (Philadelphia: Fortress Press, 1971), 28–29.

[20] Walter Wink, "Neither Passivity nor Violence: Jesus' Third Way (Matt. 5:38–42)," in Willard M. Swartley, ed., *The Love of Enemy and Nonretaliation in the New Testament* (Louisville, KY: Westminster/John Knox Press, 1992), 114–15.

[21] Ibid.

[22] N. T. Wright, *Christian Origins and the Question of God*, vol. 2, *Jesus and the Victory of God* (Minneapolis: Fortress Press, 1996), 190–91. Wright concurs with Wink that "resist" or *antistēnai* is virtually a technical term for revolutionary resistance in a military sense.

[23] Wink, "Neither Passivity nor Violence," 116.

[24] Schottroff, "Give to Caesar," 231–32.

[25] Viviano, "The Gospel according to Luke," sec.42.29.

[26] Richard Horsley, "Response to Walter Wink," in Swartley, *Love of Enemy*, 129.

[27] Ibid., 131.

[28] Walter Wink, "Counterresponse to Richard Horsley," in Swartley, *Love of Enemy*, 133–34.

[29] Richard Horsley, *Jesus and the Spiral of Violence* (San Francisco: Harper and Row, 1987), 326.

[30] Wright, *Jesus and the Victory of God*, 290n178.

[31] Wright, *Christian Origins*, vol. 1, *The New Testament and the People of God* (London: SPCK; Minneapolis: Fortress, 1992), 176.

[32] Marcus J. Borg, *Conflict, Holiness, and Politics in the Teachings of Jesus* (Harrisburg, PA: Trinity Press International, 1984), 142.

[33] John R. Donahue, "Who Is My Enemy? The Parable of the Good Samaritan and the Love of Enemies," in Swartley, *Love of Enemy*, 137–56.

[34] Wink, "Neither Passivity nor Violence," 115.

[35] Schottroff, "Give to Caesar," 230.

[36] Brendan Byrne, *Romans*, Sacra Pagina Series, vol. 6, ed. Daniel J. Harrington (Collegeville, MN: The Liturgical Press, 1996), 391.

[37] Louis J. Swift, *The Early Fathers on War and Military Service: Message of the Fathers of the Church*, vol. 19, ed. Thomas Halton (Wilmington, DE: Michael Glazier, 1983), 34.

[38] Justo L. González, *The Story of Christianity*, vol. 1, *The Early Church to the Dawn of the Reformation* (San Francisco: HarperSanFrancisco, 1984), 35.

[39] G. E. M. de Ste. Croix, "Why Were the Early Christians Persecuted?" in Everett Ferguson with David M. Scholer and Paul Corby Finney, eds., *Studies in Early Christianity: A Collection of Scholarly Essays* (New York: Garland, 1993), 16–48.

[40] Thomas L. Schubeck, "A Love That Does Justice," *Horizons* 28 (Spring 2001): 9.

[41] Ste. Croix, "Why Were the Early Christians Persecuted?" 24.

[42] Herbert Musurillo, *The Acts of the Christian Martyrs* (Oxford: Clarendon Press, 1972), 173.

[43] Justin Martyr, *First Apology*, 39.2–3. Quoted from Swift, *Early Fathers on War*, 34–35.

[44] David G. Hunter, "A Decade of Research on Early Christians and Military Service," *Religious Studies Review* 18, no. 2 (April 1992): 87.

[45] William Le Saint, "Tertullian," *New Catholic Encyclopedia* (New York: McGraw-Hill, 1967), 1019–22.

[46] Tertullian, *Apology*, trans. T. R. Glover (Cambridge: Harvard University Press, 1953), chap. 37.5.

[47] Ibid., 30.4.

[48] Ibid., 37.10.

[49] Adolf Harnack, *Militia Christi: The Christian Religion and the Military in the First Three Centuries*, trans. David McInnes Gracie (Philadelphia:

Fortress Press, 1981); John Helgeland, Robert Daly, and J. Patout Burns, eds., *Christians and the Military: The Early Experience* (Philadelphia: Fortress Press, 1985), 48.

[50] Origen, *Contra Celsum*, ed. and trans. Henry Chadwick (Cambridge: University Press, 1953), 8:68–69.

[51] Helgeland, Daly, and Burns, *Christians and the Military*, 31–34.

[52] Tertullian, *On Idolatry* 17.3.

[53] Tertullian, *De Idololatria: Critical Text, Translation and Commentary* by J. H. Waszink and J. C. M. Van Winden, partly based on a manuscript by P. G. Van Der Nat (Leiden: E.J. Brill, 1987), 266.

[54] Swift, *The Early Fathers on War*, 45–46.

[55] Robert D. Sider, *Christian and Pagan in the Roman Empire: The Witness of Tertullian* (Washington, DC: The Catholic University of America Press, 2001), 54.

[56] Lisa Sowle Cahill, *Love Your Enemies: Discipleship, Pacifism, and Just War Theory* (Minneapolis: Fortress Press, 1994), 45.

[57] Clement of Alexandria, *The Teacher* 1, 7.54. Quoted from Swift, *Early Fathers on War*, 51.

[58] Cahill, *Love Your Enemies*, 54.

[59] Washington, *A Testament of Hope.*

[60] Gunnar Jahn, "The Nobel Peace Prize 1964," http://nobelprize.org/peace/laureates/1964/press.html (accessed on August 21, 2006).

[61] Martin Luther King, Jr., *Stride toward Freedom: The Montgomery Story* (San Francisco: HarperSanFrancisco, 1986), 60.

[62] Ibid., 62.

[63] Ibid., 63.

[64] King, "A Christmas Sermon on Peace," 256n5.

[65] Ervin Smith, *Studies in American Religion*, vol. 2, *The Ethics of Martin Luther King, Jr.* (New York: Edwin Mellen Press, 1981), 100.

[66] King, *Stride toward Freedom*, reprinted in Washington, *A Testament of Hope*, 19.

[67] Ibid.

[68] King, "A Christmas Sermon on Peace," 256–57.

[69] Ibid.

[70] Juan Williams, *Eyes on the Prize* (New York: Penguin Books, 1988), 190.

[71] King, *The Strength to Love*, quoted from Washington, *A Testament of Hope*, 492.

[72] Martin Luther King, Jr., *The Autobiography of Martin Luther King, Jr.*, ed. Clayborne Carson (New York: Warner Books, 1998), 281.

[73] King, "Behind the Selma March," in Washington, *A Testament of Hope*, 127.

[74] Emmanuel Charles McCarthy, "Christian Just War Theory: The Logic of Deceit" (Wilmington, DE: Center for Christian Nonviolence, 2002), sect. 1.6.

[75] King, "Who Is Their God?" quoted from Smith, *The Ethics of Martin Luther King, Jr.*, 102.

[76] King, *Where Do We Go from Here: Chaos or Community?* (New York: Harper and Row, 1967), quoted from Washington, *A Testament of Hope*, 627.

[77] Luise Schottroff, "Non-Violence and the Love of One's Enemies," in Luise Schottroff et al., eds., *Essays on the Love Commandment* (Philadelphia: Fortress Press, 1978), 13.

[78] Helgeland, Daly, and Burns, *Christians and the Military*, 2.

[79] Reinhold Niebuhr, *Love and Justice: Selections from the Shorter Writings of Reinhold Niebuhr*, ed. D. B. Robertson (Cleveland: The World Publishing Company, 1957), 300.

[80] Martin Luther King, Jr., "*Why We Can't Wait*, quoted in Washington, *A Testament of Hope*, 546.

[81] Ibid., 547.

[82] Williams, *Eyes on the Prize*, 190.

4

LOVE AND JUSTICE IN WAR

St. Augustine

*Love and you cannot help doing good. You may chastise but
it is love that does this, not cruelty. You may strike but you
do it for disciplinary reasons because your love for love itself
does not permit you to leave the other person undisciplined.*

—St. Augustine,
Commentary on the First Letter of John (10.7)

Speaking to the cadets graduating from the Michigan Military Academy
in 1879, Civil War General William Tecumseh Sherman concluded his address with these ominous words: "You don't know the horrible aspects of
war. I've been through two wars and I know. I've seen cities and homes in
ashes. I've seen thousands of men lying on the ground, their dead faces looking up at the skies. I tell you, war is hell!"[1]

Like Sherman, World War II correspondent Ernie Pyle tried to awaken his
audience to the true nature of war by describing to the folks back home how
it looks from the trenches:

> But there are many of the living who have had burned into their brains
> forever the unnatural sight of cold dead men scattered over the hill-
> sides and in the ditches along the high rows of hedge throughout the
> world. Dead men by mass production—in one country after another—
> month after month and year after year. Dead men in winter and dead
> men in summer. Dead men in such familiar promiscuity that they be-
> come monotonous. Dead men in such monstrous infinity that you come
> almost to hate them. These are the things that you at home need not
> even try to understand. To you at home they are columns of figures, or
> he is a near one who went away and just didn't come back. You didn't
> see him lying so grotesque and pasty beside the gravel road in France.
> We saw him, saw him by the multiple thousands. That's the differ-
> ence.[2]

Pyle's depiction of war's victims—"cold dead men scattered over the hill-
sides in one country after another . . . lying so grotesque and pasty"—reinforces Sherman's judgment that war is hell.

86

St. Augustine called the horrible evils committed by humankind "hell on earth,"[3] but he never said that *war* is hell, because both the tormentor and the tormented in war are temporary, but in hell their misery is everlasting.[4] Moreover, the hell metaphor implies that war has no redemptive qualities; not so for Augustine. Even with its barbarous behavior, suffering, and death in "such monstrous infinity," Augustine asserted that war can be redemptive. God chastises by means of war the warmongers' love of violence, their revengeful cruelty, and their lust for power. These malicious desires, or what Augustine calls the "lust of domination," are far worse than the tragedy of dead bodies strewn across the battlefields.[5] Sherman's metaphor also suggests that war, like hell, has no moral limits, that "all is fair in love and war," implying that the voices of justice and charity are muted when war is being considered, declared, and waged.

JUST WAR MOTIVATED BY RIGHT LOVE

Augustine countered this way of thinking, arguing that war could be defended morally, but only when the decision to go to war *(jus ad bellum)* and when military conduct during the war *(jus in bello)* were motivated by rightly ordered love. His assertions may strike us as odd, if not contradictory to what we have already learned from the New Testament teaching and from the practice of the first Christians. Jesus reaffirmed the commandment found in the Torah—"Thou shall not kill"—then cautioned his listeners against even being angry with their neighbor, because anger is the emotional prelude to murdering the neighbor (Mt 5:21–22). He also enjoined his followers to resist nonviolently the evil deeds committed by their enemies so that their resistance would express love, not hatred. Paul urged the Christians at Rome: "Bless those who persecute you; bless and do not curse them" (Rom 12:14). How then could Augustine justify war by "a love rightly ordered"? In what way could love possibly participate in the massive killing, torture, and pillage that warfare inevitably produces?

Augustine's moral perspectives on the use of violence and engagement in war generate a host of questions about his ethical framework, political world, method of interpreting the Bible, and moral arguments. Four questions will serve as guideposts as we journey through the complex mind of Augustine. The first question asks about his ethics of virtue and how the virtues of love, justice, and peace shape his thinking about how we should live, especially in the face of conflict. His ethics places great emphasis on interiority; that is, it gives a prominent role to a person's disposition, intentionality, and motivation when judging how one should act. The second question asks about the political context, specifically about the sociopolitical and theological events and ideas in the early fourth century that influenced the thinking of this brilliant theologian on issues of violence. The third question asks about Augustine's method of interpreting the Bible, or hermeneutics. This question is pivotal because Augustine's ethical reasoning on issues like self-defense and war was much more dependent on biblical interpretation than are the ethical arguments of contemporary moral theologians.[6] The fourth question invites us to examine Augustine's arguments on self-defense and public defense against the enemy in light of his ethics of virtue, especially in light of the virtues of love, justice, and peace.

The chapter concludes with an assessment of Augustine's just-war thinking and with two inserts for reflection. The first links Augustine's just-war criteria with contemporary just-war criteria. The second is a case involving the U.S. government's decision to invade Iraq on March 19, 2003. It invites the reader to assess, in light of Augustine's or of contemporary just-war principles, whether the United States government should have launched a preemptive attack against Iraq.

AUGUSTINE'S ETHICS OF VIRTUE

We return to the paradoxical question raised above: How could Augustine justify war by "a love rightly ordered"? Could any love that intentionally kills or maims the enemy be considered "right love?" We begin our search for an answer to this question by examining Augustine's ethics of virtue. His ethics emphasizes the theological virtues of faith, hope, and charity and the moral virtues of prudence, temperance, fortitude, and justice, which transform the character of the person. Augustine's virtue ethics has a distinctive characteristic: it gives a central role to the interior disposition of moral subjects, that is, to their intentions and motives, which determine whether their acts are virtuous. Focusing on the subject, Augustine's ethics of virtue considers a person's identity, asking, "Who am I, what is my final goal, and how will I get there?"[7] In answer to "Who am I?" Augustine says that we are persons made in God's own image with a soul endowed with reason, intelligence, and free will.[8] Our ultimate goal is to love and worship God and finally to rest peacefully in God's love, in a blissful existence that continues beyond our earthly existence. We get there by following the teachings and example of Jesus, especially by living the virtues. The grace-infused virtues shape our character, giving us the capacity and facility to make good moral choices. A prudent monarch will make a prudent decision about war, a loving husband will care for his spouse with deep affection, and a just teacher will evaluate the work of students justly.

If we were to ask St. Augustine, "What is virtue?" he would reply succinctly, "It is the order of love."[9] This means that love in its many expressions functions as the foundation of all virtue and virtuous living. Love understood as charity assumes this key role, drawing the person of faith to the supreme good. Addressing God in his *Confessions*, Augustine writes: "You stir man to take pleasure in praising you, because you have made us for yourself, and our heart is restless until it rests in you."[10]

Charity also directs the other virtues toward the person's final goal, union with God or eternal happiness. We might liken love's relationship to the other virtues as a coach's relationship to the players on a basketball team. Like a coach who insistently points to the team's goal (winning the championship) and inspires the team members to work together to achieve it, so love as charity fixes the sights of the companion virtues on the ultimate good, always motivating them to achieve that end.

Conversely, the virtues contribute something to love. Let us consider justice in relation to love. Augustine refers to justice in two ways. Borrowing Aristotle's definition, he says that justice renders to each what is due. And so we have a duty in justice to give to God, neighbor, and self what is properly due them. But Augustine also speaks of justice as a virtue that puts an order into our various loves. It does this by establishing a hierarchy among the objects of our love. God as the supreme good is at the top of this hierarchy, followed by love of ourselves and love of our neighbors (who are in turn ranked).[11] We love ourselves best, Augustine says, by loving God. We love our neighbors as ourselves when we help them to be more closely united with God.[12] Augustine's second definition of human justice, then, is a function of love; it establishes right relationships with God, neighbor, and self, loving them according to a divinely ordered love.[13]

In contrast to human justice, God's justice makes persons just; God justifies human persons by forgiving them, thus reconciling them to God by empowering them through grace to live a virtuous life. Whereas human justice is a power that enables persons to rightly order the way they love and whom they love, God's justice empowers them to love and to act justly toward all.

PRIDE VERSUS CHARITY

We have been examining Augustine's concept of love that is virtuous or benevolent, a love that wills good for another. But the sin of pride causes a disorder in a person's will, moving a person away from God and neighbor and toward one's own interests. Prideful persons may selfishly or unjustly pursue great wealth, power, honors, and status, which in effect become their gods. They may also prefer material things to friendship or spiritual values. Augustine wrote:

> When the miser prefers his gold to justice, it is through no fault of the gold, but of the man; and so with every created thing. For though it be good, it may be loved with an evil as well as with a good love: it is loved rightly when it is loved ordinately; evilly, when inordinately.[14]

Here Augustine identified two types of love: a disordered love, or pride; and a rightly ordered love, or charity. In *The City of God*, he uses the metaphor of a city to contrast these two irreconcilable loves, each of which creates a different network of human relationships: "The earthly [city] by the love of self, even to the contempt of God; the heavenly by the love of God, even to the contempt of self."[15] Whereas the earthly city pursues glory from and for itself, the heavenly city seeks its glory from God. The first city lifts up its head in a prideful stance, while the other city utters, "Thou art my glory and the lifter up of mine head" (Ps 3:3). Augustine traces the history of the earthly city from the fall of Adam to the end of time, illustrating how the princes of this city are ruled by the love of ruling and then the history of the heavenly city in which God creates new relationships in order to repair the damage done by Adam's sin. Princes and subjects of the heavenly city are restored to friendship with God by the new Adam or Christ and serve one another in love.

In his *Confessions* Augustine graphically described this unruly selfish desire, which he, as a young man, mistakenly confused with true love; only later did he discover that it was lust:

> What was it that delighted me? Only loving and being loved. But there was no proper restraint, as in the union of mind with mind, where a bright boundary regulates friendship. From the mud of my fleshly desires and my erupting puberty belched out murky clouds that obscured and darkened my heart until I could not distinguish the calm light of love from the fog of lust. The two swirled about together and dragged me, young and weak as I was, over the cliffs of my desires and engulfed in a whirlpool of sins.[16]

Augustine came to see that sin, including his own transgressions, was influenced by the sin of our first parents. As a result of this original sin, all human beings are fallen creatures in need of redemption. He described the human struggle as an interior battle in which flesh lusts against the spirit and the spirit against the flesh without any letup. Try as we might to rid ourselves of this lust, we cannot blot it out. Insofar as God gives us the capacity to resist its force, we can refuse consent and try to keep it under control. Upon being justified by God through the cross of Christ, we receive the gifts or virtues of faith, hope, and love. Yet we remain fallible with a strong tendency to sin, due to the lasting effects of original sin and our own sinful past.

Sin as pride craves for excessive self-exaltation, expressed by living for oneself and by dominating other human beings.[17] Augustine's shorthand description of sin is *libido dominandi*, the lust for domination. Even those justified by God's grace remain seriously flawed human beings. Their weakened condition manifests itself through self-absorption, lustful desires, lies, inordinate competitiveness, and violence. Viewed theologically, these selfish desires, words, and actions are idolatrous because they regard riches, prestige, and power as their gods.

Lustful desires of pride cause war. The real evil in war, Augustine says, is not the massive deaths of warriors and of noncombatants caught in the crossfire. "The real evils in war are love of violence, revengeful cruelty, fierce and implacable enmity, wild resistance, and the lust of power."[18] War is not only a consequence of sin but a remedy for sin. God uses war, even when wicked individuals wage it, to punish the warring people's lust to dominate.

Charity, by contrast with pride, has its origin in God. Augustine describes charity as God's initiative and the individual's response: "With your word you pierced my heart, and I loved you."[19] Love begins with God who utters the "word" that breaks through human beings' defenses and allows them to hear God's love. In response, they profess to love God with their whole heart and the neighbor as themselves. Persons are able to love God because God first loves them and gives them sufficient grace whereby they may enjoy happiness by resting in God to a certain degree in this life and fully in the next.

No one has spoken of God's persistent love for human beings more powerfully and more beautifully than Augustine. Toward the end of his *Confessions*, he summarizes in lovely, lyrical lines the central themes of the dark and painful journey that led him down dark alleys and dead ends before he finally found the path where he encountered the true lover, who was in fact pursuing him throughout the journey. In the following passage he speaks of God trying to break through all five of his spiritual senses, which had for many years remained impenetrable. When he finally opened himself to God's word, he experienced deep consolation:

Late have I loved you, beauty so old and so new: late have I loved you. And see, you were within and I was in the external world and sought you there, and in my unlovely state I plunged into lovely created things which you made. You were with me, and I was not with you. The lovely things kept me far from you, though if they did not have their existence in you, they had no existence at all. You called and cried out loud and shattered my deafness. You were radiant and resplendent, you put to flight my blindness. You were fragrant, and I drew in my breath and now pant after you. I tasted you, and I feel but hunger and thirst for you. You touched me, and I am set on fire to attain the peace which is yours.[20]

Augustine acknowledges here that two loves marked his tempestuous journey. The first love missed the mark ("in my unlovely state, I plunged into lovely created things which you made. . . . The lovely things kept me far from you"). The second love set a fire within him and gave him an abiding peace.

Augustine called this dearest of all the virtues charity: "There is no gift of God more excellent than this. . . . Other gifts, too, are given by the Holy

Spirit; but without love they profit nothing."[21] Charity empowers human beings to love God above all other creatures and to love their neighbors in God. Loving someone "in God" means bringing the person in closer union with God by prayer, kindness, and good example. True friendship does not exist unless God is the source of the bond between the two friends. Augustine speaks from personal experience. As a young man he had a friend who, he said, "was half of my soul. . . . My soul and his soul were one soul in two bodies."[22] Shattered by the death of his friend, he found no comfort or peace for a long time. He had loved him as though he were immortal and never entertained the idea that God was part of the relationship. He would later learn that the origin and final destiny of charity is God, in whom human beings find freedom, rest, and happiness.

Charity is what Augustine means by "love rightly ordered." It is this meaning of love that prompted Augustine to write:

> Love, and do what thou wilt: whether thou hold thy peace, through love hold thy peace; whether thou cry out, through love cry out; whether thou spare, through love do thou spare; let the root of love be within, of this root can nothing spring but what is good.[23]

Augustine's famous moral directive—"Love and do what thou wilt"—implies that the motive of love is central in ethics. If love is the compelling force in a specific human act, the act is good; if love is absent, the action is bad.

CHARITY, INTENTION, AND MOTIVE

Augustine said that the agent's intention determines whether a human act is morally good or evil. It is not what a person does that is decisive for virtuous action, but the state of the mind and will with which a person acts. "The diverse intention therefore makes the things done diverse."[24] Intentions affect the morality of an act. He invites the reader to consider two actions that on the surface fail to reveal the true situation: "A father beats a boy and a boy-stealer caresses [a boy]."[25] If one judges the two acts simply on the basis of blows and caresses, one would blame the father and praise the boy-stealer. But if you learn that the father beats his son out of love in order to make him a better person, and that the fondler caresses the boy in order to kidnap and exploit him, then you would judge the acts of the two men quite differently.[26]

Augustine's example would be clearer if he were to distinguish between intention and motive. Intention generally refers to what the will aims to realize by a designed action. Motive is that which determines the person to aim at the objective. It answers the question, "Why do you wish to do it?" In Augustine's example, the father intends to punish his son; his motive for doing so is love for the boy. As we shall later see, motive is crucial when

Augustine talks about the right intention for going to war. Motive, more than intention, manifests the interior disposition of the person. When charity is the true motive for punishment, then the action, which on the surface seems wrong, is rightly ordered.

AUGUSTINE'S WORLD

Before examining how Augustine applies his ethics to warfare, we should consider important events and theological perspectives on war during the Constantinian era, which influenced Augustine's thinking. Christians in the first three centuries generally followed the nonviolent teaching and practice of Jesus, although, as noted in Chapter 3, nonviolence was neither an explicit church teaching nor a universal practice. Augustine, born in the mid-fourth century, would qualify the nonviolent teaching of Jesus by persuasively arguing that the sovereign of a state should defend the people against hostile groups that threaten their lives, religious practice, or material possessions.

CONSTANTINE AND THE EDICT OF MILAN

Early in the fourth century the political situation in Europe and North Africa changed drastically and so did Christian thinking and practice about military service. Emperor Constantine converted to Christianity in 312, and in the following year he signed the Edict of Milan, which officially ended the persecutions of Christians. Almost overnight Christianity became the dominate religion, and by the end of the fourth century, it was accepted as the official religion of the empire.

This change heralded good news and bad news. The good news was that the terrible persecutions by Constantine's predecessors ceased; the edict permitted Christians to practice their religion without fear of reprisals. Civil law also protected the personal property of Christians as well as church property. Furthermore, laws safeguarded the office of the bishop and the life and liberty of the Christian citizens throughout the empire. Christians became jubilant over their new freedom and citizenship. They no longer felt the tension in trying to balance loyalties between church and state. Formerly regarded by the Romans as a marginal sect, Christians rapidly became members of an established church and full members of civil society. This political and cultural transformation invested them with a new outlook, hope, and responsibility.[27]

The bad news was that Christians uncritically accepted the emperor and the many changes that his regime brought about, which significantly compromised the church and its mission. The church, which had faithfully proclaimed good news to the poor in the first three centuries, came to accommodate the rich and to regard wealth and pomp as signs of God's favor.[28]

Church historian Eusebius wrote enthusiastically about the new ornate churches and their elaborate liturgies. The church very subtly came to be a church of the powerful, modeling its beautiful buildings, liturgy, and style of governance on the empire.[29] Another negative outcome was that Christians could be conscripted and were expected to use arms in order to repel foreign aggressors as well as heretics within their borders.[30] The transition from the Christians' earlier nonviolent stance to their becoming the core of a powerful militia was rapid. By 416 only Christians could serve in the military.

THREE THEOLOGIANS ON WAR

During and after Constantine's reign, theologians increasingly began to defend Christian involvement in military service and war. Three important theologians in the fourth century—Eusebius, Athanasius, and Ambrose—helped prepare a new outlook on war and peace that influenced Augustine. Eusebius (260–339), bishop of Caesarea, expressed this new vision as he effusively praised Constantine for bringing peace to the church: "God made him [Constantine] such a consistently triumphant ruler and glorious victor over his enemies that no one ever heard the like of him in human memory. Beloved by God and supremely blessed, he was so reverent and fortunate that he subdued with the greatest ease more nations than any previous emperor, and he kept the realm intact up to the very end."[31] Eusebius's appraisal of Constantine failed to mention his serious limitations, such as his outbursts of temper and bloodthirsty disposition and his serving other gods, especially the Unconquered Sun.[32] Implicit in Eusebius's accolade of Constantine was his full acceptance of the emperor's military victories over many nations, which Eusebius assumed were just conquests.

St. Athanasius (296–373), famous for his contribution in defending the divinity of Jesus against Arius, was quite explicit in his defense of war:

> One is not supposed to kill, but killing the enemy in battle is both lawful and praiseworthy. For this reason individuals who have distinguished themselves in war are considered worthy of great honors, and monuments are put up to celebrate their accomplishments. Thus, at one particular time, and under one set of circumstances, an act is not permitted, but when the time and conditions are right, it is both allowed and condoned.[33]

Athanasius, however, did not identify the conditions that justify killing in war, leaving this task for later prominent teachers of the church, especially Ambrose and Augustine.

St. Ambrose (339–97), while serving as governor of a province in Northern Italy, converted to Catholicism and in 373, while still a catechumen, was elected bishop of Milan. Both his distinguished political career and the theological studies following his conversion influenced his position on military defense. He praised the courage of soldiers in battle as a great virtue, "because it prefers death to slavery and disgrace."[34] While he condemned personal self-defense, he supported national defense, a position that Augustine later would adopt. Although he taught that Christians should never harm an intruder in order to protect their own property or life, Ambrose held that Christians must protect a third party threatened by an assailant. A Christian who refused to do so would be as much at fault as the perpetrator.

Ambrose made a second distinction that Augustine would also incorporate as part of his own teaching. Christians, in accordance with the gospel command to love one's enemies, should hate the evil deed but love the evildoer. This distinction between the evil action and the evildoer encouraged Christian soldiers to convert the enemies whom they had captured. In sum, Augustine was greatly influenced by these theologians and bishops in the church's early tradition, including their moral teachings on war and other uses of force. Although he is sometimes called the father of just-war teaching, Augustine was certainly not the first Christian to defend the use of military force.

WAR BY DIVINE COMMAND

A steady stream of reports involving heretical teaching and violence landed on the desk of Augustine as he assumed office as bishop of Hippo in 395. The attacks of heretical and militant groups demanded his immediate attention, reflection, and response. These attacks included, first of all, the criticism by the Manichees, whose teaching on the problem of evil had earlier moved Augustine to espouse their teaching. After separating himself from this group, he converted to Christianity and was baptized by Ambrose in 387. Eight years later he was consecrated bishop of Hippo in North Africa.

Shortly thereafter, Faustus, a leading intellectual among the Manichees, challenged Augustine's use of the Old Testament as a resource for God's commanding war. Augustine responded with a lengthy defense of the Old Testament (*Contra Faustum*, c. 397–99). Second, the Visigoths, led by Alaric, moved militarily against the Christian Roman Empire and finally sacked the city of Rome in 410, causing non-Christian Romans to blame Christianity for Rome's demise. Augustine addressed this critique in his classic work *The City of God*. Third, he encountered the Donatists, who espoused heretical views on the nature of the church and its sacraments. He also had to deal with the Circumcellions, the radical wing of the Donatists, who used violent means to achieve their ends. As these conflicts escalated into severe crises, Augustine wrote lengthy manuscripts and letters, advising Christian monarchs, military officers, and the people of his diocese on how they should respond to these attacks. He answered questions about how to deal with military aggression, including that of the violent Circumcellions, who murdered clergy, vandalized churches, and forcibly rebaptized Catholics.[35] He deliberated over how to protect a fragile peace in cities about to be sieged and how to restore order and security in the churches.

ANGUISHING OVER WAR

Throughout his life Augustine labored over these painful questions about Christians using force. Should criminals be executed for killing other citizens? Should armed force be used against the heretical Donatists who were desecrating the church and murdering its leaders? Or should Christians fight the Vandals, who were intent on conquering Hippo during Augustine's last years?

Scrutinizing the biblical writings, Augustine faced the tough moral dilemma: Would it be loving and right for his Christian peoples to defend themselves militarily? If so, what biblical warrant could be invoked to support the claim that the loving and just action would call for doing battle with the adversary? He knew from the Old Testament that God commanded Moses and Joshua to wage war against the Egyptians, the Amorites, and the people of Ai. But how could he reconcile these divine commands with the teaching of the nonviolent, gentle Jesus, who told his followers to return good for evil?

INTERPRETING THE BIBLE

In the course of searching for answers in response to the Manichean Faustus, Augustine developed his method of interpreting the Bible in his book *Teaching Christianity (De doctrina Christiana)*. The first group that challenged his interpretive principles was the Manichees, a pacifist religious sect named after its founder Mani. They held a dualistic doctrine that separated spirit from matter and good from evil. Manichean doctrine had attracted the young Augustine, because it claimed to solve the problem of evil, a problem that had been tormenting him.[36] Manichees held that God was a totally good and benevolent being who reigned in a kingdom of light. Evil came from a hostile force that ruled the kingdom of darkness. The evil force was eternal and equal in power to God.

As bishop, Augustine rejected this heretical teaching, as well as the Manichees' literalist method of reading the Bible that gave each passage a single meaning. They demeaned the Old Testament because they felt it presented God as a vengeful warrior and the patriarchs (Abraham, Jacob, and Moses) as immoral. They judged as false any biblical passages that depicted a stern, vengeful, warrior God who commanded the Israelites to destroy the enemy. Such qualities characterized the malevolent demon, not God, the Father of Jesus. They questioned whether the patriarchs ought to be considered righteous because they had many wives, and killed human beings, and offered animal sacrifices.[37] Finally, the Manichees rejected the Old Testament because, in the words of their spokesman Faustus, "it contained shocking calumnies against God Himself."[38] God could do no evil, yet the Old Testament frequently spoke about God commanding his people to engage in war. God did not punish Moses for slaying the Egyptian (Ex 2:11–15). Moses, supposedly under God's command, waged war against the Amalekites (Ex 17:8–13), and later Moses ordered the sons of Levi to kill three thousand of his own people because of their idolatrous practices (Ex 32:25–29). Faustus claimed that the Old Testament misrepresents God when it makes Yahweh the commander of these killings. It also portrays God as one threatening to come with a sword, sparing neither the righteous nor the wicked. Consequently, Faustus and the Manichees spurned the god of the Old Testament while continuing to believe in the suffering Christ of the New Testament, who was a savior also being saved.[39] Faustus challenged Augustine: "Either your writers forged these things, or the fathers [Moses, Joshua] are really guilty."[40]

Dismayed by the Manichean teaching on the origin of good and evil and by Faustus's literalist interpretation of scripture, Augustine developed an allegorical method for interpreting scripture that gave him deeper insight into the problem of evil. He held that the true meaning of scripture—one that is inspired by the Holy Spirit—is the meaning that the author intended. Like most of the church fathers, he taught that sacred scripture has multiple meanings, especially in figures of speech (metaphors, allegories and parables) that are meant to be interpreted on a symbolic level.[41] It is the task of the interpreter to distinguish between a text's literal and figurative meanings.[42]

A second criterion for interpreting the Bible is charity, which is linked to Augustine's theology and ethics of love. Charity, with its twofold command to love God and neighbor, should guide the interpreter in trying to understand difficult or unclear passages. Charity, for example, would caution one not to be bound by one's own self-interest or narrow view, but rather to try to understand what the Spirit-inspired author of a biblical work meant.

Augustine countered the literalist and erroneous interpretation of Faustus, calling it a perverse distortion of the Old Testament: "You understand neither the symbols of the law nor the acts of the prophets, because you do not know what holiness or righteousness means."[43] In his critique of Faustus, Augustine contended that the God of the New Testament is the same deity as the God of the Old Testament, who works in various ways to punish both the righteous and the wicked. Augustine asked Faustus, a believer in the New Testament, whether he and his fellow Manicheans held that Paul was a righteous person, even though Paul humbly and openly confessed his past sins and gave thanks for being justified by faith in Jesus Christ.[44] God, Augustine said, did not spare the righteous Paul, who confessed, "Lest I should be exalted above measure by the abundance of the revelation, there was given me a thorn in the flesh, a messenger of Satan to buffet me" (2 Cor 12:7b). Like the God of the Old Testament, the God of the New Testament punished Paul for his sins, which Paul accepted as a salutary act keeping him from becoming proud. Augustine implied that if the Manichees were consistent, they should also reject the Pauline writings, because they too, like the Old Testament, depict a God who punishes people for their sins.

Here we see two methods of interpretation at loggerheads: Faustus's literalist interpretation of God actually using the sword and Augustine's allegorical reading where the sword represents God's punishment administered indirectly by means of other agents. In response to Faustus's rejection of the Old Testament, Augustine maintained that both testaments together reveal the one true God. The Old Testament texts in which God, through Moses and Joshua, commanded the Israelites to wage war are the inspired word of God.[45] Yahweh did indeed command his people to wage war, and because God issued the command, the war should be accepted as just. Augustine does not allegorize God's command to fight the enemy; he viewed it as a historical event. He did, however, interpret God's command on a spiritual-moral level. Listen to Augustine's own words:

> When war is undertaken in obedience to God who would rebuke, or humble, or crush the pride of man, it must be allowed to be a righteous war; for even the wars which arise from human passion cannot harm the eternal well-being of God, nor even hurt His saints; for in the trial of their patience, and the chastening of their spirit, and in bearing fatherly correction, they are rather benefited than injured. No one can have any power against them but what is given him from above.[46]

God's war commands are always just because they help the righteous as well as the unrighteous. They humble the evildoers and chasten the spirit of the saints. Even wars that human leaders initiate for the wrong reasons, Augustine contended, cannot hurt the virtuous participants because they benefit through their patience in bearing correction. Thus, Augustine interpreted war on a higher spiritual-moral level, showing how, even in the atrocities that war invariably brings, men and women can grow in virtue and can be saved by surrendering themselves to God's providence.

Augustine's response to Faustus raises two questions: first, how does God's command to kill the enemy in war fit with the Decalogue's prohibition of murder? Second, how can it be reconciled with Jesus' opposition to violence? In answer to the first question, Augustine said that murder is a clear violation of charity, but he then distinguished between different kinds of killing. The Decalogue's prohibition, "You shall not murder," rules against suicide and even killing in self-defense.[47] As for capital punishment, Augustine permitted it in theory, but opposed it in practice except for extreme cases. Up to this point, we see Augustine's leanings toward pacifism.

Regarding war, he pondered over whether Christians should ever be permitted to kill in war. But in his debate with the Manichees, he confidently stated that God commanded the people of Israel to fight against certain adversaries and chastised them for their failure to do so. Killing the adversary in this context was not murder. This mode of ethics, in contemporary parlance, is known as divine-command theory. Something is morally right if it is commanded by God and morally wrong if it is prohibited by God. Few theologians today would espouse this theory in its pure form, which holds that rightness and wrongness depend exclusively on God's will and not on any intrinsic evil in the act itself. In its pure form, divine-command theory says that something is right simply because God commands it, not because it is also objectively right in itself. Hence, God could command persons to lie, or order a father to sacrifice his son, as God is reported to have done—first commanding Abraham to sacrifice Isaac and then rescinding the order (Gn 22:1–19).

Augustine, however, was not a pure divine-command theorist who held that rightness and wrongness depended simply on the will of God. On the contrary, he held that God is good and true and so provided good reasons for commanding the people of Israel to engage in a particular battle. Goodness is not derived from God's commands but from God's nature and natural law. Thus, divine revelation provided a precedent for Augustine's thinking that some wars, even in the absence of God's command, would be just if supported by good reasons. This faith conviction moved Augustine to search for reasons or causes that would justify such a war.

Reconciling the Old and New Testaments

Augustine also had to reconcile Yahweh's commands to wage war with Jesus' command not to retaliate against enemies. He first developed an "argument from silence" based on two scenes where John the Baptist and Jesus carried on dialogues with men in the Roman army. On these occasions neither John the Baptist nor Jesus suggested that the soldiers should leave the military. After being baptized by John at the Jordan River, soldiers asked the prophet what they should do as part of their repentance. He told them not to extort money from the people and to be satisfied with their wages; he did not command them to resign from the military (Lk 3:14). Similarly, when Jesus healed the Roman centurion's servant, he did not suggest that the centurion should leave the military (Mt 8:5–13). Augustine argued that if John and Jesus thought that military service was wrong, they would have made this known to the soldiers. But because they said nothing about their military status, Augustine concluded that neither John nor Jesus opposed service in the military, and by implication, did not oppose armed force.

The example of John's dialogue with soldiers is more convincing than Jesus' dialogue with the centurion. Given the context of repentance and conversion, it would have been appropriate for the Baptist to urge the soldiers to quit the army if he thought it were wrong to serve in the military. In the second dialogue, however, Jesus may have felt that it would be inappropriate to raise the question about the centurion's military profession. Moreover, the centurion and the other soldiers were likely serving as police officers keeping the peace and not military personnel engaged in military operations. Their role as keepers of the peace may not have been a problem for John or Jesus.

A more difficult New Testament text to reconcile with the Old Testament "war passages" is Matthew's Sermon on the Mount, in which Jesus calls on his followers not to resist the evildoer's buffeting or bullying a disciple (Mt 5:38–48); they should instead offer the other cheek or carry the bully's back-pack an extra mile. Augustine interpreted this passage in a manner similar to the early Christians, but he restricted this teaching to conflicts between indi-viduals, not to be applied to groups or city-states. Individual Christian citi-zens, he said, should be willing to suffer the loss of temporal goods in order to teach the assailant how little value they possess in comparison with eter-nal goods. By practicing patience, the victim would teach the assailant that "temporal goods ought rather to be valued less than eternal ones."[48] Augus-tine cautioned victimized persons to be careful lest a desire for vengeance cause them to lose patience, a virtue that they should value more than any material goods, including their temporal lives, which Christians should be willing to surrender. If the victim demonstrates good will and patience under oppressive situations, the evildoer may be won over to harmonious unity and contribute great benefits to the city. Christians should not employ vio-lence by returning a blow, or worse, by killing the oppressor who threatens them, because Jesus refused to do so when he was struck by a guard. Augus-tine commented, "He [Jesus] was prepared not only to be struck on the other cheek for the salvation of all, but even to have his whole body nailed to a cross."[49] Applying Jesus' teaching to the issue of self-defense, Augustine says, "I do not approve of killing another person in order to avoid being killed yourself."[50]

WAR BY LOVE'S COMMAND

Augustine's teaching on violence and warfare manifests many paradoxes. First, while he justified soldiers at war killing the enemy, he ruled against private citizens killing an assailant in self-defense. Second, Christian ethi-cists today regard him as the father of just-war theory, although some would say that he was more a theologian of peace.[51] Around the year 428, Augus-tine wrote Count Darius, who had been sent to Africa to negotiate with a rebellious general named Boniface, asking him to obtain peace by negotia-tion: "It is a mark of greater glory to slay wars themselves by the word rather than human beings by the sword, and to win and obtain peace by peace, not by war."[52] To better understand the paradoxical Augustine and his ethics of warfare, we must return to his ethics of virtue to see how love, justice, intention, and motive guide his thinking.

RIGHT LOVE PROHIBITS SELF-DEFENSE

Violence was a pressing problem for Augustine and many Christians of his day, mainly because it threatened to destroy a peace that was as fragile at the dawn of the fifth century as it is at the beginning of the twenty-first.[53] Publicola, a Catholic layman and Roman senator, wrote to Augustine, asking a series of questions, including one on the morality of self-defense:

> If a Christian sees that he is going to be killed by a barbarian or a Roman, should the Christian himself kill them so that he is not killed by them? Or is it permissible to fight them or repel them without killing, since scripture says, "Do not resist someone evil"? (Matt 5:39).[54]

In his response, Augustine distinguished between killing in self-defense and killing in defense of one's country as a soldier:

> I do not approve of the advice about killing human beings for fear that one might be killed by them, unless one is perhaps a soldier or is obligated by public office so that he does this, not for himself, but for others or for the city where he himself also lives, after he has received lawful authority, if it is appropriate to his person. Perhaps, however, those who are deterred by fear from doing something evil also receive some benefit. But the reason it was said, "Let us not resist someone evil" (Matt 5:39), is so that we do not take delight in vengeance that feeds the soul with the evil of another, not so that we neglect the correction of human beings.[55]

Killing in self-defense is morally wrong, first of all, because a private individual lacks lawful authority, either from God or from a civil authority. Augustine grounded his claim in Romans 13:1–5, where Paul says that governing officials receive their authority from God and may use the sword to "execute wrath on the wrongdoer." Private citizens who kill without lawful authority commit murder.

Self-defense is wrong for a second reason. An individual under attack will very likely act out of a vengeful spirit. But for Augustine, the only permissible motive for punishing another is desiring the other's good or trying to bring the evildoer closer to God. In a situation where one is about to be robbed or killed, the victim is least likely to act out of a spirit of love. More likely, the one under attack will be driven by the passions of anger or vengeance. In the words of Jesus, the victim should "resist not an evildoer," or as Augustine expressed it, "Do not take delight in vengeance that feeds the soul with the evil of another." Our passions sway us to act out of an impulsive and disordered will. "Therefore, the law is not just which grants the power to a wayfarer to kill a highway robber, so that he may not be killed [by the robber]; or which grants to anyone, man or woman, to slay an assailant attacking, if he can, before he or she is harmed."[56] The assailant should be punished, not by the victim, but by the appropriate official, who possesses lawful authority and who would likely be more objective and fair in punishing the assailant. The only other person suitable for punishing another for a crime is one whose love has removed hatred from his or her heart. Augustine frequently appeals to the example of the father, who punishes his child because he loves him and wishes the child to refrain from doing bad things.[57]

In examining Augustine's argument against self-defense, we begin to see elements from two ethical modes operating: the first mode is a deontological mode of ethics that prohibits killing unless the command to do so is authorized by God or God's human delegate; the second is a virtue ethics that says an act is virtuous or good based on disposition, or the readiness to respond in accordance with virtues. Augustine's charity and justice are key determinants in judging the morality of an act. Charity calls Christians to love their neighbor, including the hostile neighbor. Deliberately killing the assailant in self-defense, Augustine argued, arises out of an inordinate desire for the goods of this world, including one's earthly existence. Killing in self-defense goes against charity because the defensive action is motivated by unruly passions. It is unjust because it is a disordered love.

On the issue of individual self-defense, Augustine appeals more to his ethics of virtue that emphasizes charity than to his deontological ethics that emphasizes obedience to the sovereign's command. Apparently civil law in Augustine's day regarded self-defense to be a reasonable action, although the law did not force individuals under attack to kill the assailant. Speaking to his disciple Evodius, Augustine said that the law simply left the matter up to the citizen's own discretion. Most important for Augustine was charity, which ought to motivate Christians to choose eternal life over temporal life, persons over things. Rightly ordered love urges Christians not to hold on to things that are really not theirs. Augustine says:

> In short, whatever the violent assailant who is slain was going to take from us is not completely in our control, and for this reason I do not understand how it can be called our own. Thus, while not blaming the law for allowing such assailants to be killed, I cannot find any way of justifying those who take such action.[58]

The assailant can only rob the victim of goods, including life, which any human being will have to give up eventually. One should not kill in order to protect something that is not completely in one's control and therefore is not one's own. Therefore, Augustine argues, one should never kill a human being in order to defend goods or values that at death must be relinquished. By doing something evil, like killing the assailant, one risks losing the one good that the robber cannot take: one's virtue. Killing another human being to protect temporal goods makes one culpable before God and erodes the person's virtue.

RIGHT LOVE DEMANDS PUBLIC DEFENSE

It may come as a surprise to some that Augustine forbade self-defense in the name of charity and justice, but then, on the basis of the same virtues, defended the right of the state to wage war and kill the adversary. A partial explanation of this paradox is found in what has come to be known as Augustine's just-war criteria. He defended a state's right to wage war when (1) the lawful authority declares a war against another sovereign state or social entity, (2) when there is a just cause, and (3) when the lawful authority has a right intention.

The first criterion of lawful authority fits with Augustine's hierarchical ordering of reality, in which the sovereign God has authority over all things, earthly sovereigns over their subjects, and husbands over wives and children. Lawful authority is an extension of Augustine's divine-command ethics that calls for obedience to the divine sovereign. In time of conflicts between city-states, only God's earthly delegate may declare war.[59] In authorizing war the earthly sovereign delegates authority to the soldiers through their military commanders to follow orders and to kill the enemy when commanded. William Stevenson accurately sums up Augustine's thinking on obedience of subjects to their rulers:

> Subjects ought to be both passive and obedient in the face of superior human power. For them, too, power equals authority. If the subjects are soldiers, they are obliged to carry out the orders of their commanders even if those orders require fighting and killing. If they kill under military orders they are not guilty of murder; on the contrary, if they do not kill when ordered, they are guilty of treason. Soldiers ought therefore to obey even the possibly unrighteous commands of infidels, such as Julian the apostate. Even in such a case, "the soldier is innocent, because his position makes obedience a duty."[60]

Like Moses, Joshua, and the Israelites acting in obedience to God's command to fight, military commanders and soldiers incur no guilt for killing or injuring the adversary.[61] They fight, destroy, and kill with virtual impunity. Soldiers serve merely as instruments of the sovereign; they are passive moral agents who do not concern themselves with the rightness or wrongness of the war. As Christians, however, Augustine says, they must love the enemy, even though the soldiers may be instructed to think that it is the wrongdoing of the enemy that has compelled their commander-in-chief to wage the war.[62] Once authorized by the ruler and military commander, soldiers may kill the enemy without moral guilt, even if the cause for waging the war is unjust.

The sovereign, however, must prudentially determine whether there is a just cause before declaring war. Augustine borrowed this second criterion from Cicero, who said that no war is just unless it is waged to avenge injuries, that is, to recover lost goods, such as property and rights, or to repel an attack.[63] This meant for Cicero and Augustine that just cause permits both offensive and defensive wars. Just cause prohibits wars of conquest, however, because they arise out of lust for domination.

Augustine's third and final condition for establishing a just-war is the most problematic. The head of state must have a right intention, which for Augustine means a just peace. He defines peace as the tranquility of order, which in its highest form is the fruit of love and justice: "The peace of the celestial city is the perfectly ordered and harmonious enjoyment of God and of one another in God."[64] But an earthly or temporal peace falls far short of that ideal. At its best, temporal peace entails a well-ordered concord between those who rule and citizens who obey. But in Augustine's lifetime, temporal peace was marred by wars and rumors of wars, as noted earlier. Civilization never enjoyed perfect peace, but only what poet Gerard Manley Hopkins, a Jesuit poet writing in the nineteenth century, calls "piecemeal peace":

> When will you ever, Peace, wild wooddove, shy wings
>   shut,
> Your round me roaming end, and under be my boughs?
> When, when, Peace, will you, Peace? I'll not play hypocrite
> To own my heart: I yield you do come sometimes; but
> That piecemeal peace is poor peace. What pure peace
>   allows
> Alarms of wars, the daunting wars, the death of it?
>
> O surely, reaving Peace, my Lord should leave in lieu
> Some good! And so he does leave Patience exquisite,
> That plumes to Peace thereafter. And when Peace here
>   does house
> He comes with work to do, he does not come to coo,
>   He comes to brood and sit.[65]

Hopkins addresses the Spirit of Peace, or the Holy Spirit, who is traditionally symbolized as a dove. The poet admits that the Dove of Peace comes some time, but the Dove brings only "piecemeal peace"; pure peace does not allow war and rumors of war. In accord with Augustine's thought, Hopkins believes that pure or perfect peace comes in the world hereafter. Meanwhile, the Holy Spirit gifts us with patience, which is the forerunner to pure peace ("Patience . . . plumes to peace thereafter"). The wooddove does not simply come to console us, but to work—"to brood and sit," implying that the Spirit is actively hatching or creating little wooddoves as he contemplates the world.[66]

Augustine, like Hopkins, believed that true peace was the labor of the Spirit of Peace. Augustine the realist knew that unwise or corrupt sovereigns often sought "piecemeal peace" for reasons of self-aggrandizement and territorial expansion. Nonetheless, Augustine the idealist insisted that Christians, including rulers and the military, should strive for peace, however imperfect, by loving the enemy and by pursuing a peace based on justice.

Although he did not distinguish between intention and motive, Augustine implied that charity must be the driving force, or motive, behind right intention and true peace.[67] He illustrated how good deeds can be done from the motive of pride as well as of charity:

> Charity feeds the hungry, and so does pride: charity, that God may be praised; pride, that itself may be praised. Charity clothes the naked, so does pride: charity fasts, so does pride: charity buries the dead, so does pride. All good works which charity wishes to do, and does; pride, on the other hand, drives at the same, and, so to say, keeps her horses up to the mark. But charity is between her and it, and leaves not place for ill-driven pride; not ill-driving, but ill-driven. Woe to the man whose charioteer is pride, for he must needs go headlong![68]

The difference between a charitable deed and a prideful one lies not in intention, because both agents intend and perform ostensibly good deeds, but in motive. If a just peace is sought through warfare, it must be motivated by authentic love or charity, which in turn must be ordered by justice; peace motivated by pride or the lust to dominate one's opponent is poor peace.

Robert Holmes perceptively identified the problem in Augustine's ethics of virtue as applied to war:

> Because rectitude is tied to virtue, and virtue to love, we can know whether someone acts rightly only by knowing that person's motivation. And that, according to Augustine, is hidden from us—often even in the case of our own actions. We presumably know when we are deliberately acting pridefully. But when we think we are acting lovingly, we may unwittingly be motivated by pride.[69]

This poses a difficult problem. Because, for Augustine, right intention issues from the motive of love, and because we cannot know our true motivation (whether it stems from charity or pride), then we cannot know with certainty whether the sovereign declares war with a right intention. Holmes suggests that we have to determine right intention on the basis of a negative calculus: whether the sovereign is *not* acting from love of violence, revengeful cruelty, desire for conquest, and lust of power.[70] To minimize the evils of war, he suggests, we (and our political leaders) should purge ourselves of those sinful motivations that lie behind our desire to wage war.

One difficulty with this suggestion is that the negative actions of the sovereign that should be exposed may be identified only after the war has begun. This would include actions aimed at gaining control over land and natural resources (for example, gas and oil fields) and demanding unconditional surrender. The citizens minimally should insist that right intention be consistent with the reasons expressed by just cause. In today's society, which allows for rapid communication by means of technology, people can more quickly know a leader's intentions, if not his or her motives, based on public statements sometimes made far in advance of declaring war (see Box 4–2 below).

REFLECTION ON AUGUSTINE'S ETHICS

Trying to grasp Augustine's teaching on war is challenging, first because he did not treat war and violence in a systematic way but addressed issues as they arose historically. Second, as mentioned earlier, Augustine discusses issues of violence from two modes of ethics: a divine-command ethics, which is a deontological ethics based on obedience to God; and a virtue ethics, in which charity and justice guide persons to their final goal of pure peace and eternal happiness. In his deontological ethics the obligation comes as an external command; in his virtue ethics the obligation arises from the interiority of the moral agent. When Augustine considers the morality of individual acts of violence, he operates more out of his ethics of virtue supported by Jesus' teaching on nonviolence. But when he addresses the morality of war, he assumes that some wars are truly just because God, who is just and good, would only command the people of Israel to wage war against their enemies for good reasons, even though the human mind may be unable to know these reasons. Where there is no clear divine command, Augustine recognizes the sovereign's right to declare war because the political leader receives authority from God and therefore can rightly command obedience from his subjects. The sovereign is to be obeyed, even when he or she declares war for the wrong reasons. The heavy emphasis on legitimate authority seems to overshadow the criterion of right intention motivated by love, which suggests that Augustine's deontological argument, at least within his social ethics, has the upper hand over his virtue ethics.

As a result, a tension exists between the social issue of war and the individual issues of homicide, self-defense, suicide, and capital punishment (where

---

Box 4–1. Contemporary Just-War Criteria

Thomas Aquinas (1225–74) organized and reiterated with some adaptation Augustine's three conditions under which a war could be just: (1) It must be *declared and waged by the sovereign* charged with the care of the common good; (2) for a *just cause* (fault or *culpa* committed by adversary); and (3) with the *right intention* (advancement of good). Whereas Augustine stressed God's authority as the basis of the sovereign's right to declare war, Aquinas emphasized the monarch's service of the common good as the standard.* Unlike Augustine, Francisco de Victoria (c. 1487–1546) and Francisco Suárez (1548–1617) distinguished between a defensive war as a response to armed attack upon a peaceful people, and an offensive war launched because of injurious actions such as infringement of rights. They also added two other conditions: the war should be fought as a *last resort (jus ad bellum)* and in a *proper manner (jus in bello)*. Both theologians struggled over the morality of the offensive war, especially over how a Christian nation could reconcile the will's love of peace with pursuing the enemy's death.** In 1983 the National Conference of Catholic Bishops published a pastoral letter on war and peace, *The Challenge of Peace: God's Promise and Our Response,* in which the bishops stated that just-war doctrine shares with Christian nonviolence a presumption against war. They also listed seven conditions, including Augustine's three criteria, to help determine when and why recourse to war is permissible.

1. *Just cause:* Permissible only to confront a real and certain danger, such as protecting innocent life or securing basic human rights.
2. *Competent authority:* Declared by officials responsible for public order.
3. *Comparative justice:* Do protection of rights and values justify killing?
4. *Right intention:* Pursuit of peace and reconciliation.
5. *Last resort:* When all peaceful alternatives have been exhausted.
6. *Probability of success:* No nation should resort to force if the expected outcome of the war will clearly be disproportionate or futile.
7. *Proportionality:* The foreseen damage and costs of the war must be in proportion to the good expected (see nos. 85–100).

---

* Thomas Aquinas, *Summa Theologica* (New York: Benziger Brothers, 1947), 2–2, 40.1.

** Richard A. McCormick and Drew Christiansen, "War, Morality of," *New Catholic Encyclopedia,* rev. (Washington, DC: Catholic University of America, 2003), 14:635–44.

Augustine leans toward pacifism). Augustine justifies war almost entirely on the basis of legitimate authority and just cause, and he prohibits self-defense, suicide, and nearly always capital punishment on the grounds of love rightly ordered. Whereas his virtue ethics brings him closer to the nonviolent tradition of the first Christians, his divine-command ethics and, in a minor motif, his natural-law thinking move him to embrace the beginning of a just-war theory.

Augustine argues against self-defense because the victim is motivated by unruly passions. But a similar argument could be made for prohibiting soldiers from killing on the battlefield. Although soldiers should not kill out of lust to dominate or love of killing, the passions of warriors are no less unruly on the battle lines, especially when members of one's platoon are blown apart. Finally, Augustine seems to assume that rulers have greater expertise and objectivity in determining just cause than anyone else. Granted that the sovereign should have say about involving the nation in war, heads of state are strongly swayed by the lust to dominate.

BOX 4–2. IRAQ INVASION: A JUST WAR?

President Bush wrote Congress on October 2, 2002, requesting a joint resolution authorizing him to use U.S. armed forces against Iraq. He made his case based on the following reasons: (1) to defend the national security of the United States against the continuing threat posed by Iraq; and (2) to enforce all relevant United Nations Security Council Resolutions regarding Iraq. These resolutions aimed to halt Iraq's possession and development of chemical and biological weapons, its active seeking of nuclear weapons, and its support for and harboring of terrorist organizations, including Al Qaeda.

Congress granted President Bush authorization based, first of all, on his claim that further diplomatic or other peaceful means alone would not adequately protect U.S. national security or lead to the enforcement of U.N. Security Council Resolution 1441 regarding Iraq. In just-war language, Bush claimed that using force was the last resort. Second, Bush asserted that this resolution was consistent with the efforts by the United States and other countries to take necessary actions against international terrorists and terrorist organizations.

Two weeks later the U.N. Security Council unanimously approved Resolution 1441, which imposed stronger arms inspections on Iraq, requiring Iraq to declare all weapons of mass destruction and to account for known chemical weapons stockpiles—or pay serious consequences. Iraq accepted these terms and invited back the U.N. inspectors, Hans Blix and Mohamed El Baradei, who reported to the

U.N. on January 27, 2003, that no banned weapons had been found. The inspectors, however, did criticize Iraq for not giving them full access to facilities and scientists and for not providing clear accounts of certain materials.* In spite of Secretary of State Colin Powell's attempt before the U.N. to prove that Iraq was evading the inspectors, continuing to produce weapons of mass destruction, and was linked to Al Qaeda, neither Powell nor the White House was able to provide hard evidence to support these claims.** President Bush in a news conference on March 6, 2003, criticized Iraq's government for not complying with the U.N.'s inspection teams and for failing to disarm. In speaking about the likelihood of war, Bush stated:

> Saddam Hussein has a long history of reckless aggression and terrible crimes. He possesses weapons of terror. He provides funding and training and safe haven to terrorists, terrorists who would willingly use weapons of mass destruction against America and other peace-loving countries. Saddam Hussein and his weapons are a direct threat to this country, to our people and to all free people. If the world fails to confront the threat posed by the Iraqi regime, refusing to use force even as a last resort, free nations would assume immense and unacceptable risks.

Vice President Cheney reiterated the same claims ten days later on "Meet the Press": (1) that Saddam Hussein's regime was on the verge of acquiring nuclear capabilities, (2) that he had already amassed stockpiles of chemical and biological weapons, and (3) that his regime had significant links with Al Qaeda and that he might have had sometime to do with the terrorist activities of September 11, 2001. Cheney said, "We know he's out trying once again to produce nuclear weapons and we know that he has a long-standing relationship with various terrorist groups, including the al-Qaeda organization."*** Three days later the war began. Was the United State justified to attack Iraq on March 19, 2003?

---

*Hans Blix, "The Security Council, 27 January 2003: An Update on Inspection," http://www.UN.org/Depts/unmovic/Bx27.htm, 1–9 (accessed on August 28, 2006).

** Editors, "The Talk of the Town," *The New Yorker* (November 1, 2004), 37–38, 40–42.

***Editor, *The New York Times* (March 18, 2005), A25. Following the invasion of Iraq, no weapons of mass destruction were ever found, and Iraq's alleged link to Al Qaeda was proven false.

RESOURCES

DISCUSSION QUESTIONS

1. Civil War General Sherman said that "war is hell," and others who saw war from the trenches, like Ernie Pyle, seem to be in accord with him. Although Augustine stated that "war is hell on earth," he never said that war simply is hell. Why do you suppose he would refrain from using Sherman's metaphor to describe war?
2. What does Augustine mean by virtue? How does an ethics of virtue differ from other types of ethics, like a mode that presents formal guidelines for making moral decisions or a mode that decides what to do on the basis of foreseen consequences?
3. What is Augustine's general understanding of love? How does love become sinful? How does it become virtuous?
4. Augustine said that love as charity relates to all virtues by directing them to their final goal, which is union with God and happiness. What role does justice play in relation to love?
5. How would you respond to the statement that Christianity was a non-violent and pacifist religion until Augustine compromised its gospel values by replacing nonviolence with just-war thinking?
6. How does Augustine resolve the paradox in which charity prohibits private self-defense while obliging a lawful sovereign to employ force to protect the common good?
7. Although we have not discussed contemporary just-war doctrine in this chapter, do you think that additional criteria found in the U.S. bishops' statement (Box 4–1) makes war harder to justify than Augustine's just-war criteria? Explain.
8. Do you think that Augustine's just-war theory with its emphasis on order, hierarchy, and lawful authority makes soldiers too passive and unquestioning about what they should or should not do during combat?

SUGGESTED READINGS

St. Augustine. *Confessions.* Translated with an introduction and notes by Henry Chadwick. Oxford: Oxford University Press, 1991.

St. Augustine. "Chapter XIX." In *The City of God,* translated by Marcus Dods and introduced by Thomas Merton. New York: The Modern Library, 1950.

Brown, Peter. *Augustine of Hippo: A Biography.* New edition with an Epilogue. Berkeley and Los Angeles: University of California Press, 2000. Originally published in 1967.

McCormick, Richard A., and Drew Christiansen. "War, Morality of," s.v. *New Catholic Encyclopedia.* Rev. ed. Washington, DC: Catholic University of America, 2003.

National Conference of Catholic Bishops. *The Challenge of Peace: God's Promise and Our Response.* Washington, DC: United States Catholic Conference, 1983.

NOTES

[1] Charles O. Brown, *The Enquirer and News* (Battle Creek, MI), November 18, 1933. Dr. Brown heard the remark of General Sherman's address to the cadets at the Michigan Military Academy on June 19, 1879.

[2] Ernie Pyle, *Ernie's War—The Best of Ernie Pyle's World War II Dispatches*, ed. David Nichols (New York: Simon and Schuster, 1986), 419.

[3] St. Augustine, *The City of God*, trans. Marcus Dods (New York: The Modern Library, 1950), XXII.22.

[4] St. Augustine, "Sermon: The Sacking of the City of Rome" (410/411), in E. M. Atkins and R. J. Dodaro, eds., *Augustine's Political Writings* (Cambridge: Cambridge University Press, 2001), 209.

[5] St. Augustine, *Contra Faustum* XXII.74, http://www.gnosis.org/library/contf2.htm (accessed on June 7, 2004).

[6] Robert Dodaro, "Ethics: Lying and War," in Alan Fitzgerald, ed., *Augustine through the Ages* (Grand Rapids, MI: Eerdmans, 1999), 328.

[7] James F. Keenan, "Proposing Cardinal Virtues," *Theological Studies* 56 (1995): 711.

[8] St. Augustine, *The City of God* XII.23.

[9] Ibid., XV.22.

[10] St. Augustine, *Confessions*, trans. Henry Chadwick (New York: Oxford University Press, 1991), I.i.

[11] St. Augustine, *The City of God* XIX.14.

[12] John E. Rotelle and Boniface Ramsey, eds., *The Works of Saint Augustine: A Translation for the 21st Century,* Part II, vols. 1–4 (letters 1–99; 100–155; 156–210; and 211–270, 1–29), *Letters,* trans. Roland Teske (New York: New City Press, 2001–2005), letter 130.14. All references to Augustine's letters are from this series.

[13] Robert Dodaro, "Justice," in Fitzgerald, *Augustine through the Ages*, s.v., 482.

[14] St. Augustine, *The City of God* XV.22.

[15] Ibid. XV.28.

[16] John E. Rotelle and Boniface Ramsey, *The Works of St. Augustine: A Translation for the 21st Century,* Part I, vol. 1, *The Confessions*, trans. Maria Boulding (New York: New York City Press, 2002), II.1.

[17] St. Augustine, *The City of God* XIV.13.

[18] St. Augustine, *Contra Faustum* XXII.74.

[19] St. Augustine (Chadwick), *Confessions* X.vi (8).

[20] Ibid. X.xxvii (38).

[21] St. Augustine, *On the Trinity*, in *Basic Writings of Saint Augustine*, vol. 2, ed. Whitney J. Oates (New York: Random House, 1948), XV.18.

[22] St. Augustine (Chadwick), *Confessions* IV.vi (11).

[23] St. Augustine, *Ten Homilies on the Epistle of John* in *Nicene and Post-Nicene Fathers of the Christian Church*, ed. Philip Schaff (New York: Charles Scribner's Sons, 1908), VIII.9.

[24] Ibid. VII.7.

[25] Ibid.

[26] Robert L. Holmes, "St. Augustine and the Just War Theory," in Gareth B. Matthews, ed., *The Augustinian Tradition* (Berkeley and Los Angeles: University of California Press, 1999), 326.

[27] Louis J. Swift, *The Early Fathers on War and Military Service* (Wilmington, DE: Michael Glazier, 1983), 81.

[28] Justo L. González, *The Story of Christianity*, vol. 1, *The Early Church to the Dawn of the Reformation* (San Francisco: HarperSanFrancisoco, 1984), 132–33.

[29] Ibid.

[30] Atkins and Dodaro, *Augustine's Political Writings*, xii.

[31] Eusebius of Caesarea, *Life of Constantine*, quoted from Swift, *Early Fathers*, 87.

[32] González, *The Early Church*, 122–23, 134. The author states that in spite of his attempts at diminishing the power of ancient aristocratic Roman families, "Constantine continued functioning as the High Priest of paganism. After his death, the three sons who succeeded him did not oppose the Senate's move to have him declared a god. Thus the ironic anomaly occurred that Constantine, who had done so much to the detriment of paganism, became one of the pagan gods."

[33] Athanasius, in Swift, *Early Fathers*, 95.

[34] Ambrose of Milan, *On the Duties of the Clergy* 1.27.129, quoted from Swift, *Early Fathers*, 98.

[35] Donald X. Burt, *Friendship and Society: An Introduction to Augustine's Practical Philosophy* (Grand Rapids, MI: Eerdmans, 1999), 209.

[36] Peter Brown, *Augustine of Hippo: A Biography*, new ed. with epilogue (Berkeley and Los Angeles: University of California Press, 1967, 2000), 35–37.

[37] St. Augustine (Chadwick), *Confessions* 3.7.12.

[38] St. Augustine, *Contra Faustum* XXII.3.

[39] Brown, *Augustine of Hippo*, 42.

[40] St. Augustine, *Contra Faustum* XXII.5.

[41] Robert M. Grant with David Tracy, *A Short History of the Interpretation of the Bible*, 2nd ed., rev. and enl. (Philadelphia: Fortress Press, 1984), 78–79.

[42] St. Augustine, Letter 55.21.38. Augustine gradually moved beyond a simple allegorical method to one that was more sophisticated and that included a dynamic literal interpretation (in contrast to the static literalism of the Manichees).

[43] St. Augustine, *Contra Faustum* XXII.5.

[44] Ibid. XXII.20.

[45] See Nm 21; Dt 1; and Jos 8.

[46] St. Augustine, *Contra Faustum* XXII.75.

[47] St. Augustine, Letter 47.5. "I have a hope in the name of the Lord," he explains, "that will not be fruitless, because I have not only believed my God who said that the whole law and the prophets depend on those two commandments, but I also have learned this by experience, and experience it every day, since no sacrament or any more obscure passage of the sacred writings is disclosed to me where I do not find the same commandments."

[48] Ibid. Letter 138.11.

[49] St. Augustine, *Commentary on the Lord's Sermon on the Mount,* in vol. 11 of The Fathers of the Church Series, trans. Denis J. Kavanagh (New York: Augustinian College, 1951), 85.

[50] St. Augustine, Letter 47.5.

[51] Frederick H. Russell, "War," in *Works of Saint Augustine* (New York: Cambridge University Press, 1975), s.v.

[52] St. Augustine, Letter 229.

[53] Atkins and Dodaro, *Augustine's Political Writings,* xvii.

[54] St. Augustine, Letter 46.12.

[55] Ibid., Letter 47.5.

[56] St. Augustine, *The Free Choice of the Will,* trans. Robert P. Russell, The Fathers of the Church (Washington, DC: The Catholic University of America Press, 1968), I.5.

[57] St. Augustine, *Commentary on the Lord's Sermon on the Mount* 1.20.63.

[58] St. Augustine, *Free Choice of the Will* 1.5.

[59] St. Augustine, *The City of God* 1.21.

[60] William R. Stevenson, Jr., *Christian Love and Just-war* (Macon, GA: Mercer University Press, 1987), 69.

[61] St. Augustine, *Questions on the Heptateuch,* 6.10, in Swift, *Early Fathers,* 138.

[62] St. Augustine, *The City of God* 19.7.

[63] Frederick H. Russell, *The Just War in the Middle Ages* (Cambridge: Cambridge University Press, 1975), 5.

[64] St. Augustine, *The City of God* 19.13.

[65] Gerard Manley Hopkins, "Peace," in Peter Milward, *A Commentary on the Sonnets of G. M. Hopkins* (Chicago: Loyola University Press, 1969), 102.

[66] Ibid., 105.

[67] St. Augustine, "Homilies on the First Epistle of John," in Schaff, *Nicene and Post-Nicene Fathers of the Christian Church,* VIII.9.

[68] Ibid.

[69] Holmes, "St. Augustine and the Just War Theory," 332.

[70] Ibid., 335.

5

LOVE AND JUSTICE
IN FRIENDSHIP

St. Thomas Aquinas

Just as love of God includes love of our neighbor,
so too the service of God includes rendering
to each one his due.
—St. Thomas Aquinas,
Summa Theologica, II-II, 58, 1 AD 6

Love and justice in today's Western society are distant cousins. While they sometimes appear together, more often they stand apart. Each establishes different objectives and elicits contrasting responses. Modern Western culture generally confines the language of love to interpersonal relationships and the language of justice to political relations and business transactions. While persons use words of love and endearment to nurture their friendships and family relationships, they employ words of justice and rights to establish boundaries with consumers and clients. Many contemporary theologians and philosophers claim that acts of love are optional and that acts of justice are mandatory and backed up by sanctions.[1] Whereas Western culture often associates love with emotions, compassion, and sentimentality, this same culture insists that justice be emotionally detached, impartial, and rational.

DUALISM OF LOVE AND JUSTICE

Intimate friends, spouses, and families express affection and care for one another; rarely do they speak of justice in their conversations. If a spouse should appeal to justice or rights, the conversation often becomes tense and even hostile. The other spouse may infer that something has gone awry in the relationship, for example, that he or she has been caught cheating on the other or is perceived to be avoiding household tasks or caring for the children. In such instances the offended person may raise an outcry: "That's not fair!" Following Hegel, philosopher Jeremy Waldron contends that spouses ideally relate to each other on the basis of love. He holds that appeals to rights should occur rarely in a marriage. When partners claim "their right to be relieved of child care or domestic chores once in while, their equal right to pursue a career, their right to draw equally on the family income . . . as an entitlement that one party presses peremptorily, querulously, and adversarially against the other—that would lead to our misgivings."[2] Waldron would prefer to see these values upheld and conceded not as rights but as outcomes issuing spontaneously from "intimate and mutual concern and respect."[3] In response to Waldron's contention, Kantian philosopher Pauline Kleingeld argues that discussing issues of justice within marriage can be more irenic than Waldron's analysis suggests. She makes a strong case for viewing "marriage as not merely a relationship of love, but as *also* a commitment to justice."[4]

As for relationships in civic institutions and businesses, the language of justice and rights assumes a prominent role. In courts of law, Themis, the Goddess of Justice, overshadows Aphrodite, the Goddess of Love. Themis appears in prominent places on courthouses throughout North and South America and Europe, wearing a blindfold symbolizing her unbiased way of proceeding. Her right hand aims a sword at the head of a serpent, the symbol of evil; her left hand holds a scale that measures exactly what was taken by the offender and is owed to the state. Thus, the goddess symbolizes impartial justice, no matter whether the defendants or plaintiffs are rich or poor, are of low social status or from the upper class, black or white. While many citizens approve of this symbol of evenhanded justice, others might wonder why no symbol of love or mercy appears alongside the symbol of justice. Some citizens might respond, "Because criminals must get what they deserve, that's why!" Retributive justice must be done, as the deputy in Shakespeare's "Measure for Measure" makes clear to Isabella, who pleads with him to commute her innocent brother's death sentence:

Isabella:	Yet show some pity.
Angelo:	I show it most of all when I show justice,
	For then I pity those I do not know
	Which a dismissed offence would after gall,
	And do him right that, answering one foul wrong,
	Lives not to act another. Be satisfied.
	Your brother dies tomorrow.[5]

Like many American citizens today, Angelo thinks that pity should be shown to victims and law-abiding citizens of the commonwealth, and not to the offender, who, if pardoned, might repeat the offense.

Nor is mercy or love found in the marketplace. Recent surveys have indicated that American consumers want to see companies "demonstrate more goodwill toward customers, employees and the communities where they do business."[6] Although the people surveyed do not mention a lack of compassion or love in their business dealings, they have identified values often associated with love: good will, respect, openness, and truthfulness.

The great divide between love and justice in contemporary society raises an important question for our ethics of virtue: Do love and justice operate apart or do they work as partners on the interpersonal and social levels? To answer this question we turn to the great thirteenth-century theologian Thomas Aquinas, to learn from him how he integrates love and justice on the interpersonal and social levels and to determine where his teaching can help us overcome the dualism between these two virtues in today's Western culture.

Why study the works of a thirteenth-century Dominican theologian for an answer to a twenty-first century problem? There are many reasons for selecting Aquinas. Four reasons may suffice. First, his greatest work, the *Summa Theologica (ST)*, comprehensively and coherently addresses moral issues on both the social and interpersonal levels. He discusses personal issues related to friendship, fair hiring practices, and truth-telling as well as social issues related to war, capital punishment, and property rights. Second, he thinks about these issues in relation to the Creator-Redeemer-Sanctifier God, who gifts the human family with life, justifying and forgiving love, and grace that help the human beings reach their final destiny. Third, he brings together closely reasoned arguments to support faith claims within the Christian tradition. Fourth, Aquinas, in his profound search for truth and a new synthesis, carries on a lively dialogue with the word of God and with the masters. He debates with Aristotle among the philosophers and St. Augustine among the theologians and church fathers. These conversations stated in a dialectical type of conversation give his teaching a universal and comprehensive dimension that has application beyond the thirteenth century.

This chapter examines, first, how Aquinas constructs the theological foundation of love and justice; second, how he defines these two virtues and their subtypes; and finally, how he connects them. The investigation presents examples from Aquinas's writings, especially from the *Summa Theologica*, and from contemporary stories or cases that illustrate the working of love and justice in both interpersonal and sociopolitical relations. Although this study presents Aquinas's various types of love and justice, it concentrates on charity and legal justice. Charity is the type of love that the New Testament calls *agape*; legal justice is the type of justice that contemporary Catholic social teaching calls social justice. The chapter concludes with a brief reflection on what Aquinas's model of ethics of virtue teaches us about integrating love and justice.

FOUNDATION OF LOVE AND JUSTICE

"Where is love?" Oliver Twist sang mournfully after being beaten and imprisoned in the basement of an undertaker.[7] Given his miserable social situation, this "humble half-starved drudge—to be cuffed and buffeted through the world" might also have asked, "Where is justice?"[8] Whereas Oliver posed the question from within a bleak nineteenth-century capitalist society, the Dominican theologian Thomas Aquinas asked about the meaning of love and justice from within a relatively peaceful thirteenth-century feudal society.

Aquinas developed a remarkable set of propositions that asserts that justice and love constitute part of God's essence. Whereas we might sometimes think that we mortals invented the concepts of love and justice and then projected them onto God, as nineteenth-century philosopher Ludwig Feuerbach[9] contended, Aquinas held the opposite perspective. He claimed that primordial love and justice are the very ingredients that make up the deity, and that human love and human justice are mere images or faint reflections of God's attributes. Because God is thoroughly different from human beings, Aquinas interpreted the meaning of these concepts by using analogies. Human love is like God's love, and human justice is like God's justice; yet, they are immeasurably different. He felt confident using analogies because divine revelation affirmed that God created human beings in the image and likeness of God (Gn 1:27). The Bible also revealed that God is the ground and exemplar of justice and love: "God is just" (Is 45:21), and "God is love" (1 Jn 4:16).

Supported by these and many other biblical passages, Aquinas presented arguments demonstrating that God possesses an omniscient intellect and so knows all being and all good. God also possesses a will, the faculty by which God chooses the good (ST I, 19, 1). Aquinas then showed that both love and justice are operations of God's will and that both relate to an "other." Love, he said, means "willing good for another" (ST I, 20, 1 ad 3).[10] Justice "renders what is due to another" (ST I, 21, 1 ad obj. 3). God expresses love for all finite beings by the very act of willing their good: creating and sustaining inanimate things, plants, animals, and human beings, and helping them realize their ends (ST I, 21, 1 ad 3).

Aquinas probed the meaning of divine justice using Aristotelian categories. When he began to relate Aristotle's concept of justice to God (rendering to each what is due), he encountered a problem. Aristotle had developed a type of justice called commutative justice, which is a reciprocal exchange between two more-or-less equal persons, such as an employer paying a worker a certain wage in exchange for so many hours of labor. Surely, God cannot be a debtor like the employer who owes something to human creatures in exchange for the work the hired hands do. Aquinas knew, of course, that God, strictly speaking, owes nothing to anyone and that therefore divine justice cannot be likened to commutative justice. So he again dipped into Aristotle's bag of concepts and pulled out another type, called distributive justice, which he found better describes how God does justice. God, the Just Distributor, freely and generously gives to human creatures what is due them, not in payment for what human beings have done for God, but because of what their nature must possess if they are to realize the purpose for which God created them. If God wishes to create human beings so that they freely give the Creator glory and praise and in so doing attain eternal happiness, then God *must* provide them with those faculties and gifts that enable rational beings to realize this purpose. In this sense God "owes" something to human creatures and so distributes to mortals the things necessary to accomplish the divine plan (*ST* I, 21, 1 ad 3). These "things" or goods that human persons have to possess in order to attain their ends minimally include a body that possesses an intellect and a will as well as divine assistance that helps compensate for moral weakness. Aquinas compared God's justice to that of a generous sovereign who distributes goods to his subjects in accordance with their nature, rank, and need (*ST* I, 21, 1).

MEANING OF LOVE

Aquinas first reflected on love's general meaning and then deliberated on three specific kinds of human love. In its most general sense, love *(amor)* means "willing good for another." This basic definition encompasses three types: love of friendship, love of self, and charity, which will be examined below. Love as *amor* comes alive when a real person, whom Aquinas calls a *subject,* notices something special, suitable, and attractive in another live person, or *object,* who awakens and catches the wholehearted attention of the subject.[11] Aquinas called the person's capacity for receiving this affection a *passion.* Love is the human passion par excellence; it operates as the energizer for the other passions or dispositions, such as pleasure or grief. "For Aquinas," writes theologian Paul Wadell, "the passions and affections are the linchpin of moral living because ultimately what becomes of us turns on what we love and how we love, on what we choose to make us happy and what will make us sad. Love informs all we do."[12] Love provides the motivation and guidance for human desires, pleasures, hopes, and fears (*ST* I-II, 23, 2).[13]

Aquinas described love's dynamic structure as a three-stage process that begins with what he calls complacency, or affective consent, in which the subject actively opens the self to receiving something fitting and attractive from another person.[14] At the second stage the subject loves the other in a twofold movement: loving or affirming the other for who he or she is, and loving by willing something good for the other, whether or not the subject's willing the good can actually bring it about (*ST* I-II, 27, 4).[15] At the third stage, when the relationship has jelled, the two persons experience a spontaneous joy that arises from their resting in their mutual love for each other (*ST* I-II, 26, 2; I-II 27, 4).

In the first or consenting stage the subject's passion opens itself to the object. Aquinas emphasized that love does not begin with the subject doing something to the object. Quite the reverse; the subject begins by opening himself or herself to the other—the object rouses something in the subject. Falling in love captures the sense of an active receptivity, that something good happens to the subject, who is not in full control of the situation. Harry, awakened by Harriet's dazzling smile, may choose to entertain powerful and joyous feelings that her warm smile and her lovableness elicited.[16] If Harry opens himself to Harriet, he in turn wills good to her, that is, Harry affectively affirms the goodness of Harriet.[17] Having been stirred by Harriet, Harry not only affirms her as a person but also wishes good things for her (freedom, health, and happiness).[18] He wants to be with her, and if the feeling is mutual, they develop a friendship in which they both experience bliss and joy.

This general description of love can be applied, with certain qualifications, to other kinds of relationships: love for God, love for one's spouse, and love for a needy person. Doctors, for example, who participate in the organization Doctors without Borders, put themselves in a challenging and even dangerous position in order to serve the needs of the underserved. A particular patient may be touched by the actions and the attitude of a particular doctor who has worked hard to bring the patient back to health. The patient responds by developing a deep appreciation and affection for the caregiver. They now have mutual feelings of care and perhaps even friendship. In each particular relationship, love has a different level of intensity, commitment, and responsibility. Yet the basic structure remains the same, even as the nature of the relationship changes. As affection for the other increases, love deepens, and correspondingly so does the commitment. Moving from the general notion of love, Aquinas then examined three particular kinds of love: (1) friendship, (2) love of self, and (3) love of God.

LOVE OF FRIENDS

Aquinas borrowed many ideas on friendship from Aristotle in conceptualizing his own view of the love of friendship. The ancient Greek philosopher (384–22 B.C.) said that it would be odd indeed if an individual were to seek happiness by trying to live alone: "For no one would choose the whole world on condition of being alone, since man is a political creature and one whose nature is to live with others."[19] He also taught that friendship, arising out of mutual love, was essential for the good society. Aquinas incorporated both ideas into his theology: first, human persons are by nature social beings; second, they cannot be truly happy without friendship. In friendship, both partners accept and affirm the other simply for the other's sake and not out of love for themselves. The first friend, or the "lover," respects the freedom of the second friend, or the "beloved." Three characteristics distinguish this kind of love: mutuality, autonomy, and the relationship itself. Mutuality involves reciprocity in which both partners share virtually everything: feelings, likes and dislikes, ideas, and desires. Autonomy, which literally means "self rule," respects the other's independence and freedom; it allows both parties in the relationship to be a free self in one's unique otherness, even as each person gives oneself to the other.[20] "When I am with John," the partner says, "I can be myself without any fear that he would think I'm quirky or stupid." Third, the love relationship is a bonding that connects two or more persons. Aristotle called this reciprocal love relationship *philia*, a Greek term that more or less captures Aquinas's notion of love of friends.

LOVE OF SELF

Aquinas distinguished two types of love of friendship from love of self. He called love of self *concupiscent love* (*ST* I-II, 26, 3), or what Aristotle called *eros*. In English-speaking countries today, concupiscent love generally refers to a person's strong sexual feelings for another. Similarly, the Greek equivalent *eros* connotes a sensual and sexual kind of love. Aquinas, however, meant something quite different by concupiscent love *(amor concupiscentiae)*. Concupiscent love desires its own good by seeking the good of another. A little child, for example, obeys and respects the parent so that he or she will be loved and rewarded with a hug; students may show great esteem for their teachers because the latter have helped them grow in wisdom and understanding. Concupiscent love, as Aquinas conceived it, enables human beings to attain their natural end; hence, it is good. He wrote, "Since every nature desires its own being and its own perfection, it must be said also that the being and the perfection of any nature is good" (*ST* I, 48, 1).

Moreover, he emphasized that human persons should love themselves more than their neighbor. He gave two reasons for asserting that love of self comes before love of another. First, we are more like ourselves than we are like another. Aquinas expressed it in the following way: "The lover, properly speaking, loves himself, in willing the good that he desires. But a man loves himself more than another; because he is one with himself substantially, whereas with another he is one only in the likeness of some form" (*ST* I-II, 27, 3). Second, the love with which we love ourselves is the form and root of how we love others. "We do unto others as we do unto ourselves" (*ST* II-II, 25, 4). In Aquinas's order of charity that establishes priorities of one's love objects, he ranks these natural loves not in terms of status or need of the neighbor, but in terms of their relationship to oneself. Among others the subject should first love spouse, children, and parents; then close friends before neighbors; near neighbors before distant neighbors (*ST* II-II, 26, 1–12).

Now the reader may wonder whether persons who desire and pursue their own good are egoists. How do individuals transcend their own interests to love another if their primary desire revolves around seeking their own good? Is Aquinas's theological ethics a kind of egoism in which individuals make decisions based on promoting their own good, even doing God's will so that they may flourish in this life and attain full happiness in the next? His ethics is not egoism, first of all, because he understands that true love of self esteems others, like the teacher or a parent, with a love that is authentic, even though the primary object of the love is oneself. While one could say that the teacher was a means to the person's end, the teacher was never a mere means. Second, charity helps human persons to transcend their love of self by loving God more than themselves and in God to love their neighbor as themselves. Aquinas's concupiscent love is not sensual, sexual, or narcissistic, although love of self could assume those qualities if God's grace were absent. Third, Aquinas regarded love of self as essential for loving God and one's neighbor.[21] To love one's neighbor as oneself, one must have genuine regard for oneself. In Chapter 1, we heard Grace tell how she struggled to accept herself as an African American before she could reach out to others.

Consider a woman who works as a counselor at an outreach center. She works long hours and deals with heavy situations daily. However, she becomes so engulfed in the lives of her patients that she fails to attend to her own relationships and her own well-being. Will she continue to be able to serve the needs of her clients without taking time to attend to her own health and well-being? It seems unlikely. Receiving God's love helps persons to love themselves in a balanced and proper way.

A JUST FRIEND

A contemporary example may clarify Aquinas's distinction between love of friendship and love of self.

Two college students, Gina and Marie, were assigned to the same room in a residence hall and soon became close friends. During their first year they studied together, played on the same soccer team, and became mutually supportive. They were so alike that often they could intuit what the other was thinking or feeling. They had a wonderful relationship. Not only did they communicate easily, but they also shared everything from their thoughts about guys they liked, to joking about their professors' idiosyncrasies, to sharing dreams of what they might do later in life.

During the fall semester of their sophomore year Gina began to grow very anxious, fretful, and physically quite thin. Marie, of course, noticed the weight loss as well as her friend's growing anxiety, and she spoke to her about it. Gina fretted over mathematics and physics. She also criticized the way she looked. "I'm too fat," she said to Marie. At first Marie thought that Gina's pre-med studies were getting the better of her. As Gina's anxiety heightened and she became thinner, Marie became more deeply concerned. She urged Gina to speak to her parents about getting professional help. Gina replied that she would be okay after she finished the difficult courses. As for the weight loss, she blamed it on the poor quality of food in the university's dining room. Yet Marie's intuition was that her friend had anorexia. She ate very little, frequently vomiting after her meals. She grew increasingly nervous, was critical of her appearance, became far less friendly with friends, and slept poorly. "Do your parents know?" Marie asked Gina. "No, and I want you to promise me that you will not call them." Marie spontaneously promised that she would not tell Gina's parents. During a sleepless night she mulled over what she should do, thinking, I love Gina; she's my best friend. But if I don't act, Gina will get sicker, and it could be fatal. Yet I don't want to lose her as a friend. If I talk to her parents or the guidance counselor, Gina will find out and will stop talking to me. I don't want to lose her trust and her friendship. After much deliberation she decided that for Gina's sake, she had to phone her parents.

This was a difficult dilemma. On the one hand, if Marie were to hold to her promise not to inform Gina's parents, her friend's health would likely get worse. But if she told them what was going on, she feared that she would lose her friendship with Gina. At first, she yielded to this fear and was overly concerned to have Gina's approval. At this point we see Marie's insecure love of self—wanting to be liked, especially by Gina—taking higher priority over her love of friendship (focusing more on Gina's good and the relationship). Later, when Marie came to realize that by remaining silent she was not being loving either to herself or to Gina, she decided to act. She decided to talk to Gina's parents, no matter how angry her friend might be with her for breaking her promise. By letting the parents know what was going on, Marie felt that in the long run she would be helping Gina and she would be true to herself. She might even strengthen the friendship.

Although Aquinas never spoke directly to this specific kind of dilemma, he addressed the issue of fraternal correction. He said that out of love for one's friend, a person must correct or admonish the other and encourage him or her to stop doing something that is wrong. If a person failed to correct the friend from sinning, Aquinas said, that failure would be a worse evil than the sin the friend was committing (ST II-II, 33, 2). Marie's confronting her friend and then taking action when Gina failed to seek help was this kind of fraternal correction. Marie's intervention demonstrated what members of Alcoholics Anonymous call "tough love," that is, love that challenges an addicted friend to acknowledge the problem and to get help. When Marie failed to persuade Gina to do something about her anorexia, she decided to talk to Gina's parents so that they might get professional help for their daughter.

CHARITY

The discussion of Aquinas's concupiscent love leaves unanswered the question of how the love of self becomes self-transcendent by affirming the other primarily for the other's sake. The answer, suggested earlier, lies in a third type of love, which Aquinas called charity. Aquinas moved Aristotle's friendship between human persons to a higher level: friendship with God. He called it charity *(caritas)*, derived from its Latin root, *carus*, which means "high-priced" or "dear." Like Augustine, Aquinas regarded charity as a dear or high-priced virtue; indeed, he regarded it as the supreme virtue because God is its primary object and because it directs all the other virtues. Aquinas called it an *infused* virtue, a gratuitous love that the Holy Spirit "pours into" persons; or, to use a more felicitous expression, infused charity is a good that God freely communicates to and affirms in the believer. It is a forgiving and reconciling love that enables the person to form a friendship with God and to love the neighbor in God. In response to God's communication, the beloved accepts Jesus Christ and God's Spirit and returns God's love (*ST* I-II, 55, 4). Charity, in its best expression, involves affective, mutual self-communication between God and human persons. As the subject in the relationship, God invites human persons to share in God's goodness. By accepting the offer, human persons are changed into new beings. They become what they love, Christlike persons in a process likened to a kind of transfiguration.[22]

God's love justifies human beings, transforming unjust persons into righteous ones, who now have the capacity to love God above all else and the ability to love others as themselves. Thomas expressed this as follows:

> Therefore it must be said that charity loves God for His own sake; and because of Him, it loves all others according as they are ordered to God. Thus, in a way, charity loves God in all men, for our neighbor is loved by charity because God is in him or God might be in him. It is evident that it is the same habit of charity by which we love God and our neighbor.[23]

Aristotle thought that human beings lacked the capacity to form a friendship with God because of the great inequality that separated them. For a similar reason he excluded the possibility of free persons becoming friends with serfs.[24] While Aquinas agreed with Aristotle that human beings are not in any sense equal to God, they are capable of friendship with the deity because God chose to create man and woman in God's own image and justified them through faith. As a consequence, human persons are able to relate to the trinitarian God in a grace-inspired love of friendship (*ST* II-II, 23, 1). Through Christ's redemptive, loving action of dying for humankind, all human persons can undergo a transformation and live in friendship with God, a relationship that brings joy, peace, and bliss. This mutual and benevolent relationship makes human beings like God and gives them the capability to be united eternally with God.

CHARITY AND THE CARDINAL VIRTUES

Spirit-guided charity serves as the cornerstone of Aquinas's theological ethics. As a theological virtue it bonds persons in friendship with God and with neighbors near and far. Charity accomplishes this by motivating, empowering, and guiding persons through their dispositions and virtues. The four cardinal virtues—prudence, justice, temperance, and fortitude—play decisive roles in helping persons to flourish. Theologians call them cardinal moral virtues (derived from the Latin *cardo*, meaning "hinge") because all four virtues operate like hinges on a door, securing persons and helping them to do morally good acts with relative ease. Prudence, for example, guides persons through their deliberations and facilitates their choosing the right means to achieve a desired end. Aquinas said that on a natural level, persons can develop these virtues by habitually trying to act prudently, justly, temperately, and courageously. He also taught that in the absence of God's love, persons cannot transcend their limited human powers and so would be incapable, even with their natural virtues, of achieving their final supernatural end (*ST* I-II, 23, 8).

Charity is the central theological virtue that helps persons achieve their immediate objective and their long-term goal. Aquinas called charity the *form* of the virtues, by which he meant that charity first strengthens each of the virtues to do what it is supposed to do. Charity inspires prudence to help persons discern and judge wisely. Charity moves justice to make persons aware of their obligations and to fulfill them. Second, charity in its informing capacity "tags" each of these virtues with a form that directs them to their final destination. Prudence, directed by charity, takes into account the movements of the Holy Spirit.

Charity also directs justice, which promotes the earthly common good, to pursue God and God's righteousness as the ultimate common good. More concretely, charity may inspire a wealthy person to do justice by funding the education of the poor, an act that promotes the common good; even more, charity makes the benefactor aware that doing justice on behalf of the poor is integral to the person's friendship with God and to God's reign. Theologian Jean Porter expresses it well: "The charitable person does the right thing for the right reason, that is, the love of God. . . . Furthermore, the charitable person will exhibit capacities that the ungraced person will not have, most important, the ability to grasp intuitively what devotion to God requires in a particular instance and to act accordingly."[25] Through charity the person experiences the consolation of God's love, which reduces egoism and opens the heart to friendship and to a willingness to act justly toward the neighbor.

WHEN CHARITY TURNS TO JUSTICE

In today's society people frequently connect charity with almsgiving and philanthropy. They regard such actions as completely voluntary, something that one does simply out of kindness, not out of obligation. Aquinas called such charitable acts "gratuitous," that is, good deeds freely done without any expectation that the beneficiary give something back in return. Even though doing charitable deeds involves gratuitousness, Aquinas insisted that certain acts, such as giving alms, may also be obligatory (*ST* II-II, 23, 3). How can acts, ordinarily viewed as voluntary, like almsgiving, become obligatory? Aquinas posed the question in this manner: Are we bound to do good to those closely related to us, like hosting a dinner for our close friends or members of our family? If we listen to Luke's account of the gospel, it seems that we are obligated to prefer strangers and needy persons over one's kin and friends:

> When you give a luncheon, or a dinner, do not invite your friends or your brothers or your relatives or rich neighbors, in case they may invite you in return, and you would be repaid. But when you give a banquet, invite the poor, the crippled, the lame, and the blind. And you will be blessed, because they cannot repay you, for you will be repaid at the resurrection of the righteous. (Lk 14:12–14)

Aquinas answers this objection first by noting that Christ did not forbid his followers to throw a dinner party for their family and relatives. He was more interested in their motive for doing so. One should never invite people out of greed, that is, throwing a party for friend or stranger for personal profit. As a general rule, Aquinas taught, charity, not greed, commands us to follow the order of nature, an order rooted in God's law, which calls us to care first for those who are closest to us: family before friends, and friends before strangers. However, in special situations where greater need exists, one should invite the hungry strangers in town before one's family and close friends. But in either instance—feeding one's friends or feeding hungry strangers—Aquinas implies that the host has an obligation in charity, which he calls a moral debt. Like almsgiving, hosting a party should observe the order of charity, "which requires that, other things being equal, we should in preference help those who are more closely connected with us"—those bound to us by ties of blood and common household (*ST* I-II, 32, 9). Aquinas gave a very high priority to those in great need, including widows and orphans, for the very reason that they lack familial connections.[26] We are not bound in justice to help all in need, but we are obligated in justice to help those needy who otherwise would have no one to turn to. He applied St. Ambrose's words to this situation: "Feed him that dies of hunger; if thou has not fed, thou hast slain him" (*ST* II-II, 32, 5).

Ambrose and Aquinas were referring to situations of extreme need, and in such situations obligations in charity become obligations of justice. Aquinas called these latter obligations "legal debts" (*ST* II-II, 99, 5).[27] In these situations, justice, and not simply charity, calls the wealthy to feed the hungry. Yet charity, Aquinas added, remains with justice as its companion, commanding and perfecting it as it directs it to charity's end (*ST* II-II, 32, 1 ad 2).

Both types of debt (moral and legal) flow from the rule of reason. In summary, moral debt obliges persons to do something because it is fitting; legal debt obliges persons absolutely and according to law.

MEANING OF JUSTICE

Although love has primacy over all other virtues, justice is the most excellent of the cardinal moral virtues in two basic ways. First, justice does not look to the subject's own perfection, as temperance and fortitude do, but rather extends itself to other persons or groups. If a person has borrowed money from another, justice requires that the money be returned. In this way justice is like charity in doing something for the sake of another. Just as charity gratuitously affirms the good *(bonum)* of the other, justice renders a right *(jus)* to the other. The second reason for justice's superiority over the other cardinal virtues is that justice is born out an excellent part of the soul, namely, the rational appetite or will that commands the subject to follow right reason in its obligation to another (*ST* I-II, 66, 4).[28]

While justice works with all the moral virtues, it collaborates closely with prudence, which assists justice in finding out what is due another in the concrete situation. Prudence acts by determining whether and in what way the law (of God, the church, or the state) applies in the concrete situation. It considers alternatives that may fulfill the obligation of justice. Justice, for example, would require that an oil company that has damaged the environment by an oil spill make restitution to the communities adversely affected. Using practical reason, prudence would consider the best ways of cleaning the environment and taking safety measures to prevent a reoccurrence of oil spills. The prudent person consults experts on what should be done, sorts out the alternatives, and determines the best alternative. Justice then makes the final determination to act on the best means to fulfill the debt.

Aquinas defined justice as "a habit whereby a man renders to each one his due by a constant and perpetual will" (*ST* II-II, 58, 1). Because justice operates through the rational will, it functions as a free power. As a virtue, it acts habitually, with relative ease, and with constancy. Aquinas identifies three types of justice: commutative, distributive, and legal (also called general justice). The subject and object in each of these three types may be individual persons or private groups and the common good (usually represented by the state) involved in some kind of transaction. Commutative justice, for example, would guide a real estate agent (representing the owner) as he or she sells a house to a buyer for a price acceptable to all concerned. The parties negotiate over something that is relatively easy to measure, for example, a three-bedroom colonial-style house sold at market price with a certain percentage of the sale going to the agent. In the other two types of justice (distributive and legal), one of the actors represents society and the other is a citizen or group in that society. Legal justice, for example, would direct private individuals and corporations to pay taxes to the state in proportion to their income, property, and number of dependents. The state, acting on behalf of the common good, would distribute goods and services (public education and garbage pickup) to individual households and corporations. Justice in both instances is more complex than commutative justice because what each party pays or receives varies considerably according to needs and income.

COMMUTATIVE JUSTICE

Commutative justice refers to an exchange between two private parties. It is a one-to-one relationship involving two individual persons, such as an employer and employee; or a transaction between two private companies, such as Microsoft and Apple. Commutative justice requires that both parties participate in a free and fair exchange. Aquinas refers to this type of justice as a mutual transaction between two private persons (*ST* II-II, 61, 1). Reciprocity requires that both sides carry out their part of the bargain. The consumer, for example, agrees to pay the tailor six hundred dollars for making a two-piece suit. Commutative justice shares this quality of reciprocity with the love of friendship or *philia*. In addition to honoring reciprocity, justice and love both call the two parties to respect each other. The tailor takes special care to make the suit according to specifications; the consumer pays the bill promptly. Pope Leo XIII, in his encyclical *Rerum novarum,* applied Aquinas's principle of commutative justice to the relationship between the wealthy entrepreneur and the poor laborer, emphasizing that the relationship calls for harmony, pleasantness, and reciprocity: "Each requires the other; capital cannot do without labor nor labor without capital. Mutual agreement results in pleasantness and good order; perpetual conflict necessarily produces confusion and outrage" (no. 15).[29] For the worker, mutual agreement requires that the laborer work efficiently to produce a reasonable amount of goods each day; for the employer, it calls for paying an amount of money in exchange for the labor as well as establishing a healthy working environment. Pope Leo then added that religion teaches the entrepreneur and the employer that they should never treat the laborers as though they were their slaves, but "that they must respect in every man his dignity as a man and as a Christian" (no. 16). Respect is generally associated more with justice than with charity.[30] As Pope Leo uses the term, respect obliges persons to recognize the other's dignity (no. 43).

The element of reciprocity in commutative justice raises the question whether wage contracts are made in freedom, that is, whether workers are sufficiently free to negotiate with the employer for a fair wage. Many workers are vulnerable and therefore lacking sufficient freedom. The vulnerable include immigrant workers who lack citizenship and thus are unable to negotiate for a higher wage, workers who are poor and physically handicapped, those with a criminal record, and laborers who are forbidden by law to engage in collective bargaining. For these workers, reciprocity and freedom are absent. They either must accept what the employer offers or look elsewhere. To address this problem, it is necessary to appeal to distributive and legal justice as guides.[31]

DISTRIBUTIVE JUSTICE

Distributive justice operates within a whole-to-part structure. Society (the whole) does justice by proportionately allocating public goods and services to individual citizens and to groups (the parts). Unlike commutative justice, which measures what each party owes the other according to strict equality, distributive justice calculates what each citizen or private group should receive according to a relative equality that is determined by one's rank or need in the society (*ST* II-II, 61, 1). Contemporary Catholic social teaching drops Aquinas's word *rank* and simply states that the state should give greater assistance to those whose needs are greatest.[32] Society, represented by a sovereign or parliament, distributes those goods and services held in common, such as clean water, fuel, affordable housing, health care, quality education, police protection, and public transportation. Distributive justice shows special concern for the poor, the elderly, the sick, the disabled, and others who are unable to work.

LEGAL JUSTICE AND THE COMMON GOOD

Aquinas called the third type of justice legal justice.[33] It obliges persons to work for the good of the whole of society, the common good. He calls legal justice and charity general virtues because they direct specific virtues to their penultimate and ultimate goals respectively: "For just as charity may be called a general virtue insofar as it directs the acts of all the virtues to the Divine good, so too is legal justice, insofar as it directs the acts of all the virtues to the common good" (*ST* II-II, 58, 6).

Legal justice directs charity to the penultimate goal, which is the common good; charity directs legal justice to the ultimate goal, which is union with God. What does Aquinas mean by the common good and how does it relate to the ultimate good? Although both are goods in an analogous sense, Aquinas makes important connections between them. First, the true and ultimate common good, like Augustine's city of God, consists of that final communion of persons united with one another in God. This heavenly common good expresses the full realization of the two love commandments: loving God with one's whole heart, soul, and strength; and loving one's neighbors as oneself.

Both Augustine and Aquinas compared the human common good to the heavenly common good. The earthly common good stood between God (the uncreated common good) and the collective good of lower animal life, like a beehive or apiary. The polis (symbol of the human common good) goes beyond the apiary, where worker bees slave for the sake of the colony without receiving individual recognition or gaining opportunities for personal growth.[34] The human common good involves more than efficient labor for the sake of another, like bees in an apiary. It must also establish through consensus and cooperation those conditions in which persons thrive and friendships develop. Even though the good of the whole is more perfect than the good of the parts, Aquinas taught that the common good cannot be realized unless each of its citizens develops as a human person by mutual communication of knowledge and love (*ST* II-II, 64, 2). Unlike a nonrational creature, the human person is viewed as a microcosm that embodies the value of a whole because of its divinely conferred dignity. A human person, therefore, cannot be used as a mere instrument. The state, for example, should never use a human being merely as an instrument to achieve high productivity at the expense of the person's freedom. Hence, justice and the common good rule out slavery and slave labor as morally evil institutions (*ST* II-II, 104, 5 obj. 2).

Legal justice obliges citizens, both individually and corporately, to contribute to the common good (*ST* II-II, 58, 5). They do so, for example, by supporting good legislation, by voting for the candidates they think are best qualified for political office, and by educating and training citizens to be productive through their labor and entrepreneurial skills. Owners of industrial plants and oil refineries contribute to the common good by keeping the water and air clean by constructing adequate filtering systems. Because legal justice focuses on obligations to produce goods and services and thus contribute to the good of the whole society, contemporary Catholic social teaching sometimes calls it contributive justice.[35]

Legal justice moves in a direction opposite to that of distributive justice. It requires that the parts (citizens and private groups) fulfill their debts to the whole (society or the common good). Like distributive justice, legal justice renders to the other what is proportionally due, and so its members contribute to the common good in a relative way, depending on their endowments, talents, wealth, and income. The gifted are obliged to contribute more than the less gifted, and the wealthy more than the poor.

Legal justice also calls for subordinating the goods of individuals and private groups to the common good. This does not mean, however, that individuals are regarded as mere means to the common good, but rather that individual acts of a moral nature must always take into account the good of the whole. Neo-Thomist Jacques Maritain developed a position called *personal communitarianism* in which he argues that the common good ought to include the service of the human person, who possesses natural rights.[36] The Second Vatican Council reaffirmed this personal communitarianism. Speaking in *Gaudium et spes* of the widening role of the common good in an age of growing human interdependence, the council emphasized "the sublime dignity of the human person, who stands above all things and whose rights and duties are universal and inviolable" (no. 26).[37]

Yet in special circumstances Aquinas argued that the state should subordinate the individual's good to the good of the community when an individual person threatens the community. In addressing the question of capital punishment, Aquinas said that "every part is directed to the whole" and "every part is naturally for the sake of the whole." He likens a murderer in the community to a diseased organ of a body. The health of the whole body demands surgically removing the diseased body part so that the person may live. Aquinas argues that it is "praiseworthy and advantageous" to execute an individual person who had committed a grave sin, such as murder, in order to safeguard the common good. In willingly committing murder, the sinner loses the order of reason and the dignity of his or her humanity and thereby "falls into the slavish state of the beasts." Consequently, the state may execute murderers because they are like a beast (II-II, 64, 2 ad 3). Critics have rightly pointed out an inconsistency in Aquinas's thought when he argues in favor of the death penalty for those convicted of murder.[38] On the one hand, he strongly defends the dignity of the human person, but then he argues that when an individual murders an innocent person, the killer thereby loses his or her dignity and becomes like a beast. He concludes that the state may execute the person because by committing such a heinous crime, the murderer has become subhuman.

CHARITY AND JUSTICE IN PARTNERSHIP

This section examines how charity and justice work together as partners in addressing issues on the interpersonal and the social levels. Aquinas distinguishes between acquired moral virtues, which persons can gain through their own efforts, and infused virtues, which God gives directly to each person as a gift. Although charity is always an infused virtue, justice may be either an acquired virtue (by repeatedly acting in a just manner) or an infused virtue (by receiving the grace of God). Charity and justice converge at two points: First, they come together on the level of causality, where charity and justice act as efficient causes, both directing each other and both directing other virtues to their respective ends. Second, they come together in the loving and just actions of persons working for the common good. Here we return to the question raised earlier in the chapter: Do love (charity) and justice work apart or as partners in addressing issues on the interpersonal and social levels of ethical discourse?

ARCHITECTONIC VIRTUES

The first linkage is found on the level of causality where charity and infused justice function as architectonic virtues by helping other virtues arrive at their objectives.[39] The term *architectonic* generally refers to qualities of architecture, but it also has a second meaning, the "function of something that is directive or controlling."[40] Aquinas's interpretation of charity and justice are architectonic virtues in this second sense. Like air-traffic controllers who guide international flights from country to country and then to their final destination, justice and charity direct and help move the moral virtues to their immediate objectives and finally to their ultimate destination. Charity works with the cardinal virtue of temperance by first directing it to its immediate goal of happiness that comes from acting and living well by using and enjoying food, drink, and sexual relations. Charity also points to the happiness that comes by being united with God in the next life and by being friends with God and with one's neighbors in this life.[41]

As an architectonic virtue, charity influences justice in three principal ways. First, it motivates justice to fulfill its immediate object—rendering to each what is due. Second, charity moves justice to be generous and merciful as it works to establish right relationships (*ST* II-II, 23, 8 ad 1). Third, charity, by engraving its own form of loving God and neighbor on justice, widens the focus of justice to include God and groups of people that were previously passed over.

Aristotle's justice did not require rendering to God what was due, but Aquinas's justice does. Because charity is essentially a centrifugal power, it is diffusive of itself. It calls persons to a life of ever-deepening and ever-expanding, self-giving love (*ST* I-II, 107, 1). Morally speaking, charity helps people to see and embrace all people as brothers and sisters. By enlarging the meaning of the common good, it expands the focus of justice. As charity widens a person's perspective to love the stranger, the distant neighbor, and even the enemy, it broadens the person's horizon to include the rights of others who have been ignored. Informed by charity, persons are moved to act justly, not simply because it is the reasonable and right thing to do (justice's distinctive objective), but also because the Holy Spirit calls them in friendship to worship God and in relationship with God to regard their neighbors as brothers and sisters.

Similarly, legal justice functions in architectonic fashion by directing the other cardinal virtues to the service of God and to the common good (*ST* II-II, 58, 1 ad 6). It relates to charity first of all by directing persons to love the common good, lest charity concentrate too much on a small circle of friends and ignore the stranger and the poor. Within a family, for example, justice might call a couple's deep love for each other and for their children to reach out to needy families in the neighborhood or to help single parents care for their children.

Second, justice makes charity concrete by establishing institutional policies and laws that express love in specific and lasting ways, thus allowing love to have a more permanent impact. Consider a situation in which neighbors welcome two black families into their previously all-white neighborhood against the protests of other neighbors. Their expression of love through hospitality to African Americans and other minorities could be made even more concrete and enduring by lobbying the village council to outlaw realtors' racist practices that work to prevent African Americans from living in their village.

VIRTUES OF MARTYRS

Aquinas's discussion of Christian martyrdom shows concretely how he relates charity to justice and then links both virtues to fortitude. Aristotle restricts fortitude to courage on the battlefield, where soldiers constantly face death. He excludes from the circle of the courageous the men and women who act bravely in dangerous situations like shipwreck and disease. Aquinas, however, expands this cardinal virtue to include courageous actions in the face of death of all kinds, that is, whether persons are threatened for pursuing or defending a good (for example, fighting in a just war and martyrdom) or courageously accepting the immediate possibility of dying when they are mortally wounded in an accident or are threatened by a terminal disease.[42] For Aquinas, the essence of fortitude consists in resolutely pursuing a good in all situations where one's life is threatened.

He considered Christian martyrdom to be a special form of fortitude when witnesses are willing to face persecution and death for upholding truth, for doing good works, or for defending justice out of love for Christ and God's kingdom. "Martyrdom," Aquinas wrote, "consists essentially in standing firmly to truth and justice against the assaults of persecution" (ST II-II, 124, 1). Truth is the truth of faith; it is a firm belief in the reality of God's kingdom, which includes witnessing to justice and upholding the common good.

Faith, love for God, and justice are the principal reasons that Christian believers risk exposing themselves to dangerous situations that are likely to end their lives. Aquinas emphasized that fortitude or courage must be present if Christians are to persevere. Grace-inspired fortitude gives Christians mental strength to hold fast to their faith commitment as they face the horror of a torturous death (ST II-II, 124, 2). Fortitude strengthens the person to walk a middle path between paralyzing fear and heroics. But persons in such dire circumstances need more than courage; they must have reasons of the mind and heart to be truly courageous. This means having a profound experience of God's love, a strong commitment to truth, and a love for justice. Each of these virtues—charity, fidelity to truth and justice, and fortitude—plays a key role in helping a Christian persevere through persecution, torture, and death.

Aquinas uses the example of Herod's execution of John the Baptist to illustrate the important part that justice plays in martyrdom. John was arrested because he delivered a prophetic indictment to Herod Antipas: "It is not lawful for you to have your brother's wife" (Mk 6:18). John suffered martyrdom, Aquinas said, not because he refused to deny the faith, but because he denounced the sinful practice of adultery, which Herod committed by marrying his brother Philip's wife, Herodias (*ST* II-II 124, 5). This second marriage violated justice because it wrongly severed her commitment to Philip. Aquinas argues that adultery is unjust chiefly for two reasons: first, it violates the trust that ought to bind the husband and wife, and second, it works contrary to the good of raising the children of both parties (*ST* II-II 154, 8).

Oscar Romero, former archbishop of San Salvador, exemplified to an extraordinary degree the qualities of a martyr that Aquinas presented. In the midst of constant threats he continued to identify with the poor Salvadorans and victims of oppression. He denounced the army's torturing and killing of the innocent until the day that an assassin took his life as he celebrated Mass for the Carmelite sisters. Romero had a strong premonition that he would be killed. Shortly before his assassination he asked a Carmelite sister to pray for him because he knew his life was in danger and felt that he would be unable to withstand torture and death. Yet in spite of his fears, he continued to criticize the powerful Salvadoran elite and resolutely carried out his duties as archbishop. Moreover, fear never diminished his love for the Salvadoran poor, who were uppermost in his mind, as his exchange with Colonel García attests:

Colonel García: "Monsignor Romero, there are rumors that you're going to be killed. I've come to offer you an armored car and security guards."

Monsignor Romero: "Colonel García, as long as you don't truly protect the people, I can't accept any protection from you."

García looked at him angrily.

Monsignor Romero: "Why don't you use those armored cars and security guards for the family members of people who have disappeared, been killed or put in jail?"

García stomped out furiously without so much as giving him another look.[43]

GOD AND THE COMMON GOOD

A second location where charity and justice converge in Aquinas's ethics is the common good. He concurs with Aristotle that the pursuit of the common good is greater and more godlike than the good of the individual.[44] Both Aristotle and Aquinas hold the principle that the whole is greater than any of its parts. This principle would affirm that the good of the nation is greater than special interests of private groups. As seen earlier, Aquinas altered Aristotle's idea of the common good by grounding it in God, who, as the supreme good, is the foundation of the common good.[45] "God's own goodness," Aquinas says, "is the good of the whole universe" (*ST* I-II, 19, 10, 1). Hence, the full common good comprises the communion of all human persons with God and with each other united in God. Placing God at the center of the common good has important implications. First, it rejects any theory that tries to establish the good of the nation as the highest good. Second, it opposes any ideology that gives absolute authority to a sovereign of a state.[46] The Creator governs and wills the good of the whole universe. This teaching implies that the command to love God calls for *loving* the common good, not just working for the common good because it is the reasonable thing to do. Coming at this from the side of justice, one contributes to the common good in order to give God what is due.

In today's global society, and even within individual nations, people disagree on what constitutes the common good. Aquinas claims that friendship and peace are two important constituents of the common good, a claim few would dispute even in the most pluralistic society.[47] Both charity and justice contribute to building friendships within families, neighborhoods, and in society, and to forging a peace among people within a nation and between nations. Charity's willing the good of God and neighbors builds and solidifies friendships and right relations among groups.

Charity makes an extraordinary contribution to peace by building friendships, while justice helps bring about peace by establishing just relationships and by removing obstacles that hinder peace. "Peace is the work of justice indirectly, insofar as justice removes the obstacles to peace; but it is the work of charity directly since charity, according to its very nature, causes peace" (II-II, 29, 3 ad 3). Peace and friendship, however, often develop in precarious circumstances, especially in situations where war erupts, dashing people's hope for peace and destroying friendships.

DILEMMA OF SULLIVAN BALLOU

The Civil War in the United States destroyed many friendships. Ignited primarily over the issue of states rights, the country was nearly split asunder forever as the armies of the North and the South slaughtered each other over a period of four years. The war took approximately 620,000 lives and tore apart families that had members fighting on both sides of the conflict. It severed longtime friendships, destroyed many towns and cities, and devastated forest and crops, especially in the South. At the outset of this war, two battles were fought near a small stream called Bull Run near Manassas in northern Virginia. Because Manassas was close to an important railroad junction, the North regarded it as a strategically significant location. The first battle began there on July 21, 1861, with the Union army attacking the Confederates, who were entrenched on the other side of Bull Run. The fighting raged back and forth until the South finally drove the North into a chaotic retreat back to Washington, D.C. About five thousand troops on both sides were lost in the first of the two battles.[48]

A week before this battle Sullivan Ballou, a major in the second Rhode Island Volunteers, wrote a letter to his wife, Sarah, informing her about the impending battle at Manassas and about how he felt about participating in the war (see Box 5–1 below). The letter expresses Major Ballou's profound love for his wife and for their two sons as he prepared to enter the battlefield where he foresaw that he would likely lose his life. In fact, he died in the battle one week later. His letter reveals a tension between his two great loves: love of his spouse and family, and love of his country. He asked Sarah, "Is it weak or dishonorable . . . that my unbounded love for you, my darling wife and children, should struggle in fierce, though useless, contest with my love of country?" He thought that the fierce struggle within his breast was "useless" because he believed, rightly or wrongly, that his "pure love of country" must be obeyed. But as he lived out the decision, his interior struggle between his love for Sarah and the children and his love for his country did not subside. Both loves were strong. His love for his country, which came over him "like a strong wind," bore him irresistibly to the battlefield and took priority over his love for his wife and family, even though that love bound them together like cables that no one but God could break.

Although Ballou's letter makes no mention of a specific religious tradition that guided his decision, he mentioned that he prays to God, tries to obey God's will, feels that he owes a "great debt" to those Americans who shed their blood in fighting for independence. He also expresses a strong belief in an afterlife in which he hopes to rejoin Sarah and his children. In Aquinas's language, Ballou's love and military service for his country arguably could be said to represent for him the common good that took precedence over his personal good. Preserving the Union was a greater good than staying behind and caring for his family. Viewed from the perspective of Aquinas's teaching, Ballou seemed to think that the common good of the nation was more godlike than the individual's good of wife and family, and that surrendering his life in defense of the nation was both loving and just (ST II-II, 31, 3 ad 2). Even with his moving and sincere expression of love to Sarah in which he sought her forgiveness and offered her consolation, he remained unwavering in his conviction that he was doing the right thing. He bases his decision on a "pure love" of his country and paying back a great debt to the soldiers of the Revolution (justice). Is Sullivan Ballou's ethics consistent with Aquinas's ethics of virtue? Assuming that the war was just (and Sullivan Ballou believed that it was), should citizens place love of their country ahead of love for their spouse and family?

BOX 5–1. THE CIVIL WAR LETTER OF SULLIVAN BALLOU

My very dear Sarah:

The indications are very strong that we will move in a few days—perhaps tomorrow. Lest I should not be able to write you again, I feel impelled to write a few lines that may fall under your eye when I shall be no more.

Our movement may be one of a few days duration and full of pleasure, or it may be one of sever conflict and death to me. Not my will, but thine, O God, be done. If it is necessary that I should fall on the battlefield for my country, I am ready. I have no misgivings about, or lack of confidence in, the cause in which I am engaged, and my courage does not halt or falter. I know how strongly American civilization now leans upon the triumph of the government, and how great a debt we owe to those who went before us through the blood and suffering of the Revolution. And I am willing—perfectly willing—to lay down all my joys in this life to help maintain this government and to pay that debt.

But, my dear wife, . . . when after having eaten for long years the bitter fruit of orphanage myself, I must offer it as their only sustenance to my dear little children—is it weak or dishonorable, while the banner of my purpose floats calmly and proudly in the breeze, that my unbounded love for you, my darling wife and children, should struggle in fierce, though useless, contest with my love of country?

I cannot describe to you my feelings on this calm summer night, when two thousand men are sleeping around me, many of them enjoying the last, perhaps, before that of death—and I, suspicious that Death is creeping behind me with his fatal dart, am communing with God, my country, and thee.

I have sought most closely and diligently, and often in my breast, for a wrong motive in thus hazarding the happiness of those I loved, and I could not find one. A pure love of my country and the principles I have often advocated before the people and "the name of honor that I love more than I fear death" have called upon me, and I have obeyed.

Sarah, my love for you is deathless. It seems to bind me to you with mighty cables that nothing but Omnipotence could break; and yet my love of Country comes over me like a strong wind and bears me irresistibly on, with all these chains, to the battlefield.

The memories of the blissful moments I have spent with you come creeping over me, and I feel most gratified to God and to you that I have enjoyed them so long. And hard for me it is to give them up and burn to ashes the hopes of future years when, God willing, we might still have lived and loved together, and seen our sons grow up to honorable manhood around us. I have, I know, but few and small claims upon Divine Providence, but something whispers to me—perhaps it is the wafted prayer of my little Edgar—that I shall return to my loved ones unharmed. If I do not, my dear Sarah, never forget how much I love you, and when my last breath escapes me on the battlefield, it will whisper your name.

Forgive my many faults, and the many pains I have caused you. How thoughtless and foolish I have often times been! How gladly would I wash out with my tears every little spot upon your happiness, and struggle with all the misfortune of this world to shield you and my children from harm. . . .

But O Sarah! If the dead can come back to this earth and flit unseen around those they loved, I shall always be near you; in the garish day and in the darkest night—amidst your happiest scenes and gloomiest hours—always, always; and if there be a soft breeze upon your cheek, it shall be my breath; or [if] the cool air fans your throbbing temple, it shall be my spirit passing by. Sarah, do not mourn me dead; think I am gone and wait for thee, for we shall meet again. . . .

O Sarah, I wait for you there! Come to me and lead thither my children.

—Sullivan

Sullivan Ballou died one week later at the First Battle of Bull Run (also called the First Battle of Manassas).

OVERCOMING THE DUALISM

We return to the question raised in the beginning of this chapter—whether charity and justice are partners in Aquinas's theology within the interpersonal and social dimensions. Thomas Aquinas consistently relates charity and justice on both levels. On the theoretical side charity collaborates closely with justice and does so in two major ways.

First, as architectonic virtues, both charity and justice direct each other, as well as the other virtues, to their respective ends. Aquinas has systematically integrated his theology of virtue by establishing charity as the principal conductor leading justice and all the other virtues to a person's final goal. His treatises on friendship, almsgiving, and martyrdom concretely manifest this integration. In his discussion of Christian martyrdom, charity and justice work closely together in directing and strengthening the witnesses' fortitude; conversely, fortitude makes persons resolute in carrying out their commitment to love God and to witness to justice. The martyrdom of Archbishop Romero illustrates Aquinas's theory that charity can impel a person to do justice and to face courageously the unjust adversary. Aquinas also showed that John the Baptist's critique of adultery is that it is not only a failure in marital love, but that it also violates justice.

Charity, by setting its own form on justice, widens the horizon of justice to include duties to God and to the "invisible" people who live on the margins of society. Justice directs charity to love God and neighbor in concrete and enduring ways. While charity is justice's inspiration and inner power, justice serves as charity's outward expression that concretely guarantees rights and establishes laws that protect relationships within families and larger institutions (ST I-II, 107, 1; I-II, 58, 2).

Second, charity and justice converge in the common good, where charity points to friendship with God and one's neighbor as the heart of common good. By placing God at the center of the common good, Aquinas forestalls any attempts to establish the good of the nation as the highest good or to give absolute authority to one aspiring to be a dictator. As for justice, it challenges charity to beam its love on the terrestrial common good and on all social relationships and not simply to restrict love to interpersonal relationships.

What does Aquinas teach us about overcoming the love-justice dualism in today's society? His ethics of virtue teaches us that charity and justice complement each other in a variety of issues, ranging from simple friendships to marital and family relationships to more complex issues dealing with the common good. By establishing the love of God and neighbor as the core of the common good and by directing all the virtues, including justice, to the ultimate end, Aquinas has avoided the ethical dualism of love and justice that presently exists in today's society. His emphasis on love as a passion that moves justice to the common good and beyond the common good to union with God provides a theoretical foundation for interpreting how and why persons like Sullivan Ballou can genuinely and passionately love country as well as family and for understanding how individuals like Oscar Romero courageously stand with the poor and oppressed even in great personal danger.

RESOURCES

DISCUSSION QUESTIONS

1. Thomas Aquinas and Aristotle both regard friendship as essential for personal fulfillment and for peace. What role does justice play in friendship?
2. Do you agree with Aquinas's assertions that human persons are by nature social and that they cannot be truly happy without friendship? What experiences have you had that either confirm or challenge this?
3. How does love of self relate to love of God and love of neighbor? Do you agree with Aquinas that love of self must come before love of neighbor? How does love of self avoid narcissism?

4. What does Aquinas mean by his statement that charity is the "form" of all other virtues? How does charity enrich justice? What does justice contribute to charity?

5. Aquinas, like Ambrose, gave high priority to helping the needy, like widows and orphans. Who are the "widows" and "orphans" in today's world whom love and justice call us to assist?

6. Thomas Aquinas says that reciprocity should be part of negotiating, including hiring prospective workers. Suppose you were the manager in charge of hiring workers for a department store. What would be your policy on hiring men or women who belong to a minority group in the region? How about amputees? Men or women who have served time for robbery? Would your practice differ from your stated policy?

7. Read the following case and answer the question at the end.

   Erin liked Jesse a lot. They had met during freshman orientation, and when school began, they began to do things together: went to a football game, took long walks in a nearby park, and saw a few movies. One Saturday night they went to a party together, and after the party Jesse invited her to his room in the residence hall. His roommate was away, and as they snuggled together, they had a few beers, became intimate, and had sex. Erin felt good about it until the morning after, when she awoke feeling guilty. She shared what had happened with her good friend Julie. She told Julie it was the first time that she had had sex. Julie comforted her, and Erin felt better.

   Later in the week, Gretchen, a friend who lived down the hall, approached Erin and asked her how she was feeling after the encounter with Jesse. Erin was aghast. Had Julie shared her secret with another? She began to get panicky. She wondered how many others in the residence hall knew about her intimacy with Jesse. She began to grow furious with Julie. What kind of friend would share something that Erin assumed was strictly confidential with another girl? The next day she called Julie. "Can we talk?" she asked. Julie said, "Yes, of course. What's happening, Erin?" "I'm crushed, that's what! Did you say anything to any of the girls on our floor about my night with Jesse?" "Absolutely not! How could I do such a thing?" After a long discussion Erin was convinced by Julie's sincerity. Only one other, she thought, could have told Gretchen about that night: Jesse!

   If you were Erin, how would you proceed?

8. Compare the virtues of charity and justice. In what ways are they alike? In what ways do they differ?

9. What is courage or fortitude, according to Thomas Aquinas? In light of what Aquinas said about the interrelationship of courage, charity, and justice, how might the virtues of charity and justice bolster your courage and your effectiveness in working for better working conditions for migrant workers in the United States?

SUGGESTED READINGS

Cessario, Romanus. *The Virtues, or the Examined Life*. New York: Continuum, 2002.

Farley, Margaret. *Just Love: A Framework for Christian Sexual Ethics*. New York: Continuum, 2006.

Pope, Stephen, ed. *The Ethics of Aquinas*. Washington, DC: Georgetown University Press, 2002.

Vacek, Edward Collins. *Love, Human and Divine: The Heart of Christian Ethics*. Washington, DC: Georgetown University Press, 1994.

Wadell, Paul. *The Primacy of Love: An Introduction to the Ethics of Thomas Aquinas*. New York: Paulist Press, 1992.

NOTES

[1] Anders Nygren, *Agape and Eros*, trans. Philip S. Watson (Chicago: University of Chicago Press, 1982), 86–91; Gene Outka, *Agape: An Ethical Analysis* (New Haven, CT: Yale University Press, 1972), 75–92; John Rawls, *A Theory of Justice* (Cambridge, MA: Belknap Press of Harvard University Press, 1971), 191–92, 476.

[2] Jeremy Waldron, "When Justice Replaces Affection: The Need for Rights," in *Liberal Rights: Collected Papers 1981–1991* (Cambridge: Cambridge University Press, 1993), 372–73.

[3] Ibid., 373.

[4] Pauline Kleingeld, "Just Love? Marriage and the Question of Justice," in Herbert Anderson et al., eds., *Mutuality Matters: Family, Faith, and Just Love* (New York: Rowman and Littlefield Publishers, 2004), 34, 39.

[5] William Shakespeare, "Measure for Measure," Act 2, Scene 2, in Stanley Wells and Gary Taylor, eds., *The Oxford Shakespeare: The Complete Works* (Oxford: Clarendon Press, 1988), 101–6.

[6] Ronald Alsop, "Corporate Scandals Hit Home," *The Wall Street Journal*, February 19, 2004, B1–2.

[7] Columbia Pictures, "Oliver," music and lyrics by Lionel Bart, directed by Carol Reed, first produced in 1968.

[8] Charles Dickens, *Oliver Twist*, Norton Critical Edition (New York: W. W. Norton and Company, 1993), 19.

[9] Ludwig Feuerbach, *The Essence of Christianity*, trans. George Eliot (New York: Harper and Row, 1957), 213–25.

[10] The primary good that God wills to the other is God's essence, and the person to whom God wills the good is God's self. God therefore does not need others in order to love. This is so because God is the source of all being and the exemplar of everything that is good. God wills good to creatures as the secondary good. Quotations from the *Summa Theologica* in this chapter are taken from the translation of the Fathers of the English Dominican Province (New York: Benziger Brothers, 1947).

[11] Edward Collins Vacek, *Love, Human and Divine: The Heart of Christian Ethics* (Washington, DC: Georgetown University Press, 1994), 162.

[12] Paul J. Wadell, *The Primacy of Love: An Introduction to the Ethics of Thomas Aquinas* (New York: Paulist Press, 1992), 79–80.

[13] Aquinas lists six affective or concupiscible passions and five irascible passions. The object of the concupiscible faculty is a sensible good or evil considered absolutely. The concupiscible passions are love and hatred, desire and aversion, delight and sadness. The irascible passions are spirited emotions that assist us when the good we seek is difficult to attain. They are fear and daring, hope and despair, and anger (*ST* I–II, 26–48).

[14] Stephen J. Pope, *The Evolution of Altruism and the Ordering of Love* (Washington, DC: Georgetown University Press, 1994), 55.

[15] Aquinas calls the affirmation of the beloved the love of concupiscence *(amor concupiscentiae)* and the good that one wishes for the beloved the love of friendship *(amor amicitiae)*.

[16] Margaret A. Farley, *Just Love: A Framework for Christian Sexual Ethics* (New York: Continuum, 2006), 169n109, 205. Farley describes love as "a response to the lovableness of the other, a lovableness that I behold or at least a lovableness in which I believe." See also Farley, *Personal Commitments* (San Francisco: Harper and Row, 1986), 29–32.

[17] Vacek, *Love, Human and Divine*, 34. Vacek's formal definition of love is "an affective, affirming participation in the goodness of a being (or Being)."

[18] Ibid., 168.

[19] Aristotle, *Nichomachean Ethics* Bk. IX, 1169b, in Richard McKeon, ed., *The Basic Works of Aristotle* (New York: Random House, 1941), 1088.

[20] Fergus Kerr, "Charity as Friendship," in Brian Davies, O.P., ed., *Language, Meaning, and God: Essays in Honour of Herbert McCabe, O.P.* (London: Geoffrey Chapman, 1987), 15.

[21] Vacek, *Love, Human and Divine*, 245–46.

[22] Wadell, *The Primacy of Love*, 90.

[23] Aquinas, *On Charity*, trans. Lottie H. Kendzierski (Milwaukee, WI: Marquette University Press, 1960); see also *ST* II-II, 25, 1.

[24] Gerald B. Phelan, "Justice and Friendship, *The Thomist* 5 (January 1943): 159, 161.

[25] Jean Porter, "Salvific Love and Charity: A Comparison of the Thought of Karl Rahner and Thomas Aquinas," in Edmund N. Santurri and William Werpehowski, eds., *The Love Commandments: Essays in Christian Ethics and Moral Philosophy* (Washington, DC: Georgetown University Press, 1992), 252; *ST* II-II, 45.

[26] Stephen J. Pope, "Christian Love for the Poor: Almsgiving and the Preferential Option," *Horizons* 21, no. 2 (1994): 295.

[27] Aquinas described "legal duty" *(debitum legale)* as a duty so necessary that to do without it would destroy the order of virtue. He gave two examples: the commands not to kill and not to steal.

[28] Josef Pieper, *The Four Cardinal Virtues: Prudence, Justice, Fortitude, Temperance* (Harcourt, Brace and World, 1965), 65–66.

[29] Quotations from *Rerum novarum* are taken from David J. O'Brien and Thomas A. Shannon, eds., *Catholic Social Thought: The Documentary Heritage* (Maryknoll, NY: Orbis Books, 1992).

[30] Vacek, *Love, Human and Divine*, 39. For a different perspective on love as respect or equal regard, see Gene Outka, *Agape: An Ethical Analysis* (New Haven, CT: Yale University Press, 1972), 12–13.

[31] David Hollenbach, *The Common Good and Christian Ethics* (New York: Cambridge University Press, 2002), 193–94.

[32] See National Conference of Catholic Bishops, *Economic Justice for All: Catholic Social Teaching and the U.S. Economy* (Washington, DC: United States Catholic Conference, 1997), par. 70.

[33] Aquinas explains that this justice is called legal justice "because thereby man is in harmony with the law which directs the acts of all the virtues to the common good" (*ST* II-II, 58, 5).

[34] Jacques Maritain, *The Person and the Common Good*, trans. John J. Fitzgerald (Notre Dame, IN: University of Notre Dame Press, 1985), 49n29.

[35] National Conference of Catholic Bishops, *Economic Justice for All*, par. 71.

[36] Maritain, *The Person and the Common Good*, 19.

[37] Austin Flannery, O.P., ed., *Vatican Council II: The Conciliar and Post Conciliar Documents*, rev. ed. (Boston: St. Paul Editions, 1988).

[38] Martin Rhonheimer, "Sins against Justice" (IIa IIae, qq. 59–78), in Stephen J. Pope, ed., *The Ethics of Aquinas* (Washington, DC: Georgetown University Press, 2002), 295–96; E. Christian Brugger, *Capital Punishment and Roman Catholic Moral Tradition* (Notre Dame, IN: University of Notre Dame Press, 2003), 169–77.

[39] Jean Porter, "The Virtue of Justice" (IIa IIae, qq. 58–122), in Pope, *The Ethics of Aquinas*, 283.

[40] "Architectonic," in Catherine Soanes and Angus Stevenson, eds., *The Oxford Dictionary of English*, rev. ed. (New York: Oxford University Press, 2005).

[41] Diana Fritz Cates, "The Virtue of Temperance" (IIa IIae, qq. 141–170), in Pope, *The Ethics of Aquinas*, 324.

[42] R. E. Houser, "The Virtue of Courage" (IIa IIae, qq. 123–140), in Pope, *The Ethics of Aquinas*, 309–10.

[43] Rafael Moreno, "Colonel García Came Looking for Him," in María López Vigil, *Romero: Memories in Mosaic* (Washington, DC: Epica, 1993), 395.

[44] Aristotle, *Nichomachean Ethics* Bk. I, 2.

[45] Thomas Aquinas, *Summa Contra Gentiles* (Garden City, NY: Hanover House, 1956), Bk. III, chap. 17.

[46] Maritain, *The Person and the Common Good*, 5; David Hollenbach, "The Common Good," in Judith A. Dwyer, ed., *The New Dictionary of Catholic Social Thought* (Collegeville, MN: The Liturgical Press, 1994), 194.

[47] There are, of course, many more elements that are components of the common good to which Aquinas did not attend, such as quality education, the environment, health care, and jobs.

[48] "Bull Run, Battles of," in *New Encyclopedia Britannica* (Chicago, 1994), http://www.britannica.com.

6

LOVE AND JUSTICE
IN POLITICS

Reinhold Niebuhr

*I would not judge a man by the presuppositions of his life
but by the fruits of his life. And the fruits—
the relevant fruits—are, I would say, a sense of charity,
a sense of proportion, a sense of justice.*
—REINHOLD NIEBUHR,
"WITHOUT CONSENSUS THERE IS NO CONSENT"

Reinhold Niebuhr (1892–1971), a Protestant pastor and professor of theology, spoke and wrote like a prophet. He had a prophet's gift for cutting to the marrow with a double-edged sword. Like the biblical prophets, Niebuhr discerned and exposed moral evils disguised as good and arrogance masked as righteousness. Responding to Henry Ford, who had publicly defended his "fair" treatment of auto workers, Niebuhr argued that Ford's laborers were both underpaid and overworked.[1] He also demonstrated that Marxist revolutionaries were wrong in their assertion that workers would no longer experience alienation once private property became common property. Niebuhr contended that alienation was rooted in egoism and not in political-economic structures, as the Marxists claimed. As Richard Kroner aptly expressed Niebuhr's prophetic gift: "There is no loyalty that would deter him from protest, when a higher loyalty seems to demand a protest."[2]

Niebuhr's prophetic thinking is dialectical. He scrutinizes diverse viewpoints, moving back and forth between opposing arguments in order to determine where the truth lies. His mind wrestles with contrasting ideas, like moral individuals and immoral societies, or justice and power; and with contradictory social structures, like tyranny and anarchy. Throughout his writings he grapples with the persistent tension between love and justice. He first scrutinizes the meaning of the gospel ideal of love and discovers that loving one's neighbor is not a simple possibility, especially when the neighbor involves groups. He then analyzes justice, which assists and challenges love by making human relationships and institutions more equal and free.

Niebuhr's dialectical mind observes how concrete circumstances, like serving in the military during wartime, often influence a person's values. A young

American Army captain during the First World War shared with Chaplain Niebuhr how happy he was to serve in the army. The captain said that "he *found* himself" in the military. Niebuhr afterward reflected on the captain's discovery, noting in his diary that what he thought really brought happiness to the captain was the military's simplification of life and the captain's love of authority. Momentary simplifications like the captain's, Niebuhr conjectured, would not be satisfying when the war ended and normal times returned. Postwar judgments often reveal a world "in all its confusion of good in evil and evil in good."[3] This story gives us a glimpse of Niebuhr's dialectical mind at work intuiting both good and evil in people's motives and actions.

Niebuhr's prophetic and dialectical thought searches for truth that lies somewhere between polar opposites. His habitual searching for ways to integrate divergent positions illustrates his sense of proportion, which takes into account both the virtues and the vices of human actors. His colleague, John Bennett, pointed out that when we try to follow Niebuhr's brilliant analysis, which so delicately draws out true elements from among divergent positions, we find ourselves unsure as to where Niebuhr stands. Bennett suggested that we remove the uncertainty by examining Niebuhr's articles and editorials, in which he more clearly states his position on controversial issues.[4] This chapter follows Bennett's suggestion by first examining Niebuhr's ethical framework and analysis, and then observing how he resolves concrete moral dilemmas in his essays.

THE LIFE AND TIMES OF REINHOLD NIEBUHR

Before investigating his framework, let us examine a few significant moments in the life of this prophetic figure. Karl Paul Reinhold Niebuhr was born in Wright City, Missouri, in 1892 to Gustav Niebuhr and Lydia Niebuhr. The family moved to a prairie town, Lincoln, Illinois, when he was just a child. This loving and devout family belonged to the German Evangelical Synod of North America, with roots in the Evangelical Church of Prussia, which had united the Lutheran and Reformed traditions in the early nineteenth century.[5] Gustav and Lydia gave three theologians to this Protestant tradition: a daughter, Hulda, and two sons, Reinhold and Helmut Richard. Reinhold did his undergraduate studies at Elmhurst College, west of Chicago, and at Eden Theological Seminary in Webster Groves, Missouri. After graduation he enrolled at Yale University, where he received a bachelor of divinity degree in 1914 and a master of arts degree in theology the following year.

PASTOR IN DETROIT

Ordained a minister of the German Evangelical Synod, he began his ministry at the age of twenty-three at Bethel Evangelical Church in East Detroit, near the Ford Motor Company in Dearborn, where many of his congregation worked. As pastor of this congregation from 1915 to 1928, he reflected on the First World War, became involved in race relations in Detroit, and criticized the exploitation of workers at Ford Motor Company. He preached every Sunday in English and in German until 1919, when the congregation abandoned all German services.[6] He found preaching to be easier than his organizational work for the congregation. "It is easier to speak sagely from the pulpit," he wrote in his diary, "than to act wisely in the detailed tasks of the parish."[7]

Although Niebuhr initially opposed the "Great War" because it was being fought over petty economic and political issues, he came to support it when the United States entered the war in 1917. The Versailles Conference (1919), which imposed terms of peace on Germany, seemed to Niebuhr to be unduly harsh and vengeful. The settlement shattered his commitment to the lofty ideals of U.S. President Woodrow Wilson that had earlier led him to support the war. Niebuhr's visit to Germany in 1923, where he saw its impoverished conditions, reinforced his pacifist views. He would remain a strong pacifist until the rise of Hitler in the 1930s.

When racial conflict broke out in Detroit in 1925, Niebuhr was appointed chairman of the Mayor's Race Committee, which produced a report that criticized the racist structures of Detroit. Afterward he continued to give talks and sermons on the race problem. In his celebrated book, *Moral Man and Immoral Society*, he argued that the Negro race in the United States would never be free from its subservient social and economic status "by trusting in the moral sense of the white race." He thought that using nonviolent resistance in the manner of Ghandi might be effective.[8] Later, in the 1960s, he supported Martin Luther King, Jr., for using Ghandian nonviolent strategy and tactics in fighting for civil rights for his people.

Following World War I, Ford Motor Company turned from making war materials to manufacturing cars. Niebuhr became an outspoken critic of Henry Ford, even allowing union organizers to use his pulpit to speak about workers' rights. He criticized Ford for his failure to pay fair wages and for not providing benefits to workers. "Not only is the Ford wage no longer a minimum subsistence wage, not to speak of a minimum comfort wage, but there is no conscience in the industry in the matters of unemployment or old-age insurance."[9] Niebuhr learned about injustices and the need for power if workers were to acquire their rights. "The industrial overlord will not share his power with his workers until he is forced to do so by tremendous pressure."[10] His reflections on the hard realities of war, class conflict, and racism moved him away from the Social Gospel Movement. This Protestant movement, which arose in nineteenth-century America, optimistically believed that a just society could be brought about simply by educational means and moral arguments. Niebuhr thought that this kind of vision was utopian and ineffective.

Professor in New York

In 1928 Reinhold Niebuhr began a long teaching career as professor at Union Theological Seminary in New York City, where he taught the history of Christian ethics and other related courses. Shortly after his arrival in October 1929 the U.S. stock market crashed. The following Great Depression shut down factories and banks and led to the loss of the life savings of many millions of people.

Around the beginning of the downturn of the economy in 1929, Niebuhr came to adopt Marxist strategy and social analysis, yet he never endorsed Marx's whole philosophy. During the decade of the 1930s he became a Christian Socialist, although John C. Bennett, Niebuhr's colleague at Union Theological Seminary, preferred to use the term *Christian Marxism* as a more accurate description of his position.[11] In fact, Niebuhr became a spokesperson for religious socialism, founding the Fellowship of Socialist Christians and running for political office in the U.S. Congress on the socialist ticket. He eventually broke with the Socialist Party because of its pacifist and noninterventionist attitudes on foreign policy. Around the time of World War II he abandoned Marxism, even though his political ethics continued to retain a residue of Marxist ideas. (Later in the chapter, we examine Niebuhr's reasons for rejecting Marxist communism.)

Subsequently, he became a left-wing, anticommunist Democrat in the 1940s, strongly opposing any cooperation with communism. He also spoke out against pacifism and supported the war against Hitler. Later, he backed the United States' opposition to the Soviet Union's expansion in Europe during the Cold War (1946–89) and supported the United States' policy of being militarily competitive with the USSR, because he saw the necessity of maintaining sufficient nuclear power to deter the Soviet Union from launching a nuclear war. At the same time, he opposed the United States relying too much on military power. As for the right of nations to wage war, he argued that using military force could only be justified as a last resort. "There cannot be war between us [the United States and the USSR] without mutual annihilation. There must not be war."[12]

Reflecting on whether the United States should have produced the hydrogen bomb after World War II, Niebuhr argued against American pacifists that the government was right to build the bomb. He laid out the following dilemma: Assuming that the Soviet Union had produced the H-bomb and the United States had not, the Soviet Union could have dropped hydrogen bombs and destroyed the nation. The other horn of the dilemma would have the United States producing the H-bomb before the Soviets and using it to liquidate its primary adversary. This latter action would have meant the *moral* annihilation of the United States. What should the American government do? U.S. pacifists argued that Americans and the enemy should together renounce making and using the H-bomb. The United States, however, would have no assurance that the Soviet Union would agree to such a renunciation. Niebuhr argued against the pacifists that no responsible statesman should risk putting the nation "in that position of defenselessness." Following the reasoning of St. Augustine, Niebuhr said, "Individuals may, but nations do not, thus risk their very existence."[13]

Although he supported the build up of nuclear arms to maintain parity with the Soviet Union, he was an early and strong critic of the American engagement in the Vietnam War in the 1960s. He retired from Union Theological Seminary in 1960 at the mandatory age of sixty-eight. He continued to reflect on the war in Vietnam and on the civil rights movement as he taught at Harvard, Barnard College, and Union. He died in his home in Stockbridge, Massachusetts, in 1971.

LOVE, JUSTICE, AND POWER

Reinhold Niebuhr views history as a dialectical process interacting with the kingdom of God. He shows how God's kingdom both affirms and judges human achievements and, conversely, how human achievements affirm and negate the ideals of the kingdom. Following Martin Luther's theology, Niebuhr espouses the former's paradoxical statement that the Christian is both sinner and righteous. Like the relation of the kingdom of God and human history, love relates to justice in a dialectical movement involving both affirmation and negation.[14] Justice also relates to power in a dialectical process. Before illustrating how these dialectical partners operate, we might reflect for a moment on the general meaning of *dialectic* and how Niebuhr understands and uses the term.

DIALECTICAL THEOLOGY

Dialectic comes from the ancient Greek word *diálectos*, meaning debate or argument. It implies conflict and opposition. When we argue over who has the best professional basketball team or who has written the best short story of the century, we are engrossed in a dialectic. We observe formal dialectical thinking in academic or political debates, in which one team or candidate argues the positive side of an issue and the opponent argues the negative side. Although there are different types of dialectic, all dialectical thinking assumes that social change and truth emerge through conflict and opposition, in contrast to Aristotelian-Thomistic thinking, which moves logically from premise to premise and finally to a conclusion, as expressed in a syllogism. Dialectic also assumes that elements which the adversaries oppose in the opponent are also present in themselves. The slave master's opposition to the slave's freedom, for example, is the very value that the master prizes above all else.[15]

Niebuhr uses a type of dialectic that involves tension between two opposite (though not contradictory) concepts or realities; the opposites focus on
difference, but at the same time they share something in common. Niebuhr's
dialectic between love and justice illustrates this dynamic. As opposites, they
vie with each other; love, which is non-coercive, judges justice, while justice,
which is coercive, tries to make love concrete. The Salvation Army, for example, may express deep concern and love for the welfare of homeless mi-
grants roaming the streets in sub-freezing temperatures; then it may persuade them to come to a shelter lest they freeze to death.

In Niebuhr's ethics, love and justice share the properties of equality and
freedom, although love as *agape* possesses these properties to a fuller degree.
Paired in dialectic, love and justice relate to each other in a creative tension.
Love fulfills justice by moving it toward greater equality and freedom; love
negates justice by showing that its achievement of equality and freedom is
only partial. Conversely, justice makes love concrete by creating relationships that are more equal and free than they were previously. Justice may
also judge the ideal of love as impractical, impossible, or utopian. The dialectic continues as love moves persons to be just and judges the shortcom-
ings of the concrete acts of justice, while justice partially fulfills love and
negates its idealism.[16] For Niebuhr, justice is a compromise that bridges the
ideal of love and the hard realities of everyday life. Metaphorically speaking,
he calls justice the plumbing that connects the house or superstructure to the
earthly reality.

Let us put flesh on the bare bones of Niebuhr's love and justice dialectic,
using a historic case to which Niebuhr often referred: the 1954 U.S. Supreme
Court ruling *Brown v. the Board of Education.*[17] Although this dialectic
historically began much earlier, we begin with the major crisis that occurred
in 1951 when Linda Brown, daughter of Oliver Brown, asked her father if
she could attend the neighborhood all-white elementary school in Topeka,
Kansas, where her friends went to school. Knowing that this would be a
difficult task, Mr. Brown, a toolmaker, took her to the neighborhood school
to register. Her application was rejected because she was black, and her father left the principal's office in an angry mood. Mr. Brown's love for his
daughter next moved him to seek justice. He filed a suit in a local court.
Combined with other similar suits involving black students, Linda Brown's
suit eventually went to the U.S. Supreme Court in 1954. The principal plain-
tiff, Oliver Brown, and twelve others were represented by the chief counsel,
Thurgood Marshall, who argued the case before the Warren Supreme Court
in Washington, D.C.

The Supreme Court handed down a unanimous 9–0 decision that stated
that "separate educational facilities are inherently unequal," thus overturn-
ing the "separate but equal" doctrine of *Plessy v. Ferguson,* which had supported segregated public education. The 1954 decision ruled that the de jure

segregation in public schools violated the equal protection under the law stated by the Fourteenth Amendment to the U.S. Constitution.[18] Aided by the legal counsel and the ruling of the Supreme Court, which gave the decision both majesty and power, justice took a giant step toward greater equality and freedom for African American children. In Niebuhrian language, justice drew closer to love under the conditions of sin. After the Supreme Court ruling, Niebuhr noted that racial prejudice persisted both in the North and in the South. He then commented: "The Court seems quite conscious of the fact that no law can be enforced if it is not generally accepted by the people."[19] Segregated schooling, however, was gradually eliminated; racial prejudice, however, still persists.

Niebuhr presents a similar dialectic between justice and power, which involves both the *fulfilling* and the *negating* of each other. Justice employs power as a tool to bring about greater equality and freedom, as the Supreme Court did by eliminating segregation in public schools. Power, understood as the capacity to influence others, is a neutral term that can be employed in a positive sense by promoting justice or in a negative sense by exploiting others.[20] Using power positively, justice is done by persons, like Thurgood Marshall, or institutions, like the Supreme Court, persuading or mandating that the state establish laws that regulate society impartially and fairly. Justice may use power negatively by changing laws that are discriminatory, such as the *Plessy v. Ferguson* "separate-but-equal" ruling. Justice may rightly affirm the use of power in an act of self-defense, or it may condemn it when, for example, a lieutenant orders his platoon to kill innocent civilians. Conversely, power might fulfill justice, by using a proportionate amount of force in order to control a crowd that is protesting a law. It might also negate justice by using a disproportionate amount of force.

As we continue our examination of Niebuhr's dialectical social ethics, we need to probe more deeply into the meaning of his key notions: (1) love as *agape* and love as *eros*; (2) sin as pride and sin as sensuality; (3) justice as *agape's* paradoxical partner; and (4) power as justice's instrument for transforming unjust structures.

Agape and Eros

Niebuhr describes *agape* as the transcendent, unmeasured love of Christ for others. Jesus' suffering and death on the cross symbolizes *agape*. During his life and in his death, Jesus emptied himself of egoism, desire for power, and divine status by freely surrendering his life for the sake of others' salvation. He commanded his followers to love God and their neighbors in the same self-sacrificing way. Neighbors include enemies as well as friends, Jews and Gentiles, the poor and the rich, people of all races, strangers and friends. *Agape* offers the highest possibility of human life. Niebuhr refers to this type of love as "disinterested" in the sense that persons love another without

taint of bias, egoism, and by "a consistent refusal to use power in the rivalries of history."[21]

Niebuhr maintains that the teachings of Jesus on love of God and neighbor are directly relevant to individual persons, but they are less relevant
when one tries to apply the love commands directly to groups. Why does
Jesus' teaching become less relevant for groups? First, Niebuhr contends
that Jesus' ethic was a personal ethic based on love.[22] Although it implies
social relationships, Jesus' ethic is "an individual ethic in the sense that his
chief interest was the quality of life of an individual."[23] Jesus considered it a
temptation that the crowd wanted him to become a political messiah, even
pushing to make him king. Second, for all of their majesty and power to
bring persons together, Jesus' love commands cannot persuade groups to
shed their egoistic and arrogant patterns. *Agape* does not force change; it
never coerces. Instead, it must work through justice. Justice analyzes, evalu-
ates, and strategizes about how to use power to change practices judged to
be unfair.

In its paradoxical relationship with justice, love aims to bring all people
to obey God's will. As justice brings individuals and groups closer to this
ideal, love shows persons that the achievement of justice, however great,
falls far short of full equality and freedom. Persons, therefore, should not be
self-satisfied with their progress but ought to move on toward greater justice. Using power generally involves asserting the interest of one ego against
another. Refusing to use coercive power, Jesus emptied himself of egoism
and transcended sinful rivalries. Jesus' love symbolized by the cross transcends all particular norms of justice and mutual love.[24]

Niebuhr contrasts *agape* with a mutual type of love that he calls *eros*.
Eros acts for the sake of the self's own happiness. Unlike *agape*, *eros* is not
sufficiently free from self-preoccupation and therefore unable "to lose itself
in the life of another."[25] This type of love strives for self-actualization but
falls short of its aim. In Niebuhr's words, "The self, by calculating its en-
largement [self-realization] will not escape from itself completely enough to
be enlarged."[26] Unlike *agape*, which focuses wholeheartedly on the other,
eros desires to win over the other's affection. It loves the other with the
expectation of being loved or of gaining something in return.

In contrast to *eros*, *agape* is disinterested, other focused, and gratuitous;
it does not expect any reward. The New Testament uses *agape* to convey
how God loves people and how human beings should love God. The Gospels reveal how Jesus loved both in word and deed, especially by sacrificing
his life for the salvation of humankind. Niebuhr writes that *agape* "com-
pletes the incompleteness of mutual love *(eros)*" because the latter always
works for the benefit of the self and the self's own happiness.[27]

It is surprising that Niebuhr, who relies heavily on biblical terms, uses the
word *eros*, which appears only in a few instances in the Old Testament and
never in the New Testament. Moreover, Niebuhr makes no reference to love

as *philia*, which New Testament authors often use to express mutual love in friendship. Sometimes the authors use *philia* to express friendship between God and human persons, and sometimes to mean friendship between two persons.[28] In addition, Niebuhr assumes that self-interest is always egoistic. But if that is so, then it seems that persons are sinning whenever they try to improve themselves by study or to care for themselves by eating well, exercising, or seeing their physician when ill. Within the Catholic tradition, a proper love of self, or *eros*, is not only non-egoistical, but it is essential for one's growth and development.[29] As Aquinas notes, one cannot fulfill the second love command to love the neighbor as oneself if one has no love for oneself.

SIN AS THE WILL-TO-POWER

In light of the human condition, where people pursue their own self-interest, the social ideal of *agape* seems unattainable. For Niebuhr, *agape* seems to be an unreachable goal. Given this perspective, many people would question whether a social ethics based on *agape* could be relevant in the world of politics, business, or in any social activity where persons and groups compete for money, honors, and power. It seems unrealistic that an ethics grounded in *agape* could have any moral influence on leaders of nation-states, who typically address issues in terms of national self-interest and strategies for increasing the nation's power in order to have the upper hand in international negotiations. It also seems unrealistic that private corporations competing for profits in the market would invoke *agape* as a standard for policymaking. If individuals and groups habitually act out of self-interest, and rarely because of self-sacrificing love for others, must not a Christian social ethics lower its standards, possibly by replacing *agape* with a less demanding love, like *eros*, which accepts self-interest as a given?

Niebuhr addresses this challenging question from within his theological framework, called Christian realism, which concentrates on love and justice within the social context where groups typically strive egoistically to gain power and wealth. He calls this framework Christian because his ethics is rooted in Christian revelation and in the mystery of the cross of Christ; he calls it realism because it takes seriously human experience with all of its complexity, sinfulness, human limits, and possibilities. In sum, Christian realism accounts for the presence of sin as well as of grace.

Niebuhr talks about two types of sin. The first type involves human persons denying their finitude by exaggerating their autonomy and freedom or trying to transcend human limits. He labels this sin pride or will-to-power. We see this most dramatically in tyrants, like the former president of Chile, Augusto Pinochet, who forcefully took control of the government and terrorized and executed hundreds of Chilean citizens. The second kind of sin denies one's spirituality by trying to escape from one's unlimited possibilities of freedom. Niebuhr calls this latter kind of sin sensuality. Within a marriage relationship, for example, a spouse could sin by allowing his or her partner to make all the decisions.

Critics have noted that Niebuhr accentuates sin as a will-to-power over sin as sensuality. Niebuhr's heavy concentration on sin as the will-to-power and his virtually neglecting the sin as sensuality may be partly due to his interest in groups (private corporations and nations), who relentlessly pursue power and rarely abdicate it. Whatever the reason for concentrating on the sin of pride, his critics think that Niebuhr's treatment of sin is imbalanced because he pays slight attention to sins of sensuality, in which persons abdicate their power by surrendering their freedom to others or by refusing to take action when their basic rights are denied.

In developing his Christian social ethics, Niebuhr first acknowledged that the social ideal of love by itself is irrelevant in dealing with groups. Niebuhr the realist constructed an ethics that begins by analyzing how egoism and the will-to-power operate in the minds of executives of corporations and presidents of nations as they try to advance their collective interests. In his *Moral Man and Immoral Society* he drew a sharp distinction between the moral behavior of individuals and of groups. The groups included nations competing with one another, conflicts between the privileged class and the working class, and tensions between races. Early in his academic work at Union Theological Seminary, he developed his famous thesis: "Individual men may be moral in the sense that they are able to consider interests other than their own in determining problems of conduct. . . . These achievements are more difficult, if not impossible, for human societies and social groups."[30] Collective egoism is more stubborn and persistent than individual egoism in the pursuit of power and wealth.[31] Why should groups be more selfish than individuals? "In every human group," Niebuhr argued, "there is less reason to guide and to check impulse, less capacity for self-transcendence, less ability to comprehend the needs of others and therefore more unrestrained egoism than the individuals, who compose the group, reveal in their relationships."[32] The key word here is *egoism,* which ignores loving others while selfishly seeking its own interests and happiness.[33] Because the ego's will-to-power is far stronger in collectivities than in individuals, the latter can do little to check or counter the dominating strategies and tactics of powerful groups in either government or the private sector.

A precondition for sin in human beings is insecurity. Persons try to overcome their insecurity by seeking power that exceeds their human capacity. For Niebuhr, the basic sin of individuals and groups is pride, expressed through their will-to-power. The Bible, Niebuhr notes, distinguishes two dimensions of the sin of pride: sin as a religious offense and sin as moral offense.[34] The religious dimension consists in the human creatures' rebellion against God in order to transcend their own creaturely limits. This prideful act, because it usurps the place of God, is an act of idolatry.[35] A nation, for example, might deify itself by glorifying its own culture or by exalting its people over all other nations. A dramatic and tragic instance of national self-deification was Hitler's Nazi Germany, which viewed its people as the master race, an Aryan race superior to all other races and religions, including the Christian faith.[36]

The moral dimension of sin is injustice. Persons and groups sin within the moral sphere when, "in their pride and will-to-power," they make themselves the center of the universe and regard others as subordinate to themselves.[37] Acting out this type of egoism may involve exploiting the neighbor or refusing to help persons who desperately need their help.

After analyzing the human condition and the sinful human tendencies of individuals and especially of groups, Niebuhr came to see that human beings could not fulfill the gospel's call by living the standard of *eros* because it is incapable of transcending its self-interest. Nor can justice, based solely on reason or social contract, rise above self-interest and cultural bias. Niebuhr reasons that only a justice rooted in *agape* can help persons to transcend their egoism so that they may fully realize themselves as human beings. Justice moves closer to *agape* and away from *eros* when persons and groups express themselves in self-transcendent acts, when they transcend their sinful rivalries, and when they act freely and treat others with equality.[38]

Niebuhr maintains that *agape* is an "impossible possibility."[39] It is impossible because no human person without God's assistance can express fully such disinterested, selfless love that seeks the good of the larger community. When individuals or groups interact, one ego frequently asserts itself against another. Yet this self-transcendent type of love may be present in human acts in at least two ways: first, agape may motivate persons to act justly. Second, love may judge the quality of the human act. When persons and groups are motivated to act justly, they move closer to *agape*. He defines equal justice as "the approximation of brotherhood under the conditions of sin." But because we live under these sinful conditions, justice effects a more-or-less type of equality and freedom and therefore never fully reaches full fellowship.

Feminist ethicists Valerie Saiving and Judith Plaskow have criticized Niebuhr's notions of sin and grace, questioning his primary emphases on pride as the basic sin and on grace as selflessness or self-sacrifice. Both ethicists maintain that Niebuhr's emphases reflect a male bias because they fail to capture the experience of most women. Saiving contends that there are significant differences between masculine and feminine experiences. She suggests using terms other than *pride,* such as *triviality, distractibility,* and *diffuseness* to express women's experience of sin. Women are tempted to depend on others for their own self-definition, and thus negate their selfhood.[40]

Building on Saiving's insight, Plaskow applies it to Reinhold Niebuhr's notions of sin and grace. As we have already seen, Niebuhr sees sin arising from persons' inordinately seeking relief from the anxiety of their finite freedom. They sin either by pride, that is, by denying the limits of their freedom by a will-to-power, or by denying freedom's spirituality by indulging in sensuality. Women can fail by refusing to live up to their responsibility of freedom, which, she claims, can be "no less a sin than pride." "If pride is the attempt to usurp the place of God, sensuality [Niebuhr's term] is the denial of creation in his image."[41] Saiving and Plaskow present an important corrective for Niebuhr's notion of sin. In discussing racism Niebuhr faults African Americans for not being more aggressive toward their white masters during the Civil War. Is he identifying the slaves' sin as one of sensuality, that is, by not asserting their freedom by rebelling against their masters? We will return to this issue below.

JUSTICE: LOVE'S PARADOXICAL PARTNER

As noted above, justice plays an important role working with *agape* in what Niebuhr calls a paradoxical and dialectical relationship. He describes justice in various ways. First, he refers to it as "the spirit of justice" in which love serves as its fulfillment.[42]

Niebuhr's justice has many meanings. In its first and basic meaning, "equal justice is the approximation of brotherhood under the conditions of sin."[43] "Brotherhood" for Niebuhr symbolizes a loving relationship. But because this relationship exists "under the conditions of sin," the love falls short of *agape* love. Hence, doing justice means establishing loving relationships in the context of egoism, pride, disagreements, prejudice, and sexist attitudes and actions. Since groups possess different degrees of power, justice must also include as part of its strategy sufficient power to bring about social change. Sin, for Niebuhr, is not an abstraction. Sinful acts become embedded in institutions as unjust policies or laws. When social transformers attempt to change them, the owners resist them with all their might.

Second, he refers to justice as structures or arrangements that restrain the conflict of wills and interests from developing into anarchy.[44] Third, Niebuhr's justice consists of principles and rules. These are abstract ideals. Rules of justice are his "middle axioms," which are more or less abstract norms that guide the distribution of goods and services. The principle of justice has two middle axioms: equality and freedom. Finally, Niebuhr's justice is a strategy or master plan for bringing about the best consequences to society. Justice as strategy includes a vision, its principle that approximates love, middle axioms, and virtues, like humility. Strategizing for Niebuhr would call for identifying more specific standards and virtues that would have greater applicability in certain situations.

Perfect justice exists in situations when brothers and sisters live in society without conflicts. At this level of perfection, justice is identical with love. Being a realist, however, Niebuhr recognizes that justice guided by love would only bring a relative peace, not a perfect harmony, to all relationships. "No, not a perfect peace," Niebuhr commented. "But it can be more perfect than it is. If the mind and the spirit of man do not attempt the impossible, if it [humankind] does not seek to conquer or to eliminate nature but tries only to make the forces of nature the servants of the human spirit and the instruments of the moral ideal, a progressively higher justice and more stable peace can be achieved."[45]

Like relative peace, relative justice only approximates perfect love, as it tries to move relationships and structures inch-by-inch toward *agape*. Niebuhr speaks of principles and systems of justice as instruments of the *spirit* of brotherhood. Justice, guided by *agape*, works with forces of nature and a whole network of relationships involving interpersonal relationships among family and friends to competing classes of rich and poor and segregated races within a nation, and among nations living in relative peace and war. These obligations extend from immediately felt obligations (for example, feeling compassion for and helping a sick person) to permanent obligations (for example, doing rational planning and consensus building in order to establish a national health-care plan); from simple relations among friends to complex relations involving three or more persons (for example, a pastor, elders, the parish council); from the obligations discerned by personal discernment (for example, deciding how to answer a calling) to the wider obligations that a civic community defines for its citizens.[46] In these diverse relationships, sometimes feelings and at other times discernment and reason play significant roles.

Love and justice work together in a dialectical tension both in positive and negative ways. On the positive side, love moves a person to want to seek justice and to free the person to act in behalf of justice by being less preoccupied with self and thus sufficiently free to lose oneself in the life of the "other."[47] Drawing grace and direction from *agape*, justice tries to move human acts and policies away from self-aggrandizing love and redirect it to self-sacrificing love. On the negative side, love illumines the limits of justice, showing by contrast how deficient the justice of a group really is and how much farther the group must advance, moving to building a more just social order.

Similarly, justice relates to *agape* both positively and negatively. On the positive side, it first brings about a greater "approximation of brotherhood under the conditions of sin."[48] Second, persons and communities, acting on the principle of justice, could redirect human communities to move closer to the social ideal of love by bringing about greater equality and freedom. Third, justice shows how love must work with power to bring about a viable balance of power. Fourth, justice makes love concrete by effecting a minimum expression of love.

POWER AS JUSTICE'S INSTRUMENT

Justice, Niebuhr would argue, takes into account the amount of power held by the contesting parties. He argues that equal or greater power must be used to overcome the power of the unjust structures created by corporations that may wield enormous control over others. Opponents seeking justice cannot hope to transform laws or policies solely by love or by moral arguments that persuasively demonstrate the rightness of their cause. To bring about institutional change or just laws in civil society, persons must work from a realistic conception of human nature. Groups invariably act out their self-interest and collective egoism to retain the status quo or to increase their power. They never yield their power voluntarily but change only when a contravening power coerces them to do so. In sum, doing what is justice on a corporate level requires not only presenting a reasonable argument, but it also necessitates exerting power to check or balance the power that organizations use in exploiting other groups.

What does Niebuhr mean by *power*? Christine Firer Hinze has distinguished two types of power that may help us better understand Niebuhr's use of the term. Like Niebuhr, Firer Hinze focuses on sociopolitical power. She identifies two types. The first type of power is superordination, or "power-over." It is control over another's decisions and has a coercive dimension. It enables the power holder to act against or in spite of others. The second type of power focuses on people's ability to effect their ends by collaborating with one another. It is a "power-to." It concentrates on "power's efficacy *with* or *because of* others."[49]

Niebuhr's twin emphases on the "will-to-power" as the basic sin of pride and on justice as "the balance of power" suggest that his primary type of power is power-over. Niebuhr's focus on Jesus as the Suffering Servant who freely shares power as he proclaims the reign of God implies power-to; he does not exert power over others. When religious leaders and the Roman procurator try unsuccessfully to control him and finally execute him, he does not respond in kind by using violence. Jesus' appeal to agapaic love and his inviting others to live as a community of love, justice, and peace in the reign of God suggest a power-to. Niebuhr, however, sees the power of love having only an indirect relation to and minimal impact on group life.[50]

Niebuhr's ethics sees love and justice working in a close but paradoxical relationship. The paradox is this: How does a Christian ethics, which seeks to bring about greater love that expresses a perfect harmony of interests, fit with justice that exerts a justified power-over in order to check or balance a sin-tainted power-over? This is a paradox that Niebuhr does not discuss. He fails to explain how using coercion to control or stop exploitation moves a community toward greater equality, freedom, and peace, and finally to *agape*. How does a justice that uses coercion to achieve its aims, move relationships closer to *agape*, which, by definition, is non-coercive?

CRITIQUE OF MARXISM

As a pastor in Detroit reflecting and preaching about the problems of industrial workers for thirteen years, Reinhold Niebuhr came to understand

the issues that Marx and Marxists had addressed about alienation, inequality, greed, and the blindness of industrial overlords. From the beginning he
made an option for the workers as he denounced unjust practices in the
automobile industry. He wrote the following in his diary:

> Look at the industrial enterprise anywhere and you find criminal indif-
> ference on the part of the strong to the fate of the weak. The lust for
> power and the greed for gain are the dominant note in business. An
> industrial overlord will not share his power with his workers until he is
> forced to do so by tremendous pressure. The middle classes, with the
> exception of a small minority of intelligentsia, do not aid the worker in
> exerting this pressure. He must fight alone.[51]

His experiences with injustices brought about by class conflict moved him
away from the liberal Social Gospel Movement and toward a Christian
Marxism. Niebuhr's conversations with industrial workers and executives
and his reading the writings of Karl Marx taught him about political-economic structures and the importance of power in addressing social issues.

MARX'S IDEAL OF EQUALITY

Niebuhr criticized Marx's political-economic theory on a number of points:
(1) Marx's idealism, (2) the cause of alienation, (3) class struggle, and (4)
communism's reductionism. Niebuhr liked Marx's principle of equality as
an ideal but did not think it would work in a complex society. He liked the
fact that the principle—"From each according to his ability, to each according to his needs"—arose from the need of the workers and because it expressed a relative equality. The Soviet Union, however, did not put it into
practice. On a practical level Niebuhr faulted the principle because it was
utopian and absolutist. He distinguished "soft utopianism" from "hard
utopianism." The former is an ideal society of uncoerced justice in which
every form of coercion, force, and power gradually becomes irrelevant. This
type could not survive in the real world. "Hard utopianism" is a real society
brought about by communism, which claims that the ideal society has already arrived and that the Communist Party assumes the right to enforce the
ideal principle. The latter deals ruthlessly with all enemies of the ideal. Niebuhr
called both types "illusory."[52]

THE CAUSE OF ALIENATION

Turning to Marx's notion of alienation, Niebuhr disagreed that the fundamental causes of alienation were private property and the social forces
operative in capitalist labor. If private property and all frictions and compe-
titions in labor were the causes, then the communist classless society, by

abolishing capitalist private property and private property, would forever eliminate alienation. But communism has not done so. Alienation and egoism spring from the ill will of human beings, not from faulty institutions and private property. The primary purpose of private property and the laws that protect it is to prevent persons from taking advantage of one another.[53]

CLASS STRUGGLE

Niebuhr witnessed the class struggle between the working class and the upper-class executives in Detroit's industrial plants. Marx attributed this struggle between classes to the capitalist system. Although Niebuhr saw many problems with capitalism, he did not think that Marx's vision of a classless society was a panacea. Marx overlooked the inevitable situation within a classless communist society in which the means of production held in common would necessarily be managed by someone who would then be responsible for enormous power. The administration of this power would inevitably tempt the managers to become dictators:

> The possession of power is sweet and the corruptions of power are great. We may assume therefore that those who exercise this power do not concern themselves too much with the dreams which originally endowed their power with moral legitimacy.[54]

When economic and political power are turned over to a single oligarchy, Niebuhr said, it increases the possibility of tyranny. His overriding concern was that power be shared and balanced, lest an imbalance bring tyranny. Applying Marx's principle—whoever controls the means of production controls society—to the inevitable situation in a communist state in which someone must manage the means of production, Niebuhr feared the probable situation of the country becoming a totalitarian state. This in fact happened to the Soviet Union under Stalin and under his successors. Sin is inherent in all persons, even in those working for justice. Communist workers, even as they strive toward an equalitarian ideal, do not by that fact become sinless carriers of the revolution. Nor would the managers of the ideal society be so disciplined and so rigorously just that they would not require checks and balances by other powers. Here we see again Niebuhr applying his Christian realism in his critique of a communist state.

MARX'S REDUCTIONISM

Niebuhr viewed Marx's analysis of society as reductionist because it narrowly focused on the means of production without attending to other social factors that weakened the capitalist political economy. In addition to analyzing how the bourgeois class controlled the means of production, Marx should have attended to other important factors, such as the power of the ruling party, racial prejudice within and between classes, and cultural bias within subcultures.[55] Although Marx did in fact include social, political, and cultural factors in his analysis, Niebuhr noted, he understood them to be the results, not the causal determinants of the economy. He also pointed out that within Marx's fundamental structure of class warfare, coalitions of power are more numerous. The competition, therefore, between functional groups is more complex than Marx understood it to be. In summing up his position, Niebuhr again returned to his Christian anthropology, which highlights human finitude and the pervasiveness of sin. The limits of reason and the dishonesty of the human heart are not confined to class warfare within the capitalist system; they pervade all relationships in which human beings interact for survival, acquiring power, and recognition.

CRITIQUE OF RACISM

Writing during the Second World War, Niebuhr said that racial conflict, next to war, was the most serious social problem that Americans have to face.[56] "Racial conflict has become the most vicious of all forms of social conflict in the nation."[57] His experience of racial bigotry in Detroit during the mid-to-late 1920s sensitized him to the magnitude of the problem and to the immense difficulty facing African American people as they try to achieve full emancipation. He writes that racial prejudice, like other types of group prejudice, issues from group pride that corrupts the group consciousness of the prevailing majority. He calls this prejudice idolatry because the white race deifies itself by assuming a stance of superiority over the black race.

Niebuhr begins his analysis of racism by identifying bad and good strategies for overcoming racial bigotry. The bad strategies consist of two extreme approaches. The first strategy calls American blacks to trust the moral sense of American whites, who will eventually emancipate them from the low-level social and economic positions into which whites had forced them. The second strategy calls for revolution initiated by black leaders who organize their people to overthrow the racist sociopolitical and economic structures, using violent tactics to free themselves from exploitative institutions and practices. The first strategy would fail, Niebuhr argues, because "the white race in America will not admit the Negro to equal rights if it is not forced to do so."[58] Power must be exerted. The second strategy would backfire because it would aggravate the violent passions of the deeply prejudiced white majority and would end in catastrophe for the black minority.

Niehuhr proposes a third and workable strategy that would require the use of power in the form of nonviolent resistance, following the method that Mohandas Gandhi had successfully employed in India. For American black people this reformist strategy emphatically insists upon nonviolent tactics. It would include boycotting banks that refused to grant them credit, stores

that refused to employ blacks, and public service corporations that discrimi-
nated against African Americans.[59] As we saw in Chapter 2, Niebuhr was
basically correct. During the 1960s civil rights movement, Martin Luther
King, Jr., and his people succeeded in achieving rights for African Americans
by using nonviolent tactics such as sit-in protests at lunch counters, rallies,
demonstrations, and marches.

RACISM AS IDOLATRY AND PRIDE

Addressing racism on a number of fronts, Niebuhr reviews the studies by
social scientists who have analyzed the nature and causes of racial prejudice.
Anthropologists, for example, have shown that racial bigots frequently link
superficial differences, like racial traits, with inferiority. For the bigot, difference spells subservience. Psychologists have empirically demonstrated that
subrational fears and hatreds arise from people's insecurity and sense of
inferiority.[60] Even though the social scientists' empirical studies have exposed
the racist ideologies and irrational feelings, racist attitudes and acts persist.
These studies show that educational means alone cannot overcome racist
attitudes and practices. Niebuhr claims that neither scientific enlightenment
nor moral argument will ever dispel the erroneous assumption that the white
race is superior to the black race.

He therefore delves deeper into the theological roots of prejudice to find a
solution. He argues that racial bigotry is a form of original sin and therefore
is "darker and more terrible than stupidity."[61] Human pride spawns bigotry,
which is more than ignorance and yet less than malice. Only repentance and
forgiveness can break its power. This comes about when the real God confronts the bigot, who undergoes repentance and hears God's words of forgiveness.[62]

RACISM WITHIN THE CHURCH

Niebuhr recognizes that churches, by and large, are part of the problem
of racial discrimination, when they should be part of the solution. The liberal churches fail to deal effectively with racism because they have relied
exclusively on educational and rational means. Churches would do better to
call people to repentance. Christian revivals are famous for doing just that.
In the revival, the leader preaches to large audiences and then invites people
to come forth in a spirit of repentance and to accept Jesus as their savior.

In the 1950s the most popular revivalist preacher in America was Billy
Graham. This renowned clergyman from Charlotte, North Carolina, was a
spiritual advisor to U.S. presidents. He drew thousands of people to his revivals in many cities throughout the United States. In 1956, two years after
the Supreme Court ruled that racial segregation in public schools violated
the 14th Amendment to the U.S. Constitution, Niebuhr published an essay

entitled "Proposal to Billy Graham." In this essay he expresses his uneasiness that Graham's evangelism seems to be "irrelevant to the great moral issues of our day," unlike the nineteenth-century American revivalist Charles Finney, who had made the abolition of slavery central in his revivals.[63] The contemporary revivalist Christianity, Niebuhr says, is ineffective because it oversimplifies moral issues and because it focuses on individual sins of drunkenness, adultery, and the violation of the Sabbath. It fails to challenge collective evil, such as racial segregation.[64]

CRITIQUE OF NIEBUHR'S PERSPECTIVES

In her book *Disruptive Christian Ethics*, Traci West analyzes and compares Niebuhr's ideas on racism during the 1930s and 1940s with the ideas and experiences of female descendants of former slaves and free blacks.[65] Although West applauds Niebuhr for his strong stance against racism, she disagrees that Niebuhr was an extraordinary visionary by recommending to the black community a Gandhian nonviolent strategy that many years later Martin Luther King, Jr., used with much success. She presents solid evidence showing that organizations like the NAACP, the New York Urban League, and the Harlem Housewives League had already been involved in nonviolent resistance against discriminatory policies in the 1930s when Niebuhr had presented his recommendations to the black community.[66] She cites the 1930s' practice of the Harlem Housewives League, who visited department stores and grocery stores (Woolworth's and the A&P), informing the owners how much money black consumers had spent in their stores and urging the owners to hire black workers. The Harlem Housewives League initiated a campaign of boycotts against merchants who refused to hire black applicants.[67] In calling upon blacks to adopt a nonviolent resistance strategy in his *Moral Man and Immoral Society*, Niebuhr failed to mention these New York black organizations already engaged in nonviolently protesting against discriminatory practices against blacks. West uses these examples to illustrate that white thinkers have been placed at the center of black "narratives of history and moral innovation." Doing this, she says, "reinforces the supremacy of whites in our understanding of how important moral knowledge is generated."[68]

Moreover, West thinks that Niebuhr's reading of black history is faulty. Niebuhr argued that African Americans practiced a form of rational objectivity, or what Niebuhr called "commitment to disinterestedness," a moral stance that he said American blacks took. This "disinterestedness" resulted in refusing to rebel against their masters during the Civil War; on the contrary, they remained quite loyal to them. Writing in 1932, Niebuhr said, "Their [African Americans'] social attitudes since that time, until a very recent date, have been compounded of genuine religious virtues of forgiveness and forbearance, and a certain social inertia which was derived not from religious virtue but from racial weakness. Yet they did not soften the hearts of their oppressors by their social policy."[69] Commenting on this passage, West interprets Niebuhr to be attributing to the African Americans "an inadequacy that stems from the character of the Negro race."[70]

West provides a reading different from Niebuhr's. She contends that black women activists in Harlem during the 1930–44 period moved away from and even confronted white control. Building on the work of historian Judy Weisenfeld, she shows how the Harlem YWCA provided "a respite space for black women and girls as well as a wedge against the burdens of social inequality, discrimination, and economic hardship."[71] This included affordable housing for black girls and women and a trade school that trained thousands of girls during the Depression. Harlem leaders also understood that trusting in the moral sense of whites would be futile and that protests would be essential for doing battle with the white racist society. Cecelia Cabaniss Saunders, for example, testified before the Mayor's Commission on Conditions in Harlem following the 1935 riot in Harlem about the lack of responsiveness of local stores to black protests against discriminatory hiring practices and the suspected brutality of the police against a black child. Saunders also criticized the discriminatory treatment of black women by white employers.[72]

In discussing blacks confronting whites as a strategy to create change, West cautions white theologians against focusing too narrowly on confrontation that ignores specifics of black struggle and black life. Ignoring the particulars—space for respite, self-nurture, and coordinating policies for resistance—means losing essential elements for altering practices.

West's critique of Niebuhr provides us with a valuable lesson: An exploited and oppressed people must be the author of its own history. No one understands the particulars of the struggle better than those involved in the struggle. They must tell their own story of oppression and liberation. While West incisively notes important elements of the black struggle that Niebuhr missed, the latter clearly stood by black people as he took a strong stance against racial bigotry. Black liberation theologian James Cone recognized that Niebuhr committed himself to the oppressed of the land. "Reinhold Niebuhr's *Moral Man and Immoral Society* moves in the direction of blackness. To verify the blackness of a particular perspective, we need only ask, 'For whom was it written, the oppressed or oppressors?' If the former, it is black; if the latter, it is white."[73] Clearly Niebuhr stood with the oppressed and with African Americans. He dedicated himself to addressing racism from his first days as pastor of Bethel Church to the day of his death. He addressed racism in his classes at Union and wrote articles denouncing the lynching of blacks in the South. He gave great support to Martin Luther King, Jr., especially when King was criticized by blacks and whites alike for connecting the Vietnam War with racism.[74]

ASSESSMENT

STRENGTHS

Reinhold Niebuhr has contributed many insights in his undertaking the enormously difficult task of formulating an adequate social ethics. Some close observers of his work would contend that Professor Niebuhr created the discipline of social ethics. They applaud his persistent concentration on groups and on the power that they possess rather than focusing on individual human acts as many previous Christians ethicists have done. His social ethics is especially credible because he began his theological-ethical reflection from the ground up; that is, he first considered the life and moral problems of individuals and groups and then, in light of revelation, developed his ethics. One of his first books—*Leaves from the Notebook of a Tamed Cynic*—grew out of his diary, written while serving as a pastor in Detroit. His parish work brought him into contact with industrial workers and African Americans who struggled for justice and basic rights.

Niebuhr's ethics has many other strengths. First, he developed a type of social analysis many years before liberation theology. Aided by social-scientific studies, Niebuhr probed the nature of institutions, identified their ideologies, and examined their dynamics of power. Using biblical and theological sources, he identified and analyzed the idols that civilizations create (deification of reason, self-deification of nations). He exposed them as idolatrous, illusory, and oppressive.

Second, he showed that certain virtues, such as humility, play important roles in moral discernment in opposition to pride and arrogance, which can blind persons to their personal prejudices operative even in their ethical systems. Humility, he said, is rooted in self-knowledge that leads to repentance and allows persons to love and to be forgiving. In writing about humility he said, "Moral idealists never forgive their foes. They are too secure in their own virtue to do that. Men forgive their foes only when they feel themselves to be standing under God with them and feel that under divine scrutiny all 'our righteousness is as filthy rags.'"[75] Niebuhr was a powerful critic but a humble one. Brilliant though he was, he publicly acknowledged his limitations. "I found it embarrassing that my moral teachings, which emphasized the mixture of self-regard and creativity in all human motives, had not been applied to my own motives."[76]

Third, Niebuhr consistently grounds his ethics in the gospel value of love that relates dialectically to justice. He uses these general principles to assess moral dilemmas or institutional policies, more like a prophet who intuits the presence of the good and the bad and less like a philosophical ethicist who makes judgments on the basis of a reasoned argument. His gospel rule of thumb, "By their fruits you will know them," suggests that Niebuhr is a consequentialist, though not a utilitarian type who tallies the greatest good for the greatest number. As John Bennett said, Niebuhr's analysis of concrete social problems gives us the best understanding of his type of justice. He stands for equal rights among the races, a relative balance of power among the branches of government, and a living wage, which for Niebuhr meant a minimum subsistence wage as well as unemployment and old-age insurance.[77] Whereas some critics see Niebuhr's failure to provide clear principles and structures of justice as a strength,[78] other critics see it as a weakness.[79]

LIMITATIONS

Like Augustine and Aquinas, Niebuhr constructed his ethics from philosophical as well as biblical sources. Niebuhr borrowed the concept of *agape* from the New Testament but took his notion of mutual love, or *eros*, from ancient Greek philosophy. Using two different sources to define love seems legitimate, but his ignoring completely an important type of love found in the New Testament, *philia*, limits his discussion of love. For Niebuhr, love is either other-focused *(agape)* or self-focused *(eros)*. He presents no in-between love that focuses on the relationship itself. As noted earlier, *philia*, like Niebuhr's *eros*, connotes a love that is mutual, but biblical *philia* differs from Niebuhr's understanding of *eros* in that *philia* does not imply that egoism is necessarily a part of the relationship. *Philia*, even in the most loving human relationships, necessarily includes self-interest. In *philia* self-interest, however, does not always involve egoism, as Niebuhr implies. Egoism certainly can and does creep into the relationship, but the presence of self-interest in *philia* does not mean that the loving relationship is tainted with egoism.

Niebuhr's dialectic presents many tensions: between the gospel and the empirical reason of human beings; between freedom and law; between love and justice. Love illumines, judges, and corrects injustice. Justice makes the ideal concrete and ensures at least a minimum of love in relationships. While Niebuhr's emphasis on rough justice as a balance of power is important, he seems to underplay empowerment of the disenfranchised; how marginal persons, both individually and collectively, can become active subjects in the polis and in the marketplace. Catholic social teachings refer to such empowerment as social justice.

As for the dialectical relationship between love and justice, Niebuhr's justice is derived from love, although the two are distinct. *Agape* is harmonious and free and therefore does not use power in a coercive manner to bring about justice. Justice, on the other hand, uses power-over to correct exploitation, to order society properly, and to defend the innocent. Niebuhr seems to be defining *agape*, the very love embodied in the person of Jesus, too narrowly. As a prophet, Jesus severely chastised those religious leaders who were oppressing people by their overly strict interpretation of the law. He also cleansed the Temple of money changers, buyers, and sellers because they were violating proper decorum in a house of prayer and because the sellers were overcharging the buyers. Were these coercive acts expressions of justice that involved egoism? Or were they authentic expressions of *agape*? Niebuhr does not say. But he seems to restrict *agape* either to motivating, guiding, and judging the justice of certain acts or policies, or to human acts where persons turn the other cheek, suffering at the hands of the persecutor, and sometimes dying for the faith. *Agape*, he says repeatedly, is expressed by the cross of Christ, where Jesus remained vulnerable to the end and forgave his executioners. Jesus, however, as we saw in the Temple, also expressed love in the manner of the prophets.

John Howard Yoder, a Christian pacifist, thought that Niebuhr made Jesus irrelevant because his ethics of love does not directly apply to the workings of groups. Yoder suggested that Jesus' death on the cross does have social application, arguing that it calls people to be pacifists. Whether or not one espouses Yoder's interpretation of the meaning of the cross, and Niebuhr did not, Yoder's question about the relevance of Jesus for social ethics suggests that Niebuhr defined the love of Jesus too narrowly and applied it too strictly. Jesus' prophetic words and actions, which chastise, forgive, and heal, express *agape*. His words and deeds are also powerful. In terms of Firer Hinze's two types of power, Jesus exercises a power-over when he heals human beings and casts out demons, and a power-to when he sends his disciples on mission to assist him in proclaiming the reign of God. Both types of power could be agapaic. Jesus' love for others is not always free of tension and powerless, as the gospel makes clear.

Finally, as feminist theologians have rightly argued, Niebuhr's descriptions of sin as primarily pride, and grace as simply a self-sacrificing type of love, are too narrowly focused. Sin as will-to-power would fall within the traditional Christian category of sins of commission, and abdicating one's responsibility to oneself and others would be classified as sins of omission.

RESOURCES

DISCUSSION QUESTIONS

1. What is a dialectic? In what sense is Niebuhr's relationship between love and justice in dialectical tension?
2. Do you agree with Niebuhr's argument that the United States was right to build the hydrogen bomb before the Soviet Union built it? Or do you agree with the pacifists' argument that the United States should have tried to make a treaty with the Soviet Union banning the manufacture of the bomb? Explain.
3. Do you agree with Niebuhr that it is virtually impossible for politicians or business persons to conduct their affairs motivated by *agape*? Give reasons to explain your agreement or disagreement with Niebuhr.

4. How does Niebuhr distinguish *eros* from *agape*? Would you identify an instance in which you have acted out of *agape*? Give a second instance in which you acted out of *eros*.

5. Niebuhr has argued that it is very difficult for groups to transcend their own self-interest and work for the good of their employees and consumers. But would this be true for all kinds of groups? Consider a for-profit company (like Macy's) or a university, or a voluntary association (like Catholic Charities). Are all called to be responsible to the same degree for the welfare of others?

6. During the Great Depression, Niebuhr was a Christian Marxist. What did he discover in Marxist thought that led him to change his mind?

7. Niebuhr was a prophetic type of theologian who spoke out strongly and effectively against social problems like racial segregation, lynchings, inadequate wages for industrial workers, and the Vietnam War. Is there a religious man or woman anywhere in the world today who effectively addresses burning social issues as Niebuhr did? If your answer is positive, talk about his or her strengths as a prophetic voice. If your answer is negative, why do you think religious leaders are reluctant to take such a stand?

Suggested Readings

Niebuhr, Reinhold. *Moral Man and Immoral Society*. New York: Charles Scribner's Sons, 1932, 1960.

_____. *The Nature and Destiny of Man*. Vol. 1: *Human Nature;* Vol. 2: *Human Destiny*. Gifford Lectures. New York: Charles Scribner's Sons, 1943, 1964.

Kegley, Charles W., and Bretall, Robert W., eds. *Reinhold Niebuhr: His Religious, Social, and Political Thought*. New York: The MacMillan Company, 1956.

Lebacqz, Karen. "A Protestant Alternative: Reinhold Niebuhr." In *Six Theories of Justice*. Minneapolis: Augsburg Publishing House, 1986.

Robertson, D. B., ed. *Love and Justice: Selections from the Shorter Writings of Reinhold Niebuhr*. Cleveland: The World Publishing Company, Meridian Books, 1957.

Stone, Ronald H. *Professor Reinhold Niebuhr: A Mentor to the Twentieth Century*. Louisville, KY: Westminster/John Knox Press, 1992.

NOTES

[1] Ronald H. Stone, *Professor Reinhold Niebuhr: A Mentor to the Twentieth Century* (Louisville, KY: Westminster/John Knox Press, 1992), 29–32.

[2] Richard Kroner, "The Historical Roots of Niebuhr's Thought," in Charles W. Kegley and Robert W. Bretall, eds., *Reinhold Niebuhr: His Religious, Social, and Political Thought* (New York: The MacMillan Company, 1956), 179.

[3] Stone, *Professor Reinhold Niebuhr*, 18–19.

[4] John C. Bennett, "Reinhold Niebuhr's Social Ethics," in Kegley and Bretall, *Reinhold Niebuhr*, 46–47.

[5] Stone, *Professor Reinhold Niebuhr*, 7.

[6] Ibid., 22.

[7] Reinhold Niebuhr, *Leaves from the Notebook of a Tamed Cynic* (Hamden, CT: The Shoe String Press, 1929, 1956), 2.

[8] Reinhold Niebuhr, *Moral Man and Immoral Society: A Study in Ethics and Politics* (New York: Charles Scribner's Sons, 1932), 252.

[9] Reinhold Niebuhr, "How Philanthropic Is Henry Ford?" *The Christian Century*, December 9, 1926, reprinted in E. B. Robertson, ed., *Love and Justice: Selections from the Shorter Writings of Reinhold Niebuhr* (Cleveland: Meridian Books, The World Publishing Company, 1957), 100.

[10] Niebuhr, *Leaves from the Notebook of a Tamed Cynic*, 94.

[11] Bennett, "Reinhold Niebuhr's Social Ethics," 72. Niebuhr, Bennett said, "went far beyond the acceptance of socialism as a social goal or as a morally preferable alternative to capitalism."

[12] Reinhold Niebuhr, "After Sputnik and Explorer," *Christianity and Crisis* 18 (March 4, 1958); reprinted in Ernest W. Lefever, *The World Crisis and American Responsibility* (New York: Association Press, 1958), 126.

[13] Reinhold Niebuhr, "The Hydrogen Bomb," in Robertson, *Love and Justice*, 236.

[14] Reinhold Niebuhr, *The Nature and Destiny of Man*, vol. 1, *Human Nature* (New York: Charles Scribner's Sons, 1949), 204.

[15] John Rowan, "Dialectical Thinking," http://www.gwiep.net/site/dialthnk.htm (accessed on December 4, 2006).

[16] Reinhold Niebuhr, *The Nature and Destiny of Man*, vol. 2, *Human Destiny* (New York: Charles Scribner's Sons, 1964), 246–47.

[17] Reinhold Niebuhr, "What Resources Can the Christian Church Offer to Meet Crisis in Race Relations?" *The Messenger* (April 3, 1956); reprinted in Robertson, *Love and Justice*, 152–54.

[18] Brown Foundation for Educational Equity, Excellence, and Research, "Brown versus Board of Education—Background Summary," http://brownvboard.org/summary/index.php (accessed on December 4, 2006).

[19] Reinhold Niebuhr, "The Supreme Court on Segregation in the Schools," *Christianity and Crisis* (June 14, 1954); reprinted in Robertson, *Love and Justice*, 149.

[20] Reinhold Niebuhr, "Christian Faith and Natural Law," *Theology* (February 1940); reprinted in Robertson, *Love and Justice*, 53.

[21] Niebuhr, *The Nature and Destiny of Man*, 1:72.

[22] Reinhold Niebuhr, "The Ethic of Jesus and the Social Problem," in Robertson, *Love and Justice*, 30.

[23] Ibid.

[24] Ibid., 74.

[25] Ibid., 82.

[26] Ibid.

[27] Ibid.

[28] John L. McKenzie, "Philia," in *Dictionary of the Bible* (Milwaukee: The Bruce Publishing Company, 1965), s.v.

[29] Pope Benedict writes, "Yet eros and agape—ascending love and descending love—can never be completely separated. The more the two, in their different aspects, find a proper unity in the one reality of love, the more the true nature of love in general is realized" (*Deus Caritas Est*, par. 7), http://www.vatican.va/holy_father/benedict_xvi/encyclicals/documents/hf_ben-xvi_enc_20 (accessed on March 5, 2006).

[30] Niebuhr, *Moral Man and Immoral Society*, xi.

[31] Reinhold Niebuhr, *Man's Nature and His Communities* (New York: Charles Scribner's Sons, 1965), 22. At the urging of a friendly critic, he thought that a better title for his book would be *The Not So Moral Man in His Less Moral Communities*. Even as he closed the moral gap between groups and individuals, he stood by his thesis that groups tended to act more selfishly than individuals.

[32] Niebuhr, *Moral Man and Immoral Society*, xi–xii.

[33] Niebuhr, *The Nature and Destiny of Man*, 2:82. Niebuhr does not consider a third form of love, *philia*, a friendship type of love that is mutual and that genuinely seeks the good of the other. Niebuhr thinks that it is insufficiently free of preoccupation with self "to lose itself in the life of the other."

[34] Niebuhr, *The Nature and Destiny of Man*, 1:178–79.

[35] Ibid.

[36] Ibid., 1:219.

[37] Ibid., 1:179.

[38] Ibid., 2:72–73.

[39] Reinhold Niebuhr, *An Interpretation of Christian Ethics* (New York: Harper and Brothers, 1935), chap. 4.

[40] Valerie Saiving, "The Human Situation: A Feminine View," *Womanspirit Rising: A Feminist Reader in Religion* (New York: Harper and Row, 1979), 37–39.

[41] Judith Plaskow, *Sex, Sin and Grace: Women's Experience and the Theologies of Reinhold Niebuhr and Paul Tillich* (New York: University Press of America, 1980), 68.

[42] Niebuhr, in Robertson, *Love and Justice*, 25.

[43] Niebuhr, *The Nature and Destiny of Man*, 2:254.

[44] Ibid., 2:192.

[45] Niebuhr, *Moral Man and Immoral Society*, 256.

[46] Niebuhr, *The Nature and Destiny of Man*, 2:248.

[47] Ibid., 2:80.

[48] Ibid., 2:254.

[49] Christine Firer Hinze, *Comprehending Power in Christian Social Ethics*, American Academy of Religion Academy Series, ed. Susan Thistlethwaite (Atlanta, GA: Scholars Press, 1995), 5.

[50] Ibid., 86.

[51] Niebuhr, *Leaves from the Notebook of a Tamed Cynic*, 94.

[52] Reinhold Niebuhr, "Two Forms of Tyranny," in *Christianity and Crisis* 8 (February 2, 1948): 3–5.

[53] Ibid.

[54] Ibid.

[55] Niebuhr, *Interpretation of Christian Ethics*, 124.

[56] Gordon Harland, *The Thought of Reinhold Niebuhr* (New York: Oxford University Press, 1960), 255.

[57] Reinhold Niebuhr, "Christian Faith and the Race Problem," in *Christianity and Crisis* (Spring 1945); reprinted in Robertson, *Love and Justice*, 129.

[58] Niebuhr, *Moral Man and Immoral Society*, 252–53.

[59] Ibid., 254.

[60] Niebuhr, "Christian Faith and the Race Problem," 125–26.

[61] Ibid., 128.

[62] Ibid.

[63] Reinhold Niebuhr, "Proposal to Billy Graham," in *The Christian Century* (August 8, 1956); reprinted in Robertson, *Love and Justice*, 154.

[64] Ibid., 158.

[65] Traci C. West, *Disruptive Christian Ethics: When Racism and Women's Lives Matter* (Louisville, KY: Westminster John Knox Press, 2006), 5.

[66] Ibid., 8.

[67] Ibid.

[68] Ibid., 9.

[69] Niebuhr, *Moral Man and Immoral Society*, 268.

[70] West, *Disruptive Christian Ethics*, 16.

[71] Ibid., 19.

[72] Ibid., 18.

[73] James H. Cone, *A Black Theology of Liberation*, 2nd ed. (Maryknoll, NY: Orbis Books, 1986), 144n4.

[74] Stone, *Professor Reinhold Niebuhr*, 234.

[75] Reinhold Niebuhr, "When Will Christians Stop Fooling Themselves?" *The Christian Century* (May 16, 1934), 659, quoted from Harland, *The Thought of Reinhold Niebuhr*, 135.

[76] Reinhold Niebuhr, "A View from the Sidelines," *Christian Century* (December 19–26, 1984), 1195.

[77] Niebuhr, "How Philanthropic Is Henry Ford," *The Christian Century* (December 9, 1926); reprinted in Robertson, *Love and Justice*, 100.

[78] Harland, *The Thought of Reinhold Niebuhr*, 28.

[79] Dennis McCann, *Christian Realism and Liberation Theology: Practical Theologies in Creative Conflict* (Maryknoll, NY: Orbis Books, 1981), 124.

7

LOVE AND JUSTICE
IN THE MARKET

Pope John Paul II

Love for others, and in the first place love for the poor, in whom the church sees Christ himself, is made concrete in the promotion of justice.
—POPE JOHN PAUL II, CENTESIMUS ANNUS

The last leg of our journey invites us to investigate how Karol Wojtyla (pronounced Voy-*tih*-wä), better known as Pope John Paul II (1920–2005), understood love and justice and how he used these virtues to address the plight of the poor in the market economy. Growing up in war-torn and tortured Poland during the Second World War, Karol Wojtyla witnessed the Nazis' systematic killing of his people, their persecution of Polish Jews, and, after the war, the Communists' oppression of industrial workers. Branded into his memory as a boy, these events influenced the young Karol as he created and directed dramas and wrote philosophical works. These horrible events continued to have an impact on the older Karol when, as John Paul II (1978–2005), he drafted many encyclical letters.

Our investigation focuses primarily on the pope's *social* encyclicals, especially on his landmark social encyclical called *Centesimus annus* (*On the Hundredth Anniversary of Rerum novarum*, 1991), together with pertinent sections from his earlier social encyclicals, *Laborem exercens* (*On Human Work*, 1981) and *Sollicitudo rei socialis* (*On Social Concern*, 1987).[1] It also examines certain philosophical and theological works written before Karol Wojtyla became Pope John Paul II.

In these encyclicals John Paul II talks about love, justice, dignity, and solidarity—all key virtues and principles that characterize human persons and guide them in their personal and social relationships. He consistently refers to these core values in his critical assessments of the socialist and capitalist economies. Our main focus is what he says about international trade and labor within the capitalist economy. He argues that just as it is right and proper that individual countries organize and direct their economies to promote the common good of their own nation, so also it is right and necessary that countries work together to promote the common good of all countries, especially of the less-developed nations (*CA*, no. 52).

Christian realists, like Reinhold Niebuhr, would likely balk at his efforts to work toward a *global* common good. Given the intensely competitive world market, the gross imbalance of wealth and power, and the pervasive self-interest of nations, Niebuhr would be skeptical of nations' willingness to collaborate with one another. But John Paul II was more hopeful than Niebuhr. As the head of the Roman Catholic Church and a frequent visitor to many countries, he had become knowledgeable of cultural differences and economic gaps between wealthy and poor nations. He believed that nations can and must build a universal culture by respecting the dignity of all people and by recognizing the basic interdependence of nations. Hence, he repeatedly called upon all nations to work together to improve their situations through trade and work (*CA,* no. 52).

With respect to trade, John Paul II identified a major problem: finding a way for poor nations to gain "fair access to the international market" (*CA,* no. 33). Countries protect businesses within their jurisdiction by subsidizing their farm products or by putting quotas and high tariffs on imported foreign goods.[2] This practice impedes trade, raises consumer prices, and crushes poor nations, who, as a consequence, are unable to sell their products at the market price.

THE WORLD OF JOHN PAUL II

Before investigating John Paul II's social ethics and how he relates it to the market economy, let us step into the world in which John Paul II lived and wrote his social encyclicals. Our cultural-political tour begins with an overview of Catholic social teaching; it then moves to specific sociopolitical and economic events that occurred during the lifetime of this dynamic and globe-trotting pope. His world also includes interaction with a theological movement called liberation theology and an important dialogue with economists before he published *Centesimus annus* in 1991. Even as these historical events influenced the perspectives of John Paul II, so also the pope had a powerful impact on the world community through his writing and speeches. The May 8, 2006, issue of *Time Magazine* identified John Paul II as one of four persons who has shaped the world both in the twentieth century and the early twenty-first century.

CATHOLIC SOCIAL TEACHING

As head of the universal Roman Catholic Church, John Paul II wrote his social encyclicals within an ecclesial tradition called Catholic social teaching. This tradition, which extends over two millennia, consists of a large body of formal writings by popes, synods of bishops, theologians, and regional conferences of bishops.[3] The corpus includes a genre of papal writings called encyclicals, which address the entire Roman Catholic Church and instruct its members on church doctrine and moral teaching. More recent encyclicals, beginning with Pope John XXIII (*Pacem in terris*, 1963), reach out to people beyond the Catholic community, addressing all men and women of good will.

Catholic social teaching began in early Christianity when Christian leaders addressed pressing issues within the church, such as whether the Christian community should invite Gentiles as well as Jews to be members. In subsequent centuries bishops and theologians addressed other urgent questions: Should Christians serve in the military? Under what conditions may war be justified? Should persons or institutions be allowed to charge interest on loans? Ought slavery be permitted?

Modern Catholic social teaching began at the end of the nineteenth century when Pope Leo XIII issued his encyclical letter *Rerum novarum*. This ground-breaking encyclical went beyond earlier official social teaching of the church by directly challenging the established political-economic capitalist order and also the socialist system, which was encroaching on capitalism. Leo XIII urged the state and private corporations in the capitalist system to reform their policies and practices while he denounced the socialists' model of a classless society as unworkable and unjust. Building on the theology of Thomas Aquinas, Leo XIII argued that the moral law, which is rooted both in the natural law and in the gospel, must guide state and corporate managers as they create their economic policies. Leo XIII followed Aquinas's ethics of virtue as he defended people's right to private property in opposition to the socialists, who establish a political economy in which private property is controlled by the collective or the state. Leo also argued for a just wage and humane working conditions in the capitalist economy. In addressing socialism, he denounced its atheism and its use of class struggle, which Marxist socialists adopt as a strategy for overthrowing the capitalist political economy. In *Centesimus annus* (nos. 12–17) John Paul II endorses Leo XIII's strong criticism of socialism.

John Paul II also supports his predecessor's critique of capitalist practices. He agrees, for example, with Leo XIII's denunciation of company managers for not paying a just wage to their employees. Like Leo XIII, he appeals to the state in the name of distributive justice to allocate goods and services to all its citizens, especially to those whose needs are unmet (*RN*, nos. 26–27). John Paul II says that in today's market economy certain wage contracts fail to do justice to workers' wages and to the working conditions of children and women. "This is the case," he writes, "despite the international declarations and conventions on the subject and the international law of states" (*CA*, no. 8).

THE COLD WAR (1946–1989)

The Cold War began shortly after World War II with the chilling, non-military engagement between the East (the Soviet Union and its allies) and the West (the United States and its allies). It ended with the fall of the Berlin Wall on November 9, 1989. The East-West conflict brought about many unfortunate consequences. First, both superpowers competed for dominance in the nuclear arms race that frightened and at times paralyzed people throughout the world. Second, both the West and the East attempted to expand their hegemony over nonaligned nations. Third, they interpreted virtually all conflicts either in terms of freedom and democracy (the West) or equality (the East), when in fact the deeper causes underlying domestic conflicts were often poverty and oppressive practices carried out by local totalitarian dictators who were not aligned with either of the superpowers. Fourth, although the Western and Eastern powers spoke of their assistance to developing nations as "foreign aid," both powers lumped together military aid with economic assistance, thus enabling these smaller nations, now armed with high-powered weapons, tanks, and helicopters, to defend or expand their territory by military conquest. Between 1980 and 1990, for example, the United States gave more than $4.5 billion in foreign aid to the government of El Salvador to combat what the United States claimed was the spread of communism, when other observers identified the major problem as an inequitable distribution of land.[4] The greater part of this so-called foreign aid was military assistance.[5] The Soviet Union provided huge amounts of foreign aid to Cuba and also secretly installed nuclear missiles there, with the result that the Soviet Union and the United States teetered on the brink of a nuclear war.

John Paul II often addressed the East-West conflict, which, he said, created the "insane arms race" and "swallowed up the resources needed for the development of national economies and for assistance to the less developed nations" (CA, no. 18). The Cold War between these superpowers, he accurately observed, exploited disagreements within the developing countries and contributed to civil wars by superpowers selling arms to dictatorial governments.

POLAND AND SOLIDARITY

The transformation of Poland's Marxist political economy in 1990 was the knell announcing the imminent death of communism in Eastern Europe. The unraveling of the Polish political economy began in 1980 with a national strike of the workers' union called Solidarity. The movement began with peaceful protests and strikes in a shipyard of Gdansk under the leadership of Lech Walesa. After nearly a decade of resistance, protests, and strikes, in 1989 the workers throughout Poland persuaded the centralized government to sit down with them for round-table talks. These talks brought about the government's acceptance of Solidarity as a political party. Shortly thereafter, members of Solidarity gained representation in parliament, winning the majority of seats both in the lower house and in the senate. Subsequently,

Solidarity became the majority party and ousted the Communist Party's control of parliament. The next year (1990) Lech Walesa was elected president of Poland.

John Paul II, who had supported Solidarity by his visits to Poland, used this organization as a model to illustrate what he meant by the virtue of solidarity. He showed how the oppressed workers could achieve justice through open dialogue with Poland's communist regime and by their appeal to human rights. Most impressive was the manner in which Solidarity gained its objectives by a nonviolent use of power rather than by employing force, as communists had often done (CA, nos. 23–24).

LIBERATION THEOLOGY

The liberation theology movement arising out of Latin America in the 1960s engaged in its reflections the people's life of faith within the struggles of oppressive living conditions.[6] It created a method and theological principles that influenced the social encyclicals of John Paul II. Although the pope criticized liberation theologians because of their sympathy with a Marxist type of social analysis, he nonetheless borrowed important concepts and principles from this theology, including the concept of liberation as a multidimensional process aimed at freeing persons on the political-economic, humane, and religious levels. In a manner similar to liberation theology, the pope viewed liberation as a process of working for the "conversion of hearts and for the improvement of structures."[7] He appropriated liberation theology's bedrock principle, the preferential option for the poor, adapting it somewhat, but affirming that "stronger nations must offer weaker ones opportunities for taking their place in international life" (CA, no. 35). In defense of poor nations, John Paul II supported the transformation of social structures, such as removing trade barriers and monopolies. Like liberation theologians, he identified certain structures as sinful. He wrote in Sollicitudo rei socialis (SR) that "sin" and "structures of sin" are categories that are seldom applied to the situation of the contemporary world. However, one cannot easily gain a profound understanding of the reality that confronts us unless we give a name to the root of the evils that afflict us (SR, no. 36).

Trained in phenomenology that describes conscious experience, John Paul II reflected on human subjectivity and on concrete human experiences, such as working and trading, and on social institutions, such as socialism and capitalism. His reading of the signs of the times in light of the gospel was also distinctive of liberation theology's method. Like liberation theologians, John Paul II appealed to biblical sources in his social teachings and rarely to natural law, which was a shift away from the social encyclicals of his predecessors, Leo XIII, Pius XI, and Paul VI.[8] Although liberation theology's method differs from John Paul II's approach in certain important respects (the pope's approach was more deductive and less analytical than the liberation theologians' method), the similarities suggest that he respected liberation theology even though he criticized it.

DIALOGUE WITH SOCIAL SCIENTISTS

As part of a process of writing pastoral letters addressing war and the economy in the 1980s, Catholic bishops from the United States and Canada introduced a process of consulting social scientists. They did this in order to better understand the economy by engaging economists in an open dialogue. This process likely encouraged John Paul II to do the same. In fact, he did consult with fifteen economists from many countries, who advised him on many aspects of the economy as the pope and his team of writers were drafting *Centesimus annus*.

The pope sent out a questionnaire to these economists in preparation for their meeting on November 5, 1990, asking a variety of questions, such as how rationality in economics affects moral considerations in economic behavior and how social cooperation might affect the conception of rational behavior.[9] In *Centesimus annus* John Paul alludes to this rich interchange with the economists: "The church's social teaching has an important interdisciplinary dimension. In order better to incarnate the one truth about man in different and constantly changing social, economic and political contexts, this teaching enters into dialogue with the various disciplines concerned with man" (*CA*, no. 59). The seminar clearly had an impact on *Centesimus annus*, which manifests greater openness to the market economy than had previous social encyclicals.

TOWARD A GLOBAL ETHICS

In light of these theological and sociopolitical influences on John Paul II's writings, we turn to his ethical perspectives, found both in his early writings and his social encyclicals. We begin with his critiques of socialism and capitalism, which indirectly reveal values and principles that form the framework of his social ethics.

CRITIQUE OF SOCIALISM

For over a hundred years Roman Catholic social encyclicals have criticized both the capitalist and the socialist economies. Whereas the popes, beginning with Leo XIII in 1891, had positive as well as negative comments regarding capitalism, their critiques consistently condemned socialism. In his social encyclicals John Paul II reaffirms the church's unequivocal rejection of socialism. In *Centesimus annus* he singles out four elements in the socialist political-economy that he claims are false: (1) its view of human freedom, (2) its atheism, (3) its strategy of class struggle, and (4) its terrorist tactics (*CA*, nos. 13–14). Although he refers to this political-economic system as socialism and not Marxism, it is clear from the social context that he is referring to the Marxist socialism that then prevailed in Poland and in the Soviet Union.

First, John Paul II says, socialism allows the state to subordinate individuals to work for the state, as though they were automatons functioning like parts of a machine. Workers in this system have little or no opportunity to take the initiative and have no say about what is to be done. The pope implies that exploitation continues within the capitalist system as well, especially in the Third World (*CA*, no. 42). In contrast to socialist teaching, Christian doctrine upholds the dignity of workers, who are regarded as autonomous subjects possessing the right to make decisions about their working situation.

Second, John Paul II attributes the suppression of personal freedom in the work place to socialism's atheism. The denial of God blocks individuals from becoming aware of their transcendent dignity and from experiencing the self-worth that comes about by hearing and responding to God's call found in creation. The systematic denial of God deprives the person of this religious experience "and consequently leads to a reorganization of the social order with no reference to the person's dignity and responsibility" (*CA*, no. 13). In addition, atheism destroys the opportunity to gain insight into what persons most deeply desire and are able to attain only through God's saving love. Consider, for example, how an atheistic society would have curbed St. Augustine's search for the ultimate, which, as a young adult, he discovered to be God.

Third, atheism permits persons to accept and to participate in class struggle. Class struggle, as Marxists use the term, does not mean that the rich and the poor classes merely have conflicts; indeed, they do. Rather, it means that groups foster and use conflicts between classes as a strategy in order to heighten the tensions, to bring about deep division, and finally to destroy the class system and usher in a classless society. John Paul II condemns this strategy not only because of its violence, but also because it fails to work for the common good.

Fourth, Marxist socialists adopt tactics that do not follow any ethics or juridical framework. They often use violent means, lies, and terror tactics—practices that amount to what John Paul II called total war aimed at destroying the capitalist system. Atheism and contempt for the human person give license to these immoral tactics (*CA*, no. 14).

This critique of Marxist socialism, by way of negative contrast, points to truths or values that John Paul II affirms as essential elements in his ethics. His denunciation of atheistic socialism implies that faith in God plays a fundamental role in his social ethics, a belief that instills in believers an awareness of their dignity, freedom, and solidarity. His rejection of class struggle indicates his high esteem for the right of workers to organize so that they might work together for the common good. Finally, his condemnation of the violent tactics of socialists manifests his support for nonviolent resistance, which he shows by backing the Polish workers' organization Solidarity.

QUALIFIED ACCEPTANCE OF CAPITALISM

Turning away from socialism and focusing on capitalism, John Paul II raises the following question: "Can it perhaps be said that after the failure of communism, capitalism is the victorious social system, and that capitalism should be the goal of the countries now making efforts to rebuild their economy and society?" (*CA*, no. 42). He then responds with a qualified acceptance of the market economy, an endorsement that depends on whether capitalism allows its participants to exercise free human creativity in a responsible manner, a freedom denied to workers in socialist Poland. He writes:

> If by *capitalism* is meant an economic system which recognizes the fundamental and positive role of business, the market, private property and the resulting responsibility for the means of production, as well as free human creativity in the economic sector, then the answer is certainly in the affirmative, even though it would perhaps be more appropriate to speak of a *business economy, market economy* or simply *free economy*. But if by capitalism is meant a system in which freedom in the economic sector is not circumscribed within a strong juridical framework which places it at the service of human freedom in its totality, and which sees it as a particular aspect of that freedom, the core of which is ethical and religious, then the reply is certainly negative. (*CA*, no. 42)

Acknowledging the positive role that private enterprise can play by its respect for private property, personal responsibility, and creativity, he insists that the capitalist economy must be guided by "a strong juridical framework." He implies that if it were not so guided, he would reject it. The word *juridical* refers to law, which suggests that laws of the nation and possibly of the international order should guide the economy. He specifies that the juridical system should defend freedom, a freedom that should be grounded in ethical and religious values. He identifies the values that he regards as crucial for dealing with the economy: love, social justice, dignity, solidarity, the common good, and subsidiarity (*SR*, nos. 21, 26).[10]

John Paul II does not intend to present a model of economy. Yet his constructive criticism of the free-market economy seems to assume that it is the best we have, at least in the foreseeable future. While he clearly calls for reform measures in this economy, he thinks that reforms should be undertaken by those directly involved in socio-political, economic, and cultural realities (*CA*, no. 43).

A Personalist Social Ethics

The pope's condemnation of Marxist socialism and his constructive criticism of capitalism manifest key values in his social ethics. First, faith in God helps people to become aware that they possess an inherent dignity, freedom, and responsibility for others. Atheism stifles that awareness. Second, he emphasizes the dignity inherent in all persons, a dignity that must be respected by all people. These two statements indicate that his social ethics is distinctively personalist. His personalism evolved out the ethical personalism of Max Scheler (1874–1928) and other personalist theologians, who developed the unique individuality of persons and the ethical significance of this uniqueness.[11] Third, while emphasizing the radical individuality of each and every person, John Paul II also relates this individuality to the person's social nature.[12] He holds that human dignity and freedom grow when persons live in solidarity with one another.[13] His personalism, in other words, is communitarian. He warns against mistaking personalism with individualism: "The human being as a person is simultaneously a member of society."[14] Indeed, dignity serves as the basis of solidarity. As social beings, persons have an innate tendency to form relationships, friendships, communities, and societies.

Human beings form a community of persons, created male and female in the image of the trinitarian God. By associating man and woman with the trinitarian God, scripture confers a profound dignity on human persons.[15] They are self-transcendent subjects who possess the capacity to know, create, discern, and love. Yet because of pride and selfishness, man and woman bring about disturbances and injustices in the social order (CA, no. 25). Yet John Paul II does not emphasize the sinfulness of human beings to the degree that Niebuhr does. He stresses more than Niebuhr the creative possibilities of human persons over their finitude and sinfulness. As God's stewards, man and woman are commissioned to work creatively and responsibly. History has manifested many examples of humanity's creative and self-transcending nature through its culture and technology.[16] In exercising this creative capacity, workers not only satisfy their basic needs, but they also fulfill themselves as persons. Through their work, human beings earn their living and actualize themselves as persons of dignity (LE, nos. 5–6). Work should always serve human persons; persons should never be enslaved by work. When workers historically have experienced oppression and exploitation because of inhumane working conditions and low wages relative to the cost of living, they sometimes have united in solidarity by critically discussing their work experiences, by organizing themselves in unions, and by voicing their discontent in protests and strikes.

John Paul II maintains that human dignity requires that employers recognize their workers as sharers with other workers throughout the productive process in the economy. As workers, *persons* want to see their work benefiting others as well as themselves. They are not simply self-interested workers.

As free and creative subjects, workers desire not only a just remuneration for what they produce, but they also think of themselves as working for themselves. They refuse to regard themselves, as oppressive employers do, as cogs in a huge machine.

John Paul II insists that all persons, including workers, are true subjects who exercise initiative and possess personal values and rights (*LE*, no. 15). The rights of workers include the right to own and use property. Yet private ownership is not an absolute right. Following the teaching of Thomas Aquinas on ownership of property, John Paul II holds that persons should respect external things not simply as their own, but as common in the sense that they are willing to share external goods to others in need.[17]

SOLIDARITY, LOVE, AND JUSTICE

Solidarity is a modern notion. It arose from labor-union movements in the nineteenth century and was adopted by Catholic social theorists in the early twentieth century.[18] Pope Pius XI's *Quadragesimo anno* (published in 1931) was the first papal encyclical to use the term to differentiate Catholic social teaching's perspective on the market economy from economic liberalism, which Pius XI views as excessively competitive, individualistic, and resistant to state intervention.[19] He also distinguishes Catholic social teaching's notion of solidarity from the socialist use of the term. The notion of the collective within socialism does not embody true solidarity. The collective tries to strengthen the workers' movement, not by collaborating on the basis of a shared common good among the proletariat, but on the basis of a "common bad" (capitalism) and a "common enemy" (capitalists). In contrast, Pius XI uses solidarity as a call for cooperation and dialogue among owners, workers, and the state, all of which promote the common good. Subsequently, John XXIII, the Second Vatican Council, Paul VI, and John Paul II adopt and develop the term.

John Paul II refers to solidarity as both a vision and a virtue. As a vision, solidarity expresses the profound truth that all members of the human species are bonded to one another. The pope proclaims the far-sighted hope that some day humankind will live in universal solidarity and peace as God's people. His vision of a people united in God assumes that all human beings are now related as sisters and brothers because they all have the same creator, redeemer, and sanctifier. He hopes that fully accepting this vision will ultimately lead people from all nations to work together as one global community.

More concretely, what is solidarity? We might think of it as a cohesiveness among persons and within a group, a social glue that helps people stick together and work together for the good of the community. John Paul II formally defines solidarity as "a firm and persevering determination to commit oneself to the common good" (*SR*, no. 38). Solidarity functions, in his theological framework, like Aquinas' architectonic virtue, charity, which motivates and guides other virtues by directing them to the ultimate good. In a similar manner solidarity strengthens people's commitment to the poor, but at the same time it directs this commitment to the universal common good. We see such determination and commitment in families, athletic teams, companies, and schools, in which each member of the group commits himself or herself to supporting the good of the whole group, or the common good. One of the attributes of solidarity is love expressed by genuine affection and caring for one another. A second attribute is social justice, which works for the good of the whole and for the active participation of its members. A third attribute is its cognitive or intellectual dimension, which means that members reach a shared understanding of their goal and the means to work together to attain the goal. The group celebrates its identity, and its members support one another and face adversity together. If one member of the family or the team does something extraordinarily well, the group celebrates the achievement; if another gets injured or sick, the others rally around the afflicted member.

Although John Paul II recognizes that solidarity should be pursued in small groups, regions, and nations, he envisions a global solidarity that links nations together on the firm foundation of love, justice, and truth. Let us first examine love as one of the components that is needed to reach a global solidarity.

LOVE AND SOLIDARITY

As we have seen in the previous chapter, Reinhold Niebuhr holds that *agape* must work through justice to change social institutions. How does John Paul II conceive of *agape* contributing to a global solidarity among nations? In agreement with Niebuhr, he sees love as *agape* working with justice. But he differs from Niebuhr in two ways. First, he sees love working *directly* in the social sphere, through dialogue between groups and nations, forgiveness and reconciliation among previously hostile groups, and a preferential love for the poor. He argues that because all people are sons and daughters of the Creator and are redeemed by the death and resurrection of the redeemer God, all people are brothers and sisters to one another. All men and women, therefore, are called to love one another in solidarity.

How does John Paul II understand the form of love that expresses the relationship among nations? He speaks of love as *agape*, which moves persons to transcend self-interest by affirming the other's goodness. Affirming the goodness in the neighbor means seeing the neighbor as "the living image of God the Father, redeemed by the blood of Jesus Christ and placed under the permanent action of the Holy Spirit" (*SR*, no. 40). This is truly a high standard of love, one that seems almost impossible on a group level. But for John Paul II, love in solidarity cannot be reduced to a commitment in justice based on the obvious truth that men and women belong to the same human species and that therefore have rights. He maintains that solidarity calls us to the profound truth to love others in communion with God. He emphasizes the unity of the human race as a reflection of the trinitarian life. All people are united in God, who is three Persons. This universal solidarity brings people together on the interpersonal, national, and international levels of communication and interaction.

Yet John Paul II does not use the word *love* in defining solidarity. He refers to solidarity as a commitment, a commitment to the common good, which is the good of all persons. It builds on Aquinas's notions of benevolence and beneficence in the sense of willing and doing good for another. John Paul II's use of commitment deepens the meaning of willing and doing good for others.

He contrasts the love that moves toward solidarity with a diametrically opposed act that inordinately desires profit and thirsts for power. The love of solidarity commits people to their neighbors "with the readiness, in the gospel sense, to 'lose oneself' for the sake of the other instead of exploiting him, and to 'serve him' instead of oppressing him for one's own advantage" (*SR*, no. 40). This is clearly the language of *agape*, a love that involves making sacrifices for another without seeking a return.

Commenting on this passage, Catholic philosopher John Langan writes that the pope is here invoking a "top of the line form of solidarity which draws on the heroic altruism of Christ's teaching and example." Langan comments that there is a need "for more mundane and less sacrificial forms of solidarity, which are not simply the polar opposites of our desires for profit and power."[20] Langan may have in mind either a reciprocal love, like *philia,* or a love of another for one's good, like *eros,* as the "more mundane and less sacrificial form."

John Paul II, however, never explicitly mentions *philia* or *eros* as the driving force behind solidarity. His concrete suggestion that rich nations and financial institutions should cancel or reduce the external debt of poor nations seems to confirm Langan's observation that *agape* ought to be the motivating force behind authentic solidarity. It would seem that a reciprocal type of love, such as love in friendship *(philia),* would be a more fitting type of love in relation to John Paul II's concept of solidarity. Reciprocal love that focuses on the relationship would be less prone to paternalism by calling for mutual trust and mutual exchange. Economists might argue that *agape,* or sacrificial love, precisely because of its unilateral nature, would lead to dependency on the part of the debtor nation and inefficiency on the part of the lending nation, which does not get paid the money lent. John Paul II says that payment of the debt is just. "However, it is not right to demand or expect payment when the effect would be the imposition of political choices leading to hunger and despair for entire peoples." In dire situations, he says, ways must be found to "lighten, defer or even cancel the debt" (*CA,* no. 35).

Yet, for all of his idealistic language of sacrificial love and solidarity, John Paul II is not naive about human beings' selfish tendency to exploit and alienate others. Alienation and sin arise, he says, when persons refuse to transcend themselves and to live the experience of self-giving (*CA,* no. 41). Instead of trying to pursue a good by cooperating with others, which often means subordinating one's own desires for the sake of the common good, people often do as they please without concern for others. An employer may either work cooperatively with employees by listening to their difficulties and suggestions in the manufacture of a certain good, or the employer may act in a tyrannical way that demeans the dignity of the workers.

JUSTICE AND SOLIDARITY

Justice is the second component of John Paul II's understanding of solidarity. He follows the basic Aristotelian-Thomistic notion of justice, which obliges persons to render to others what is due (*CA,* no. 10). But he gives solidarity a personalist perspective by focusing on a justice that requires persons to be *responsible* for one another and to work together for common objectives. This perspective focuses on both the person as subject who acts justly and on the person as object who is the recipient of the just act. A just agent may assist employees who are about to be laid off by helping them gain a new skill or an updated technology that will enable them to find another job. John Paul II calls this kind of assistance social justice (*SR,* no. 39). This dedication to social justice not only helps the individual worker but also helps the common good, because the worker contributes something to the economy in addition to caring for his or her own welfare. On the international level, rich nations help weak nations by sharing technology, giving them access to the market, trading with them, and investing in their local economy. In turn, the developing nations help the developed nations by trading with them.

John Paul II suggests that individual entrepreneurs, private corporations, and wealthy nations should take the initiative in helping other groups and nations, but that it should involve cooperation and reciprocity on the part of the needy group:

> Stronger nations must offer weaker ones opportunities for taking their place in international life, and the latter must learn how to use these opportunities by making the necessary efforts and sacrifices and by ensuring political and economic stability, the certainty of better prospects for the future, the improvement of workers' skills, and the training of competent business leaders who are conscious of their responsibilities. (*CA,* no. 35)

He does not identify the form of love that should move both the stronger and the weaker nations to take greater responsibility in international life. But he does urge all nations to participate in promoting the good of the entire international community. The stronger nations should offer weaker nations opportunities, and the weaker nations should make sacrifices and ensure political and economic stability so that they might learn how to use these opportunities. Efforts on the part of both the weaker and the stronger nations will bring "better prospects for the future," presumably for all nations who cooperate in this endeavor. He implies that doing so will foster the common good, as well as the good of the participating countries.

John Paul II seems to restrict the love that moves groups and nations to promote justice to *agape*. "Love for others, and in the first place love for the poor . . . is made concrete in the promotion of justice" (*CA*, no. 58). He does not discuss the other two forms of love that very likely could be moving nations and other economic entities to contribute to building up the economy: love as *philia*, which is a reciprocal form of love between friends; and *eros*, in which nations love other nations for the good that each nation does for itself.

Just as it is legitimate and good that we as individuals love others partly because of what they can do for us (God, physicians, teachers), so also it seems proper and good that nations love other nations partly because of what they can do for one another. The political-economic world calls this enlightened self-interest. Persons or nations act to advance the interests of others, knowing that it will serve their own interests as well. John Paul II does not mention enlightened self-interest, or *eros*, as does his successor, Pope Benedict XVI.[21] Perhaps further insight into global solidarity might be gained by including the dimensions of love as *eros* and *philia* along with *agape* as motivators of nations to bring about more just relationships.

In summary, solidarity for John Paul II incorporates the virtues of love and justice by its commitment to the good of others and by serving the common good. It assumes that all persons are responsible for and accountable to others for what they hold in common (*SR*, no. 38). All groups and societies have a common good, whether the group is a nuclear family, a nation, or the entire human family. John Paul II distinguishes two dimensions in the common good: material and spiritual. The material dimension is an extrinsic, physical entity—such as land, a home, clean air and water, technology—that satisfies basic needs. The spiritual dimension is intrinsic—including values such as dignity, freedom, trust, and friendship that bring people together to communicate, plan, and work to achieve something for the benefit of all. Both dimensions are essential for living together and flourishing.

Solidarity calls people of all nations to commit themselves to serve both dimensions of the common good. Stronger nations should work together to allow weaker nations to have equal access to the market and to help needy people gain technological expertise. Poorer nations should contribute by taking advantage of new technologies, by ensuring political and economic stability, and by participating in international trade. The pursuit of the common good involves a process that is built on trust and a commitment that move members of a community or society to make agreements on such things as property rights and trade policies. On the international level the common good involves a process involving the cooperation of many nations, a network of friendly relationships based on trust, and a security that is based on open and fair exchanges in the market.[22]

SOLIDARITY AND THE OPTION FOR THE POOR

John Paul II's virtue of solidarity involves loving and serving all neighbors, especially the poorest (*SR*, no. 46). Serving the neighbor, in other words, entails a love that brings people together to help the poor to meet their basic needs. Global solidarity excludes no one, not even one's enemies. As mentioned earlier, John Paul II relates solidarity to the principle of the preferential option for the poor. It is a love that moves people to be just by assisting them to meet their needs. Doing justice in the context of the global economy means helping poor nations, saddled with a large external debt, to reduce the debt, or perhaps even forgiving the debt. The chief problem, John Paul II wrote, was "gaining fair access to the international market" (*SR*, no. 33).

The preferential option for the poor, for John Paul II, is not an arbitrary principle; it is an integral part of commitment to the universal community.[23] But how does a commitment to a part (poor people) contribute to the whole (society)? John Paul II shows on the biblical level that God calls upon people to care for the poor and the stranger (*SR*, nos. 42–43).[24] The pope, however, does not develop an argument on the philosophical or ontological level that shows how giving priority to the needs of the poor actually promotes the common good. He does not show that when poor and marginal people move from unemployment or underemployment to gainful employment, they not only help themselves and their families but contribute to the good of society. By moving from unemployment to being producers, the poor contribute to the larger society by what they produce, sell, and trade; by their purchases as consumers; and by their personal savings, which provide security for them and their families.

John Paul II insists that the love must always be part of doing justice. Love, he says, looks directly to the interiority of person; justice concerns itself with the exteriority, that is, material goods (wages, rights) and moral goods of persons (such as reputation).[25] But he might have said more about how love and justice relate to each other.

Love motivates persons to care for and support one another financially and technologically. Justice directs groups or nations to worthwhile goals and ultimately to the common good. Justice enhances solidarity by getting people to share power with the very people they are assisting, for example, sharing technology that helps the unskilled to get jobs. Justice respects the dignity of everyone, supports the initiative of private groups over the state (subsidiarity), yet gives special concern to those with the greatest needs (the preferential option for the poor). Finally, love and justice give the group a sense of identity, and its solidarity and success in its work project deepens its dignity.

SOLIDARITY IN BANGLADESH

Encyclicals are often overly abstract. The following true story shows how solidarity can work in today's economic world.

A Bangladeshi economist, Muhammad Yunus, after studying economics at Vanderbilt University in 1974, returned to his home, where he began teaching economics at Chittagong University in Bangladesh. That same year a severe famine struck his homeland. He felt moved to do something for his people. At first he tried to persuade commercial banks to make loans to the poor, who had no assets. But the banks would do so only when he co-signed as a guarantor. One day he decided to give a personal loan of $27 to forty-two villagers living near Chittagong University without asking for any collateral. Investing the money in a business project, the group earned enough money to repay Yunus in full, even though the members had signed no contract. He recalls asking himself that day in 1976: "If you can make so many people so happy with such a small amount of money, why shouldn't you do more of it?"[26] So he founded the Grameen Bank (*grameen* means "village"), which gave small loans, or microcredit, to millions of the world's poorest, mostly women who were destitute widows, landless laborers, weavers, sweepers, and beggars. What Yunus learned was that a very high percentage of people (around 95 percent) repaid the entire loan.[27] Grameen Bank gave small loans, averaging around $100, to groups with five people in each group to ensure that each member of the group repaid his or her share, or, if one person was unable to do so, the other four would pick up that person's share. Solidarity was at work within these small groups. The borrowers made enough profit to reinvest in their own businesses and to expand their operations. Most of the people who benefited from microcredit were able to send their children to school. Most striking was the people's growth in self-esteem, especially among the poor women, who before they developed their trade or businesses were quiet, diffident, and lacked confidence. Once they succeeded in developing their business and were able to pay back the loan, they grew in confidence and looked their creditors in the eye as they negotiated new terms. Economist Amartya Sen said that Grameen's loans gave women financial clout and power, whereas, before their successful business venture, they lived cloistered lives in their homes. They no longer saw themselves as victims but as dignified micro-entrepreneurs. Skeptics and supporters both credited Yunus and Grameen Bank with "helping to fundamentally change the way the world saw the potential of poor people."[28] The Nobel Committee gave Muhammad Yunus and the Grameen Bank the Nobel Peace Prize on October 9, 2006. In conferring this award, the committee praised Yunus and his bank for combating poverty in Bangladesh and for inspiring similar structures across the developing world. "Microcredit has proved to be an important liberating force in societies where women in particular have to struggle against repressive social and economic conditions."[29] Today there are many microcredit banks in the United States and throughout the world. Solidarity has emerged among millions of people in poor countries because of the vision of one man, who took great delight in watching widows and beggars participating in his program and leaving abject poverty and begging forever.

SOLIDARITY IN THE GLOBAL MARKET

This section pursues the question raised earlier: Can John Paul II's global solidarity work in a competitive international market, given powerful private interest groups, strong nationalism across the globe, and the great inequality between rich and poor nations? While recognizing the problems that globalization brings, John Paul II focuses on positive outcomes that the global economy could create: "Today we are facing the so-called 'globalization' of the economy, a phenomenon which is not to be dismissed, since it can create unusual opportunities for greater prosperity" (*CA*, no. 58).[30] He thinks that trade, sharing technology, and investing in foreign companies can bring prosperity and peace to all nations, including developing nations. While he recognizes problems that arise from "the all-consuming desire for profit . . . and the thirst for power, with the intention of imposing one's will upon others," he hopes that people of good will will see the wisdom of transcending self-interest to work for the common good (*SR*, no. 37).

To address the problem of wealthy nations protecting their own companies and exploiting developing nations, John Paul II contends that international agencies should be given the authority to bring trading nations together in order to work out rules of trade and to settle disputes. Here the pope follows the principle of subsidiarity, which allows a larger structure, like an international organization, to assume authority when a smaller structure, like the individual nations, is unable to create and coordinate trade rules. He wisely argues that a strong nation or group of nations should not assume this responsibility because of its own nationalistic bias (*CA*, no. 58). The pope must have had in mind a multilateral organization like the General Agreement on Tariffs and Trade (GATT), which was still in existence when *Centesimus annus* was published in 1991. Four years later the World Trade Organization (WTO) replaced the GATT. John Paul II says that the agency would have to give special consideration to the less-developed nations. Keeping before us John Paul II's notion of solidarity among trading nations and his recommendation that an international agency should coordinate and establish trading rules that are fair, let us examine as a case study what problems the WTO encountered as it became the international agency that tried to stimulate economic growth for all trading nations, poor as well as rich.

WORLD TRADE ORGANIZATION

Founded in 1995, the WTO is a multilateral organization with 150 member nations (as of 2007). Its purpose is to facilitate the reduction of trade barriers, which would in turn promote freer trade for all participating nations.[31] The WTO provided a forum called *rounds* for nations to negotiate trade policies. WTO follows the GATT principle that international trade should operate according to multilateral rules (rules that affect many nations including developing nations). It endorses these trade rules based on the principle of comparative advantage. This principle, which has the widest acceptance among economists today, states that a country not only benefits financially by importing goods that it could produce more efficiently (using less labor at less cost) than other countries, but it also profits by exporting certain goods to countries that produce certain goods more efficiently.[32] A country comes to have an advantage not because a certain producer in one country has an *absolute* advantage over a foreign producer by manufacturing a commodity at lower cost; rather, the company has a *relative* advantage. Comparative advantage, however, measures relative efficiency among producers by taking into account their *opportunity* costs, not their absolute costs. An opportunity cost is a good that must be given up in order to produce a second product that makes a higher profit for the company. The producer who has the lowest opportunity cost—the one who must give up fewer goods to produce the desired good—has the comparative advantage.[33] This means that companies may gain a substantial profit by trading goods with other countries that could produce them at a lower cost.

This may seem counterintuitive: A skeptic might ask, "Why should Company A buy computer hardware from Company B when Company A can make the same product for less?" It is because Company A has lower opportunity costs. By dropping the hardware industry and by concentrating on computer software, it can reap greater profits. Based on the logic of the principle of comparative advantage, WTO assumes that international trade is good for both developing and developed nations when all these nations produce and trade goods in which they specialize and have a comparative advantage.

If this is so, why are there many disagreements within the WTO and strong attacks against the WTO? There are many reasons. A major problem is that there is another logic of the market system running concurrently with comparative advantage: self-interest. Private corporations often use power to persuade their own governments to subsidize their goods, such as grain, vegetables, or cotton. They might also try to persuade the government to impose high tariffs on imported goods, such as sugar cane, so that they cannot be undersold by imports. While these protective measures help the domestic industry, they hurt the consumers at home, who have to pay higher prices. To the extent that the United States protects its goods by keeping foreign goods, like sugar, out of the United States, world prices decrease because of an increased supply. While this helps foreign consumers, it hurts foreign sugar producers in the developing nations. Protectionism harms developing nations, who cannot compete with the developed nations because of subsidies, tariffs, and quotas. To sum up, protectionist laws hurt global solidarity, while promoting a national, or what some critics call a tribal solidarity. To see how tribal solidarity plays out in the WTO, we turn to the organization's conferences in Seattle and Doha, Qatar.

SOLIDARITY VERSUS SELF-INTEREST

In November 1999 the city of Seattle hosted the third ministerial conference of the WTO, at which trade ministers met to discuss and to create rules of international trade. The agenda included discussion on reducing trade barriers on industrial products and lowering high tariffs in less developed countries in exchange for doing trade for services, such as sharing information technology and telecommunications.[34]

The process, however, encountered obstacles both outside and inside the WTO conference. Outside the conference, people from many countries protested and debated WTO's rules of international trade. While TV cameras focused on a small group of protesters breaking windows on the streets of Seattle, almost fifty thousand men and women from many nations gathered in a stadium to hear activists and representatives of nongovernmental organizations (NGOs) voice their objections to the practices of multinational corporations because of the way they affected their economies back home. These outsiders included environmentalists and labor rights activists.[35] The issues were primarily related to fair trade, dealing with labor standards, human rights, and protection of the environment. Among the many criticisms, speakers reported that trade and foreign investment failed to improve the lives of the poor in their nations. They claimed that poverty levels increased and real wages fell.[36]

Inside the WTO conference, disgruntled trade ministers were unhappy about tariff reduction. The participants failed to come to consensus on principles that would advance international trade by making it more open to the developing countries and by reducing the tariffs.[37] The conference ended without achieving consensus about trading rules.

In November 2001 the WTO launched a new round of meetings in Doha, Qatar, where WTO repesentatives would convene two more times over the next five years. At this first round, trade ministers from the United States and Europe pledged that the final negotiations would create trade legislation benefiting the poor nations as well as the rich nations.[38] The primary issue involved establishing rules that would make trade *freer*, that is, fewer protectionist barriers. The Doha Declaration reconfirmed the long-term objective to establish a fair and market-oriented trading system. Member nations committed themselves to bringing about greater market access and substantial reductions in export subsidies. Whatever hopes the fair-trade advocates and the free-trade WTO participants may have had as the negotiations opened in Doha, were dashed five years later, again in Doha, when talks broke off without an agreement on new rules or a timetable for restarting or concluding the talks.

Why did the negotiations in 2006 collapse? Representatives blamed certain nations for refusing to reduce subsidies and tariffs and other nations for failing to give market access to potential traders. The European Union faulted the United States for its unwillingness to reduce its high subsidies for American farmers, which allowed the farmers to undersell competitors in poor countries. The United States in turn placed blame on the European Union countries, especially France, for refusing to decrease subsidies for their agricultural products, which the United States said were higher than its own. Observers cited political reasons behind the U.S.'s and the EU's unwillingness to lower these subsidies, in spite of their pledge in 2001. President Bush would not risk losing the support of farmers during a mid-term election year. Developing nations, such as Brazil and India, also put up barriers to free trade by insisting on high tariffs. Brazilian politicians wanted to protect jobs as the 2006 general elections were approaching.[39] India's Commerce Minister Kamal Nath blamed the United States for "thinking of only market access," especially for products that the United States was protecting with high subsidies.[40] Beneath the volley of criticism, observers identified a distinctive group of actors who exerted the most influence on the negotiations: farmers in France, the United States, Brazil, and India. The farm lobbyists applied enormous power to their political representatives, thus effectively bringing the trade negotiations to an unsuccessful close.[41] Each nation held fast to its commitment to protect the domestic farmers by providing subsidies and protecting other goods by tariffs.[42] Many nations or blocs of nations possessed sufficient power to block the objective of developing new trade rules. But as members of the WTO, these nations clearly lacked consensus.

Toward Global Solidarity

In the wake of the collapse of the WTO trade talks in Seattle and Doha, John Paul II's call for global solidarity around the issue of trade seems like a pipedream or at least an ideal to be realized only in the distant future. If we were to apply his principle of solidarity to rules governing international trade, what steps would have to be taken? Gaining a consensus among rich and poor nations would mean lowering if not entirely eliminating tariffs, quotas, and subsidies among all trading nations. It would also require that the United States scuttle the farm bill that protects its farmers and require that the European Union do away with its Common Agricultural Policy of protectionism. Brazil, India, and other developing nations would also have to eliminate their high tariffs on agricultural goods. Poor nations presently not part of the WTO would be encouraged to enter the market after the high tariffs were eliminated. As John Paul II states:

> Even in recent years it was thought that the poorest countries would develop by isolating themselves from the world market and by depending only on their own resources. Recent experience has shown that countries which did this have suffered stagnation and recession, while the countries which experienced development were those which succeeded in taking part in the general interrelated economic activities at the international level. It seems therefore that the chief problem is that of gaining fair access to the international market, based not on the unilateral principle of the exploitation of the natural resources of these countries but on the proper use of human resources. (CA, no. 33)

The pope's statement is clear: isolation stifles economic growth; trade fosters development. Economists have provided ample evidence in support of John Paul II's statement. In the last decade economist Jagdish Bhagwati observed that "many poor countries have begun to see the folly of their own protectionism."[43] He cites Chile and India, both of which have reduced their tariffs and made great economic gains.

But economist Martin Khor maintains that the WTO in practice has favored rich countries and multinational corporations to the detriment of poor countries. In spite of the pledges to help poor countries and the Generalized System of Preferences, which is designed to lower tariffs, the wealthy nations continue to maintain high tariffs and quotas that block certain imports (clothing and agricultural products) from developing countries. As already noted, rich countries protect agriculture while pressing the developing countries to open their markets.[44]

The protests against WTO trade rules and the disagreements among trade representatives in Seattle and Doha underscore a problem in today's world economy: for many nations, both rich and poor, global trade appears to be neither free nor fair. The thousands of activists in Seattle focused on what they perceived to be unfair international trade policies, especially among the developing nations. The WTO negotiators in Doha failed to realize the WTO's goal of freer trade because of disagreements over protectionist barriers and market access.[45]

These protests and disagreements over international trade are related to employment. Workers and politicians in developed countries, such as the

United States, claim that imports, like steel, automobiles, and T-shirts, eliminate many American jobs. And since China and many other developing nations have an abundance of labor, workers in developed nations complain that those making the T-shirts and other commodities work for low wages in oppressive working conditions. (See the case study in discussion question 6 in "Resources" below.)

For all the benefits that international trade within a capitalist economy brings to people, it raises questions about whether countries will ever realize the type of global solidarity strong enough to satisfy both rich and poor nations. Given the competing self-interests of trade ministers, environmentalists, and labor union activists within a nation as well as the economic gap between rich and poor nations, many skeptics doubt whether countries have the will to work together for the global common good. Yet, while not denying the difficulties, we should note that nations have greater communication and trade today than ever before. While the WHO may not be the best model, it is a relatively recent worldwide organization that struggles with important issues, such as how to involve more developing countries that presently have no access to the market.

ASSESSMENT

Imagine Reinhold Niebuhr sitting next to John Paul II at the 2006 WTO conference in Doha. Both are invited observers. The pope appears to be disappointed as the ministerial conference ends with very little agreement. Dr. Niebuhr turns sympathetically to the pope and says, "Whether we invoke Christian realism or personalist communitarianism, changing structures is tough work." The pope nods affirmatively, and then adds: "The WTO is young. Let us be hopeful." John Paul II's *Centesimus annus* brings hope by engaging in dialogue with political and economic leaders who daily deal with issues of international trade.

This concluding section reflects on the strengths and weaknesses of John Paul II's global ethics and its relation to trade. Creating a global ethics that deals with trade and political issues is enormously difficult. As both Niebuhr and John Paul II teach us, corporations and nations virtually always aim to protect their interests and expand their power.

The strengths of John Paul II's global ethics are many. First of all, he develops virtues (love, justice, and solidarity) and principles (respecting human dignity, promoting the common good, and subsidiarity) that are universal in scope and so are theoretically applicable to issues involving corporations and nations. His personalist social ethics balances the concerns for both the individual and society by his double emphases on the dignity of each person and the solidarity of communities and nations. By underscoring the importance of the individual as a free and creative agent, John Paul II identifies virtues that help workers to take initiative and to work with entrepreneurial ability. The intelligence of men and women enables them to discover the productive potential of the earth and the multiple ways in which they can satisfy human needs. The pope's heralding of the virtues of diligence, industriousness, prudence, and courage echoes Max Weber's listing of virtues in his *Protestant Ethic and the Spirit of Capitalism*.[46] John Paul II balances Weber's virtues of worldly asceticism (self-control, industriousness, and frugality), which are associated with individuals, with the virtue of solidarity and the principles of the preferential option for the poor and subsidiarity, which are associated with groups.

His emphasis on the dignity of persons and the solidarity of groups avoids both an individualism that rejects all intervention or guidance by the state and a collectivism that overemphasizes the authority of centralized authority (socialism). John Paul II pinpoints the reason why Marxist socialism in Poland failed: its rejection of belief in God eroded the people's sense of dignity and with it any ethics or human rights to help guide the government's and the people's policies and decisions.

Yet John Paul II's global ethics has limitations. The first limitation relates to its deductive method, or what moral theologian Charles Curran calls the pope's top-down approach. John Paul II, Curran says, first states general principles about human persons and their communities and then moves to particular issues. Curran sees a problem with using this top-down approach: "Moving from the universal to the particular, one tends to claim more universality than exists and a greater certitude than the complexity and diversity of our global existence warrants today."[47] Moreover, Curran says, one can overlook the particular and the diverse. In contrast to John Paul II's approach, Reinhold Niebuhr often begins with the concrete situation and, in light of the reality, develops his principles.

While we can commend John Paul II for his critiques of and support for trade, he might have developed reasons to support his contention that solidarity on a global level supports trade in general and calls for developing countries to work out multilateral trade agreements. He clearly states that remaining isolated from the market hurts a nation's economy. As for his general reflections on social sin, he does not apply it to concrete practices in the economy, for example, powerful nations preventing developing nations from having access to the market by establishing protectionist barriers.

Second, John Paul II talks about love as *agape*, but he makes no reference to love as *philia* or *eros*. As his successor Pope Benedict XVI has argued, *agape* needs to work with *eros;* by doing so, it helps people avoid becoming egoistical. Not all self-interest or love of self *(eros)* is egoistical or sinful, especially in instances where *agape* is also present.

Third, John Paul II does not adequately discuss power.[48] He does not show how his notion of solidarity can be efficaciously implemented. Christian realists, like Reinhold Niebuhr, would be likely to criticize John Paul II's ethics as inefficacious. His ethics fails to show how justice can be done; it simply talks about changing structures through rational discourse and moral persuasion. Yet his concepts of solidarity and work do have an implicit notion of power. For example, in discussing how work contributes to wealth, the pope said that work increasingly is becoming "work with others and work for others" (CA, no. 31). This suggests that one of the modes of power for John Paul II is a "power-to" in contrast to Niebuhr's "power-over." As Christine Firer Hinze distinguishes these two types, "power-to" involves collaboration "with others or because of others" in order to achieve the objective; in contrast, "power-over" emphasizes the "capacity to act against or in spite of other" to achieve the objectives.[49] The pope's notion of solidarity implies a power-to. Addressing the power dimension of solidarity that works toward consensus among groups and nations would strengthen his ethics. His notion of solidarity works well with his preferential option for the poor principle. Yet John Paul II does not show how the poor—as groups or as developing nations—can be active agents in their negotiating fair as well as free trade agreements.

Fourth, John Paul II often makes claims without providing a moral argument in support of his assertions. For example, he asserts that rich nations must help poor nations by giving them access to markets; that they should invest in poor countries where multinational corporations operate; and that they ought to forgive or lessen the poor country's external debt. Using his principles of human dignity, solidarity, and the preferential option for the poor, he needs to complement his biblical evidence with philosophical arguments to support his claims. Though a faith conviction about solidarity may stir the hearts of believers, global solidarity must intellectually convince people of good will who do not share the same faith tradition and sources to which John Paul II appeals. Persuasive arguments based on reason are also needed.

RESOURCES

Discussion Questions

1. Why does John Paul II totally condemn the political economy of socialism? Does his strong criticism of socialism mean that he wholeheartedly embraces the capitalist economy? Explain.
2. What does Pope John Paul II mean by *personalism*? Which values form the basis of his personalism? What does the term *communitarian* add to his personalism?
3. How does John Paul II integrate the virtues of love and justice in his principle of solidarity?
4. John Paul II recognizes that protectionist barriers, such as tariffs and subsidies, have negative consequences for poorer nations. What would be the impact on the U.S. economy if the government were to eliminate its present subsidies for American industries that produce cotton and sugar?

5. In light of the collapse of the WTO rounds of talks at Seattle and at Doha, what should the WTO do to promote the consensus that is necessary to develop new trade rules?

6. Case study: Sweatshops: For and Against

   A professor stood in the midst of a crowd of a hundred students on a cold February day in 1999 outside Healey Hall on the campus of Georgetown University listening to a young woman trying to awaken the crowd to the evils of sweatshops:

   "Who made your T-shirt?" she asked the crowd. "Was it a child in Vietnam, chained to a sewing a machine without food or water? Or a young girl from India earning 18 cents per hour and allowed to visit the bathroom only twice per day? Did you know that she lives 12 to a room? She shares her bed and has only gruel to eat? That she is forced to work 9 hours each day, without overtime pay? Did you know that she has no right to speak out, no right to unionize? That lives not only in poverty, but also in filth and sickness, all in the name of Nike's profits?"[50]

   The professor, an economist at Georgetown University, wondered how this young woman knew so much about sweatshop conditions. So she decided to investigate. After purchasing a cotton T-shirt in a Walgreen's drugstore in Fort Lauderdale, Florida, the professor inquired from the vendor where the T-shirt was manufactured. She then began her travels across three continents to trace its history. In the course of her travels she learned at first hand what sweatshops are like in China from talking with female workers like He Yuan Zhi. The workers work long hours in poor working conditions and for low pay. They are forced to do overtime and are not permitted to form unions. Professor Rivoli summarized the living and working conditions in China:

   Living quarters are cramped and rights are limited, the work is boring, the air is dusty, and the noise is brain numbing. The food is bad, the fences are high, and the curfews inviolate. As generations of mill girls and seamstresses from Europe, America, and Asia are bound together by this common sweatshop experience—controlled, exploited, overworked, and underpaid—they are bound together too by one absolute certainty, shared across both oceans and centuries: This beats the hell out of life on the farm.[51]

   He Yuan Zhi said that even with the hard working conditions and low pay (she earns a little less than $150 per month), she preferred working in Shanghai's textile mill to laboring on her family's farm with its physical and mental drudgery. The factory gave her a feeling of autonomy and choices afforded by receiving a paycheck, however small the check. Another researcher expressed this autonomy in terms of dignity: disposable cash income brought more than consumer items. "It was a resource with which women workers from the north asserted their dignity in the face of society's imposition of an image of migrant *daughters as poverty-stricken and miserable."*[52] *Her travels and studies led Professor Rivoli to appreciate what markets and trade have done to liberate some workers laboring in sweatshops. And yet wages are low, and conditions are often unsafe, dirty, and humiliating. Professor Rivoli saw exploitation, and after her research she applauded the protests by students on college campuses who pressured for U.S. apparel and shoe manufacturers to disclose the names and locations of their suppliers' factories and to audit their working conditions.*[53]

In light of her study and what John Paul II says about the dignity of labor and workers' dignity, what do you think should be done about sweatshops?

SUGGESTED READINGS

Curran, Charles E. *The Moral Theology of Pope John Paul II.* Washington, DC: Georgetown University Press, 2005.

Finn, Daniel. *"Centesimus annus."* In *Modern Catholic Social Teaching: Commentaries and Interpretations,* edited by Kenneth R. Himes et al. Washington, DC: Georgetown University Press, 2005.

Rivoli, Pietra. *The Travels of a T-Shirt in the Global Economy.* Hoboken, NJ: John Wiley and Sons, 2005.

Wojtyla, Karol. *Person and Community: Selected Essays.* Catholic Thought from Lublin Series 4. Translated by Theresa Sandok. New York: Peter Lang, 1993.

NOTES

[1] *Centesimus annus (CA)* and *Laborem exercens (LE)* are called "anniversary" encyclicals because they commemorate the ninetieth and the one hundredth anniversary of Pope Leo XIII's encyclical *Rerum novarum (The Condition of Labor) (RN).* Quotations from the encyclicals in this chapter are taken from David J. O'Brien and Thomas A. Shannon, eds., *Catholic Social Thought: The Documentary Heritage* (Maryknoll, NY: Orbis Books, 1992).

[2] A subsidy is a grant of money given by a government to a private company to help it stay in business; a tariff is a government tax usually levied on imported goods but sometimes on exports.

[3] A synod of bishops is "that group of bishops who have been chosen from different regions of the world and who meet at stated times to foster a closer unity between the Roman Pontiff and the bishops, to assist the Roman Pontiff with their counsel in safeguarding and increasing faith and morals and in preserving and strengthening ecclesiastical discipline, and to consider questions concerning the Church's activity in the world" (*Code of Canon Law* [Washington, DC: Canon Law Society of America, 1983], canon 342). A conference of bishops is a group of regional bishops within a nation or regional territory who meet one or twice a year to discuss pastoral issues pertinent to their territory (canon 447).

[4] Harold Jung, "Class Struggle and Civil War in El Salvador," in Marvin E. Gettleman et al., *El Salvador: Central America in the New Cold War*, rev. ed. (New York: Grove Press, 1986), 64–103.

[5] Major Adrian D. Hope, "El Salvador Sets the Example for Success," http://www.faoa.org/journal/Salvaodr.htmol (accessed on September 6, 2006).

[6] Thomas L. Schubeck, *Liberation Ethics: Sources, Models, and Norms* (Minneapolis: Fortress Press, 1993), 6–7.

[7] The Congregation for the Doctrine of the Faith, "Instruction on Christian Freedom and Liberation," *Origins* 15, no. 44 (April 17, 1986).

[8] Stephen J. Pope, "Natural Law in Catholic Social Teachings," in Kenneth R. Himes, ed., *Modern Catholic Social Teaching: Commentaries and Interpretations* (Washington, DC: Georgetown University Press, 2005), 58.

[9] Pontifical Council for Justice and Peace, *Social and Ethical Aspects of Economics: A Colloquium at the Vatican* (Vatican City, 1992), 13.

[10] The term *subsidiarity* is a principle that Pope Pius XI in his encyclical *Quadragesimo anno* (no. 49) used to establish the autonomy of groups within society. The state should respect this autonomy. Following this principle the state, for example, should not take over the production of certain goods, like steel or education, when private and smaller organizations are able to do the job just as well or better than the state. But it also implies that a country and international organizations sometimes should help when smaller groups or individual countries are unable to cope with certain problems, like famine, natural disasters, and international trade.

[11] John F. Crosby, "The Individuality of Human Persons: A Study in the Ethical Personalism of Max Scheler, *The Review of Metaphysics* 52 (1998).

[12] Delores L. Christie, *Adequately Considered: An American Perspective on Louis Janssens' Personalist Morals* (Louvain: Peeters Press, 1990), 12–17. Christie presents a fine overview of personalism and its various types. She summarizes the contributions of Mounier, Scheler, and Janssens, all of whom influenced the personalism of John Paul II.

[13] David Hollenbach, "The Market and Catholic Social Teaching," in Dietmar Mieth and Marciano Vidal, eds., *Outside the Market No Salvation?* Concilium Series (London: SCM Press, 1997), 71.

[14] Karol Wojtyla, *Person and Community: Selected Essays*, trans. Theresa Sandok, Vol. 4 in *Catholic Thought from Lublin*, Andrew N. Woznicki, gen. ed. (New York: Peter Lang, 1993), 146.

[15] Ibid., 166–67.

[16] Wojtyla, *Person and Community*, 178.

[17] See Thomas Aquinas, *Summa Theologica*, II-II, 66.2.

[18] Matthew L. Lamb, "Solidarity," in Judith A. Dwyer, *The New Dictionary of Catholic Social Thought* (Collegeville, MN: The Liturgical Press, 1994), s.v., 908.

[19] Ibid.

[20] John Langan, "Solidarity, Sin, Common Good, and Responsibility for Change in Contemporary Society," in Oliver F. Williams and John W. Houck, eds., *The Making of an Economic Vision: John Paul II's On Social Concern* (Lanham, NY: University Press of America, 1991), 281.

[21] Benedict XVI, *Deus caritas Est (God Is Love)* (2005), http://www.vatican.va/holy_father/benedict_xvi/encyclicals/documents/hf_ben-xvi_enc_20051225_deus-caritas-est_en.html (accessed on March 5, 2006).

[22] David Hollenbach, *The Common Good and Christian Ethics* (New York: Cambridge University Press, 2002), 8–9.

[23] Stephen J. Pope, "Proper and Improper Partiality and the Preferential Option for the Poor," *Theological Studies* 54, no. 2 (June 1993): 270–71.

[24] See also Congregation for the Doctrine of the Faith, "Instruction on Freedom and Liberation," nos. 46–48.

[25] Karol Wojtyla, *Love and Responsibility*, trans. H. T. Willetts (New York: Farrar, Straus, Giroux, 1981), 42.

[26] Cecilia W. Dugger, "Peace Prize to Pioneer of Loans to Poor No Bank Would Touch," *New York Times*, October 10, 2006.

[27] BYU Broadcasting, "Small Fortunes: Microcredit and the Future of Poverty" (2005), documentary, available on DVD.

[28] Dugger, "Peace Prize."

[29] Ibid.

[30] See also Jagdish Bhagwati, *In Defense of Globalization* (New York: Oxford University Press, 2004), 3. Bhagwati argues that economic globalization "constitutes integration of national economies into the international economy through trade, direct foreign investment (by corporations and multinationals), short term capital flows, international flows of workers and human generally, and flows of technology."

[31] Robert Gilpin, with the Assistance of Jean M. Gilpin, *Global Political Economy: Understanding the International Economic Order* (Princeton, NJ: Princeton University Press, 2001), 218–19.

[32] Douglas A. Irwin, *Free Trade under Fire* (Princeton, NJ: Princeton University Press, 2002), 24–25.

[33] N. Gregory Mankiw, *Principle of Economics*, 2nd ed. (Fort Worth, TX: Harcourt College Publishers, 2001), 53–55.

[34] Ibid., 224. The author lists eleven issues on the WTO agenda.

[35] Environmentalists argue that increased trading brings about denser industrial pollution. They also say that it expands logging and the devastation of forests, which contributes to greater soil erosion. Finally, it causes fishing industries to over-fish the oceans.

[36] Sarah Anderson and John Cavanagh, "The Battle in Seattle—How Does It affect Poor People around the Globe? *NETWORK* (Washington, DC) (March/April 2000), 3.

[37] Bernard K. Gordon, *America's Trade Follies: Turning Economic Leadership into Strategic Weakness* (London: Routledge, 2001), 8.

[38] Scott Kilman, "Talks for Global Trade Deal Collapse," *The Wall Street Journal*, July 25, 2006.

[39] Ibid.

[40] Bernard K. Gordon, "Doha Aground," *The Wall Street Journal*, July 26, 2006.

[41] Steven R. Weisman and Alexei Barrionuevo, "Failure of Global Trade Talks Is Traced to the Power of Farmers," *The New York Times*, July 27, 2006.

[42] "Doha Is Dead . . . ," *The Wall Street Journal*, July 26, 2006, editorial.

[43] Bhagwati, *In Defense of Globalization*, 232.

[44] Wikipedia, "World Trade Organization," http://en.wikipedia.org/wiki/World_Trade_organization/ (accessed on October 29, 2006).

[45] Gordon, *America's Trade Follies*. The impasse between trading nations may continue to lead to what Gordon calls "regional trade blocs," like NAFTA, which not only threaten national interests but also the international order.

[46] Max Weber, *The Protestant Ethic and the Spirit of Capitalism*, trans. Talcott Parsons (New York: Charles Scribner's Sons, 1958), chap. 2. Weber lists mental concentration, duty to one's work viewed as a calling, self-control, and frugality, all of which form the spirit of capitalism.

[47] Charles E. Curran, *The Moral Theology of Pope John Paul II* (Washington, DC: Georgetown University Press, 2005), 242.

[48] Ibid., 243.

[49] Christine Firer Hinze, *Comprehending Power in Christian Social Ethics*, American Academy of Religion Academy Series, ed. Susan Thistlethwaite (Atlanta, GA: Scholars Press, 1995), 5–6.

[50] Pietra Rivoli, *The Travels of a T-Shirt in the Global Economy: An Economist Examines the Markets, Power, and Politics of World Trade* (Hoboken, NJ: John Wiley and Sons, 2005), viii.

[51] Ibid., 90.

[52] Ching Kwan Lee, *Gender and the South China Miracle: Two Worlds of Factory Women* (Berkeley and Los Angeles: University of California Press, 1998), 135.

[53] Rivoli, *Travels of a T-Shirt*, 105–7, 215.

CONCLUSION

We began by eliciting from college students what they thought about justice by asking them to share their experiences of injustice. Reflections on their own negative experiences show by way of contrast how they think they should have been treated. Thus, the students indirectly reveal what they think justice means. They also share how the love of significant others helped them deal with the injustice. We then examined the meaning of love and justice in the writings of biblical and theological authors. We studied the relationship of love to justice, and how they work together to cast light and engender life in bearing with these issues. The issues arose from relationships involving love of God, friends, and self, and from dilemmas arising out of poverty, pacifism, self-defense, war, racial discrimination, and international trade. In conclusion, I offer a few general observations about the meaning of love and justice and about how the authors we examined perceive love doing justice.

MEANING OF LOVE AND JUSTICE

In all of the works investigated—from Deuteronomy to the New Testament, from Augustine to Aquinas, and from Niebuhr to John Paul II—the theological virtue of love, or charity, enjoys primacy among all the other virtues. Augustine and Aquinas assert that charity directs and fulfills the other virtues, including justice, by moving them to their immediate end and to their final end. Niebuhr holds that love fulfills and negates justice. John Paul II enlarges the object of love by stating that love is a commitment to the good of all others, that is, to God and to the global common good. For all these authors love's source is God, whose creative, energizing action in the lives of men and women shepherds them to their final goal.

Love acts by affirming the goodness of others: God, self, friends, even enemies. Such affirmation moves in many ways. First, it affirms by awakening in persons who have never experienced love the exhilarating feeling of being loved for the first time. We read the story of Nina, the victim of the sex-slave trade, who felt beautiful and joyful as David awakened her by affirming her goodness and by asking her to marry him. God's love awakened a ragtag, group of slaves and formed them into a free people of Israel, who pledged their love to God, sealing it in a covenant. Second, love affirms goodness in others by expressing compassion to those suffering from injury, disease, or loss of a friend. The student narratives in Chapter 1 illustrate the important role parents play as they console and help heal sons and daughters who have been victimized by unjust acts. Third, love affirms by forgiving others. The self-emptying love of Jesus moved him and his followers to affirm others by speaking respectfully to public sinners and to respond non-violently to the aggression of enemies. All of these expressions of love—awakening, feeling compassion for, and forgiving others—affirm goodness in others and in oneself. As Augustine and Aquinas both teach, persons gifted with charity, or *agape,* bring others closer to God by affirming them as sons and daughters of one God.

Whereas love affirms the other's goodness, justice affirms the other's right. As love's partner, justice renders to others what is due to them. Persons, groups, and nations owe others respect, fair wages, goods, and services for a variety of reasons: because the others are human beings possessing dignity, because of what they have earned, or because of the nature of the relationship. Justice works with love in a variety of ways. Justice helps persons to distribute love by establishing priorities among their many loves. Parents, for example, rightly give priority to caring for their own children over looking after other children. Persons of means ought to assist those whose needs are great.

Love is expressed in different forms—*agape, philia,* and *eros*—depending on the quality of the relationship. Justice also assumes three forms, depending on the actors involved and the situation. The first form, commutative justice, regulates what is due to buyers and sellers in their one-to-one exchanges. The second form, distributive justice, obliges the whole society (represented by the state) to allocate goods and services to the parts (private citizens and groups) based on needs. The third form, called social justice, calls upon citizens and private groups to contribute to the common good, which includes enabling poor citizens to participate in the economy.

LOVE DOING JUSTICE, JUSTICE SERVING LOVE

Each of the chapters has addressed how love and justice interact. Love does justice in the sense that it sensitizes, motivates, directs, and energizes persons, groups, and nations to be just and to carry out justice. Love broadens the horizon of justice by sensitizing citizens, legislators, civil courts, and heads of private corporations to the plight of the invisible poor or marginalized members of society. Love transcends justice by generously exceeding justice's strict measurements of what is due. And it urges justice to be merciful to the offender, debtor, and the needy.

Justice serves love by guiding persons in their distribution of love among their many love objects. In addition, it challenges some of love's ideals, which can appear to be infeasible. Justice complements love by making love's ideals concrete and lasting. It accomplishes this by establishing just policy and law. As we saw in Reinhold Niebuhr's social ethics, justice by doing careful analysis of unjust practices can move the hearts of people to take action. We saw how Mr. Oliver Brown expressed his love for his daughter and for all black children who were refused entrance into the segregated school. His love pursued justice by filing a suit in a lower court that eventually led to the passage of the 1954 Supreme Court decision ruling that separate educational facilities are inherently unequal.

Chapter 1 illustrated the dynamic of love and justice at work. Grace narrated how her mother helped her affirm herself as a person with dignity and honor by teaching Grace to replace the negative racist refrain that daily bombarded her psyche and caused her to hate her blackness. Each day during her first semester away at college, Grace's mother called to tell her daughter that she loved her and believed in her. Justin, a college student, after studying the working conditions of laborers in sweatshops, felt moved to help his fellow students at the university to become aware of the unjust treatment of the poor in sweatshops. He did this by sharing his historical analysis of these work places. He hoped that they might be moved to do something to transform these oppressive institutions.

Chapter 2 examined how biblical love and justice addresses the challenge involved in liberating the enslaved and the poor. In harmony with the book of Exodus, the book of Deuteronomy speaks of a God who expresses love for the poor by inviting them to be partners in a most extraordinary covenant. As part of this covenant, God inspires them to draw up an impressive set of laws aimed at justice for all people living on the land. The love of the liberating God does justice first by freeing the people from an oppressive servitude in Egypt, by caring for them "in a howling wilderness," and by guarding them as "the apple of his eye" (Dt 32:10). The covenant envisions a just society in which no one will live in poverty. "There will be no one in need among you" (Dt 15:4). It draws up laws that will eliminate poverty altogether, and it calls fidelity to these laws "justice" *(tsedeq)*. Specific laws of justice *(mishpāt)* free debtors every Jubilee Year, and as they are released, they must receive from the creditor, according to law, the means necessary to earn their livelihood (for example grain, and livestock). Addressing the creditor, the law says: "Provide liberally out of your flock, your threshing floor, and your wine press, thus giving to him some of the bounty with which the Lord your God has blessed you" (Dt 15:14). By becoming free persons with property, they are able to move to a higher social status and to participate in religious feasts. In short, covenantal love does justice by being magnanimous to the poor, establishing for them conditions whereby they may live freely and with dignity.

Chapter 3 examined Jesus' radical teaching and practice of nonviolent resistance and love of enemies. In Matthew's account Jesus instructs his followers that they should not exact vengeance or equivalency from oppressive evildoers. Instead, they should resist the enemy in nonviolent and creative ways. Even more remarkable, Jesus teaches them that they should love the enemy, including praying for hostile agents who persecute them. Although biblical scholars read these teachings differently, we interpret the first imperative—"Do not resist the evildoer!"—to mean that the followers of Christ should transcend the urge to retaliate against an evildoer by using physical force (Mt 5:39). However just the "eye-for-an-eye" standard may seem by human standards, Jesus teaches, lives, and dies with the conviction that apparently justifiable vengeance does not do true justice; God's gratuitous and merciful justice does.[1] Jesus also enjoins them to love their enemies and to pray for their persecutors (Mt 5:44). Although New Testament scholars debate whether the enemies are individuals or groups, the arguments favoring the interpretation that enemies refer to groups, like the Roman colonizers, are more persuasive.

Early Christians, like Tertullian and Justin Martyr, followed Jesus' teaching by praying for the Roman emperor while at the same time resisting the emperor's command that Christians should serve in the military. Later, Christians like Martin Luther King, Jr., interpreted Jesus' teachings on nonviolence to mean that black Christians should love their white oppressors while at the same time resisting their racist policies. King said that a nonviolent response to the oppressor is an excellent expression of *agape*. Such love refuses to discriminate between friend and foe; rather, it looks to the needs of the neighbor, as did the Samaritan who assisted the wounded victim on the road to Jericho (Lk 10:25–37).

Chapters 4 and 5 examined the virtue ethics of Augustine and Aquinas. Both theologians teach that love and justice guide persons of faith to their ultimate goal of union with God. Both emphasize the virtue of charity as the chief motivator and director of other virtues. Justice rightly orders and distributes love.

In an effort to discern whether human agents are following a rightly ordered love or a disordered love, Augustine focuses on the interior dispositions, intentions, and motives of the agents. Discussing the use of force, Augustine agrees with Jesus' teaching that individual Christian citizens must not employ violence against an oppressor, even in self-defense. However, when the issue involves national defense, he maintains that a nation's sovereign, motivated by love, aimed at a right intention, and based on a just cause, ought to wage war against an unjust aggressor. War, he says, arises from a disordered love, a lust for domination. In short, charity and justice play key roles both in justifying and prohibiting war, as well as in guiding military conduct during war. Both the individual citizen and the sovereign acting on behalf of the nation must always act out of a rightly ordered love. Because sovereigns receive their authority from God, they must defend their people out of the motive of love. Yet they should love the aggressor and seek peace based on justice.

We saw in Chapter 5 how Thomas Aquinas develops love, beginning first with a general notion of love *(amor)* and then treating two specific forms, which he calls concupiscent (love of self) and a mutual type of love between friends. Finally, he discusses the highest form of love, the theological virtue called charity, which has its origin in God. He treats justice under the cardinal or moral virtues. Aquinas borrows Aristotle's general definition of justice as well as two of its particular forms (commutative and distributive). One of Aquinas's great contributions lies in his synthesis of love and justice on both the interpersonal and social levels. Both love and justice work architectonically by directing each of the other virtues to its immediate and ultimate end. Charity motivates persons to do justice for the sake of the earthly common good, a loving and just act that brings persons closer to the heavenly common good. Thus charity ascribes an eschatological quality to doing justice and gives persons an additional motive for doing justice. Aquinas best demonstrates charity working with justice in his discussion of Christian martyrdom. Charity, he says, is the chief motivating cause for courageously witnessing to truth and justice. Aquinas's treatment of martyrdom fittingly applies to contemporary martyrs, like Archbishop Romero, whose love and commitment to the poor of El Salvador cost him his life.

Chapter 6 focuses on Reinhold Niebuhr's love and justice. Following St. Paul, Niebuhr defines *agape* as a self-emptying, sacrificial love in the manner of Jesus. He describes justice as the approximation of brotherhood under the conditions of sin. He emphasizes how the conditions of sin make it virtually impossible to base a social ethics on *agape* alone. Love needs justice to analyze the behavior of groups and nations, which act according to their powerfully protected self-interests and egoistic tendencies. Love that does justice, for Niebuhr, entails trying to find a balance of power between competing economic or political entities, such as balancing the military power between the United States and the former Soviet Union.

Whereas Aquinas's love and justice work cooperatively as they direct persons toward their ends, Niebuhr's love and justice work dialectically. In Niebuhr's paradigm love and justice affirm and negate each other. Love affirms justice's working for freedom and equality. Justice partially fulfills love by bringing about more freedom and equality; it negates love's idealism. Justice works as an interlocutor bridging the ideal of love and the hard realities of the world. When dealing with groups, Niebuhr's justice analyzes the complexity of issues and seeks solutions that involve a balance of power, a greater freedom, and a relative equality, all of which move persons closer to brotherhood under the conditions of sin. Using non-biblical sources and a sense of proportion, Niebuhr first analyzes the policies of institutions, such as the conditions of labor in the Ford automobile plant in Detroit. He then assesses opposing viewpoints (the positions of management and labor) and finally makes a judgment. Sensitive to how tenaciously groups cling to power, he emphasizes how important power alignments are in trying to establish justice.

He incisively analyzes the Marxist political economy, showing how alienation among workers, which Marx claims arises from capitalism's division of labor, really stems from human pride, not from the structures themselves. Moving to his biblical resource, he demonstrates how racial bigotry arises out of hubris in the form of idolatry and not primarily from ignorance or stupidity. Niebuhr's principle of love inspires justice to identify the sin, analyze its nature and power, and work out a solution that brings greater freedom and a relative equality to the parties involved.

Like Niebuhr, John Paul II presents a social ethics in which love and justice serve as the foci for evaluating interpersonal, social, political, and economic issues. Niebuhr's Christian realism and John Paul II's personalist social ethics both address issues on micro- and macro-group levels. John Paul II's personalism teaches that the person is a free and rational subject, possessing a dignity that must always be respected. The element of personalism emphasizes that persons flourish in loving and just relationships within a community.

John Paul II brings love and justice together as components of a third virtue called solidarity. He appeals to solidarity as a commitment of people who work for the common good in movements, such as the Polish workers' group. He also suggests that solidarity should serve as guide for international organizations that work for the global common good. The pope's two emphases on the human dignity of each person and the solidarity of groups and nations help steer movements away from a collectivism that gives too much authority to central government and from an individualism that resists state intervention. Unlike Niebuhr's notion of justice, which focuses on a balance of power, John Paul II's justice is linked to building power by consensus. In this age of globalization he challenges citizens and nations to think, negotiate, and trade on an international scale that moves people to participate in promoting the global common good. He appeals to rich nations to talk to poor nations, to trade freely and justly with developing nations, to reduce weaponry, and to support the test-ban treaty.

In the process of writing this book, I often found in my investigations another issue that urgently needs to be addressed: the bitter alienation and hatred that presently exists between many nations and the need for these nations to be reconciled. The alienation has a history that spans many generations, and in some cases many centuries. I had considered addressing the issue of the reconciliation of enemies in this book, but then I saw that the issue deserves special treatment. I have been impressed by the movement called restorative justice, which brings victims and offenders together for the purpose of reconciling and healing both parties. It has proved to be successful as an alternative to retributive justice within the judicial system in New Zealand, Canada, and parts of the United States. Can restorative justice be effective on the national level, where groups within countries and hostile countries continue to harbor resentment toward each other? I am inspired by people like Cynthia Ngewu, mother of a young man slain in the Guguletu 7 incident in South Africa, who testified before the Truth and Reconciliation Commission: "This thing called reconciliation . . . if I am understanding it correctly . . . it means the perpetrator, this man who killed Christopher Piet, if it means he becomes human again, this man, so that I, so that all of us, get our humanity back . . . then I agree, then I support it all."[2]

NOTES

[1] Christopher D. Marshall, *Beyond Retribution* (Grand Rapids, MI: Eerdmans, 2001), 85. See also Mt 5:38–42; Rom 12:21.

[2] *Long Night's Journey into Day: South Africa's Search for Truth and Reconciliation*, Study Guide, ed. Pamela Harris (Berkeley, CA: Iris Films, 2000).

INDEX

Of Related Interest

The Catholic Vote
A Guide for the Perplexed
Clarke E. Cochran & David Carroll Cochran
ISBN 978-1-57075-075-742-6

"I'm a Catholic—What should I be thinking about
before I cast my vote?"

Based on the Catholic values of life, dignity, solidarity, and proper
stewardship, *The Catholic Vote* describes 1) the importance of
participating in the political life of a community, 2) the extent to
which Catholic values influence Catholic voter choices, 3) the
significant issues, 4) how to evaluate candidates for office, and 5) how
the Catholic tradition can transform our political landscape.

Business Ethics
Gene Ahner
ISBN 978-1-57075-748-8

An essential guide to business ethics in a global economy.

"Gene Ahner's principled book is required reading for those searching
for the intersection of ethics, business and Christianity."
—*George B. Irish, Hearst Newspapers*

Please support your local bookstore or call 1-800-258-5838.
For a free catalog, please write us at
Orbis Books, Box 308
Maryknoll, NY 10545-0302
or visit our website at www.orbisbooks.com.

Thank you for reading *Love That Does Justice*.
We hope you profited from it.